Lars Tvede

The Psychology
of Finance

Lars Tvede

The Psychology
of Finance

Norwegian
University Press

Norwegian University Press (Universitetsforlaget AS), 0608 Oslo 6
Distributed world-wide excluding Scandinavia by
Oxford University Press, Walton Street, Oxford OX2 6DP

London   New York   Toronto
Delhi   Bombay   Calcutta   Madras   Karachi
Kuala Lumpur   Singapore   Hong Kong   Tokyo
Nairobi   Dar es Salaam   Cape Town
Melbourne   Auckland

and associated companies in
Beirut   Berlin   Ibadam   Mexico City   Nicosia

British Library Cataloguing in Publication Data
Tvede, Lars *1957–*
    The psychology of finance.
    1. Finance
    I. Title
    332

    ISBN 82-00-02772-4

Printed in Norway
by A.s Verbum, Stavanger

Contents

I   GREED AND FEAR   7
1   The Dark Forces of Time and Ignorance   9
2   A Few Practical Terms   20

II THE FOUR TERRIBLE TRUTHS ABOUT
    FINANCE   25
3   The First Rule: The Market is Ahead   27
4   The Second Rule: The Market is Irrational   35
5   The Third Rule: Chaos Reigns   48
6   The Fourth Rule: Charts are Self-fulfilling   60

III THE TREE OF KNOWLEDGE   67
7   An Investment Philosophy   69
8   The First Chartists   74

IV CROSS-TALK   85
9   International Investment: Three-Dimensional Chess?   87
10 Rhythm and Swing   94
11 The Importance of Money   103
12 Harmony and Resonance   117

V   INFORMATION: THE QUEST OF
    THE HOLY GRAIL   135
13 The Fastest Game in Town?   137
14 The Second Degree: Interpreting Information   145
15 Smoke Without Fire?   152
16 Little and Big Fish   158

VI   THE MADNESS OF CROWDS 171
17   Tracing the Monster's Tracks 173
18   When the Going Gets Decisive 184
19   Catching the Breath and Changing the Mind 208
20   Bungee Jumping 229
21   What's *Really* Going on When a Trend Reverses?... 239

VII   BEATING THE GUN 249
22   Strategy and Tactics 251
23   Exposure Tactics 256
24   Timing Tactics 261
25   The Road to Ruin 271

Appendix 1: Characteristics of Typical Chart Formations . 274
Appendix 2: Leading, Coincident and Lagging Indicators . 281
Appendix 3: Warning Signals of a Stock Market's Peak .. 282
Appendix 4: List of Historical Financial Crises 284

Glossary 286
Bibliography 293
Index 297

I

Greed and Fear

What registers in the stock market's fluctuations are not the events themselves but the human reactions to these events, how millions of individual men and women feel these happenings may affect the future. Above all else, in other words, the stock market is people.
Bernard Baruch

1.

The Dark Forces of Time and Ignorance

If a man will begin with certainties, he shall end in doubts; but if he will be content to begin with doubts, he shall end in certainties.

Francis Bacon

This book is about an aspect of stock trading which is often shrouded in mystery. It is about "the psychology of the market": About how the market's behavioral phenomena arise, and how we can learn to see them. It is also about how we can interpret this psychology and earn money from trading on it.

Some of the behavioral mechanisms creating price movements are rational and intelligent. Others are ridiculous and absurd. But, as we will see time and time again, they appear all the time and have all existed for as long as stock trading itself.

When It All Started

The history of the stock exchange goes back many centuries. Nobody can say for sure how many, but there are a number of indications that its origins were in 12th-century France, where the Counts of Champagne in 1114 introduced standardized forward contracts (lettre de faire) for trading in cloth, wine, fish, timber and metals (Sowards, 1965).

Although the first exchange-like markets saw the light of day in France, Italy soon came to play the most dominant role. From the 12th to the 16th century Italy led the field as a financial center, its finance houses trading gold, silver and currencies.

The European term "bourse" (meaning stock exchange) arose in the 16th century, when the house of the Dutch Van der Beurs family in Bruges became a center for local trading in finance and securities. People wanting to trade went "to Beurs", which is how the name originated. In the same century stock exchange trading spread throughout Europe, mostly trading of bonds issued by the royal houses, ever in need of funds.

After this, events followed in quick succession. The world's first official bourse building was erected in Amsterdam in 1613 and was soon followed by most European countries. At the same time the first sophisticated financial instruments arose: Option contracts were introduced in Holland prior to the famous tulip mania in 1636, and the first futures contracts were introduced on Japanese rice markets in 1679. The trading in rice futures was regulated by the Cho-ai-mai-a-kai rules, which stipulated exact standards for contracts and definitions of the various grades of rice. All trading was regulated by a non-profit clearing house and all price differences settled in cash: Physical delivery of rice was not involved (Bakken, 1953).

The Invisible Hand

For as long as stock trading has existed price movements have astounded us. Many have tried to explain the origins of these fluctuations and most theoreticians have endorsed what appears to be the most natural explanation:

> In the long term, stock exchange prices reflect real values. On the other hand, short-term fluctuations reflect small shifts in supply and demand and must be considered to be unpredictable and random.

Those who bow to this viewpoint are described in the jargon of the stock exchange as "fundamentalists" or "fundamental analysts". The fundamental analyst tries to assess the "true value" of the security, i.e. its commercial utility value or its value based on expected future yield. A skillful fundamental analyst should be able to say what the object *should* cost and therefore also how its price *should* develop.

But the market does not always behave as it should. The October 1987 crash was not exactly "random fluctuation". The fact that stock markets all over the globe could start a nose dive of such gigantic proportions at one and the same time, as though controlled by an invisible hand, served as a reminder that price fluctuations can be influenced by phenomena of a strength exceeding the wildest imaginations of most observers.

Why Not Stick to the True Value Anyhow?

We could ask why these mystical forces are so interesting. Why not just concentrate on economics? After all, stock exchange collapses are few and far between. Why aren't the intervening price movements just random, unimportant variations around true value?

The first problem for the fundamentalist is that variations around true value can be very large indeed. In *Technical Analysis of Stock Trends*, R. D. Edwards and J. Magee provide an excellent example concerning United States Steel stocks.

Table 1. Price/book value for United States Steel

Year	Book value according to accounts	Stock prices	Price/book value
1929	204	261	1.28
1932	187	22	0.12
1937	151	126	0.83
1946	117	97	0.83
1947	142	70	0.49

As Table 1 shows, over these eighteen years the price of United States Steel showed fluctuation which was impossible to explain by objective assessment of the security, even though book value naturally cannot be used as the only economic criterion.

The Value of Economic Forecasts

Now, of course, it could be said that the markets themselves are to blame if they don't reflect fundamental values. Investors could pay more attention to the forecasts of fundamentalists. The fact is, however, that the people who actually listen to the fundamentalist are often having difficulty beating the market. This is because such forecasts are rarely accurate. In fact, they are often so poor that Nobel Prize Winner Wassily Leontief has stated on the subject of economic models:

> In no field of empirical inquiry has so massive and sophisticated a statistical machinery been used with so indifferent results.

11

One reason is that in theory true value should discount the future events of many years – a sequence which it is almost impossible to predict. In *Investments*, J. P. Williams gives an example of his problems in calculating the right value of IBM stock, based on estimates of future profit growth. These calculations were made in 1968. He first estimated that the company's profits would grow by 16% annually for ten years, and then by 2% annually forever after. According to his calculations this gave a "true value" for the stock of 172.94 dollars. However, this was only half the price at which the stock was actually traded on the exchange.

Because his calculated value was far below the stock exchange price, he decided to alter his original high growth estimate from ten to twenty years, after which growth would fall to 2%. When he put these variables into his formula the result was a value of 432.66 dollars, somewhat higher than the actual stock exchange price. So this one variable alone, in reality almost impossible to predict, gave two alternative estimates of true value, one of which was two and a half times higher than the other. And, moreover, this was in a situation where the applied formula was taken for granted.

In many cases analysts vacillate between several different calculation methods, each giving very different results. Economists will often estimate the true value of a currency on the basis of a "Purchasing Power Parity" (PPP) model or a balance of payments-oriented model. The two sets of results will regularly deviate from each other by 50% or more. Which model is best? Are any of them any good?

When uncertainty is so great, it might be reasonable to assume that different economic prognoses are always very far apart, and thus at least give an indication of the extent of unpredictability. But this is not the case. Typically, fundamentalists' prognoses are very close to each other, but very far from the actual outcome. In 1980, *Euromoney* published sixteen leading analysis institutes' 12-month dollar/D-mark forecasts. The results are given in Table 2.

At the end of twelve months, the dollar/D-mark rate was neither 1.60 nor 1.72. It was 2.35!

The best example of the problems faced by economists is the case of Henry Kaufman. For a number of years Kaufman worked for Phibro-Salomon and was generally accepted as one of the

Table 2. Sixteen leading analysis institutes' 12-month forecast for dollar/ D-mark on 1 July 1981. The actual price was 2.35.

Institute	Forecast
Henley Centre for Forecasting	1.72
Economic Models	1.71
Berkeley Consulting Group	1.70
Citibank	1.70
Marine Midland	1.70
Phillips & Drew	1.70
Predex	1.70
Data Resources	1.69
Amex Bank	1.68
Conti Currency	1.68
Brown Brothers Harriman	1.67
Chemical Bank	1.65
European American Bank/Forex Research	1.65
Bi/Metrics	1.615
Security Pacific National Bank	1.61
Harris Bank	1.60

most skillful economic forecasters. But on 28 February 1983, *Business Week* published a systematic overview of Kaufman's forecasts over six years. During this period he had published twelve "large" analyses, of which seven had been accurate and five wrong. The astonishing results showed that one of the country's most prominent economic forecasters was only slightly more accurate than a coin toss. Even worse: Many of his wrong guesses turned out to be very wrong indeed.

Fundamentalists thus face no easy task when estimating what security values "ought" to be and what the market "ought" to do. Firstly, it is clearly completely unrealistic to interpret true value as anything more than a wide margin of probability. Secondly, economic scenarios can change radically – and frequently do – due to details which even the most skillful analyst could never predict.

The Art of Timing

It is even more difficult for the fundamental analyst to judge "when" predicted movements will occur. If the price lies outside the true value's probability interval, when will it slot into place?

The securities of most finance markets fluctuate considerably and if, against expectations, they are over or undervalued, this state of affairs can last for many years. Meanwhile, the true value apostle must patiently wait for time to smooth out irrational market fluctuations. Being a fundamentalist can thus equal being a "long-term investor" and can mean ignoring the crucial element called timing. The fundamentalist, ready to hold on to a security and wait for what he believes to be the true value, has another problem: While he waits the basis for his analyses can change radically.

In *The Money Game* from 1967, "Adam Smith" (pseudonym of George J. W. Goodman) describes how an American speculator, Timothy Bancroft, earned a fortune on stock trading in the mid-19th century. Bancroft's philosophy was "Buy good securities, put them away, and forget them". By "good securities" he meant "dealing in essential commodities that the Union and the World will always need in great quantities". So Bancroft was a fundamentalist.

He left a fortune on paper of 1,355,250 dollars, at that time A Lot Of Money. But when his estate had been settled and assets realized his stocks in "Gold Belt Mining", the "Carell Company of New Hampshire" and "American Alarm Clock" were worth nothing. His entire estate was worthless.

Times change, and what can appear healthy and promising one year can lose all value, while the present investor patiently waits.

An Important Complication

A complication which it is hard to ignore is that *true value fluctuates with price*. A good example is exchange rates. If a country's exchange rate starts to rise this will often mean that the country's inflation and interest rates start falling, resulting in an improvement in competition. Over a period, this will compensate for the rising exchange rate. In other words, exchange rate fluctuation is self-validating. When the price goes up the true value also rises.

The same is true of stocks. If a stock rises, the company's credit rating improves, as well as its opportunities to finance activities with loans or by issuing new stock. The company's general image among its product's users will also improve, and it will become more popular among potential executives. Price fluctuations thus have an impact on true value.

The situation is not very different on commodities markets.

On many of these markets, suppliers have formed cartels in an attempt to control prices. During price increases, cartel members have little difficulty meeting their commitments: Discipline is maintained. But if prices drop, the weakest often react by increasing production to secure a stable revenue. Consequently, the supply curve becomes distorted so that, in the short term at any rate, rising prices are an incentive for production cut-backs, while falling prices give increased supply, which in its turn exerts pressure on prices. This is also a self-validating process, where supply and demand fluctuate as a function of price movements to a degree which would surprise the uninitiated. No wonder so many people have abandoned so-called "long-term investment". One of these was John Maynard Keynes.

Keynes's Discovery

Keynes was born in England in 1883, the year of Karl Marx's death. He quickly proved to be extraordinarily intelligent. When he was six, he tried to analyze how his brain worked and when he was 28 he became editor of England's most respected financial publication, the *Economic Journal*. Throughout his life he produced a series of epoch-making economic publications, and for a period he was deputy for Britain's Chancellor of the Exchequer.

While Karl Marx's life was a personal fiasco, Keynes bathed in success, not just as a public figure, but also as an investor. Every morning he spent half an hour in bed planning his investment strategy (he preferred commodities and currencies), managing to earn over two million dollars. He also managed a fund for King's College, Cambridge, and under his financial management its capital value increased more than tenfold. Keynes's writings on investments and stock markets therefore carried great authoritative weight. What then did he write exactly? In his book *The General Theory of Employment, Interest and Money,* 1936, his description was the following:

> It might have been supposed that competition between expert professionals, possessing judgment and knowledge beyond that of the average private investor, would correct the vagaries of the ignorant individual left to himself. It happens, however, that the energies and skill of the professional investor and speculator are mainly occupied otherwise. For most of these persons are, in fact, largely concerned, not with making superior long-term forecasts of the probable yield of

15

an investment over its whole life, but with foreseeing changes in the conventional basis of valuation a short time ahead of the general public.

The social object of skilled investment should be to defeat the dark forces of time and ignorance which envelop our future. The actual, private object of the most skilled investment today is "to beat the gun," as the Americans so well express it, to outwit the crowd, and to pass the bad, or depreciating, half-crown to the other fellow.

Obviously Keynes considered stock markets to be myopic and irrational and the struggle against the "dark forces of time and ignorance" to be much more difficult than "beating the gun". In his own stock operations he put economics in the back seat and concentrated on psychology. And this, it seems, was the prime reason for his successful investments.

The Worst Problem

The worst problem faced in the hunt for the true value is not that constructing the right economic forecasting model is difficult or that true value moves with the price. The worst problem is that the better the economic simulation models describe the actual dynamics of the world, the more chaotic their behavior gets. Or, in other words, the further our economic scientists elaborate and sophisticate their models, the stronger becomes the evidence that such models can never predict the long-term development at all.

Mathematicians laugh at this, because they suspected it all along. "The reason", they say, "is that the true mathematical nature of dynamic systems such as a complex economy is Very Messy and Highly Unpredictable". In the mathematician's eyes, the economists have simply failed to realize the true nature of their task because they have failed to consider the true nature of non-linear mathematics. And "The true nature of non-linear mathematics", they say, "is that in general you can only forecast the behavior of such systems in the very short term".

The explanations for this are found in a complex of peculiar phenomena commonly described as "deterministic chaos". What chaos means is that for many or most economic systems, objective and quantitative long-term forecasting cannot be done. So, in beating the dark forces of time and ignorance, we are instead left with the alternative of sticking to personal and subjective

16

guestimates. And these will of course be entangled with our personal and subjective emotions such as hope, fear and greed.

Hope, Fear and Greed

In *The Battle of Investment Survival* the successful investor, American Gerald Loeb, describes the markets as follows:

> There is no such thing as a final answer to security values. A dozen experts will arrive at 12 different conclusions. It often happens that a few moments later each would alter his verdict if given a chance to reconsider because of a changed condition. Market values are fixed only in part by balance sheets and income statements; much more by the hopes and fears of humanity; by greed, ambition, acts of God, invention, financial stress and strain, weather, discovery, fashion and numberless other causes impossible to be listed without omission.

So, clearly, the Great Masters may not agree on how to make money on the stock exchange, but they do agree that *the market is very often irrational.* But is it possible to analyze "hopes and fears", "greed and ambition" – to predict investors' "financial stress and strain"? Or to calculate their buying-power at a given point in time? Or what "fashion" they will go for?

Yes, we can. The market lives a life of its own and many of its irrational phenomena can be analyzed.

Chartists

If we analyze markets instead of the economy we are "chartists" or "technical analysts": We pay attention to hope, fear and greed. However, the study of the markets is not *just* a study of the irrational, since chartists have the same problem as fundamentalists – they can never be sure when a market is irrational. The chartist has as little chance as the fundamentalist of answering the question "Do the others know something I don't?"

"They" – all the others – almost always know a whole lot that you don't, not necessarily as individuals, but collectively. William Peter Hamilton acknowledged this, writing in the *Wall Street Journal* in 1929: "Everything that everybody knows about anything with even a remote bearing on finance finds its ways into Wall Street, in the information: The stock itself, in its fluctuations, represents the sifted value of all this knowledge."

The market holds a fantastic store of knowledge. This knowledge is constantly being discounted in stock exchange prices, with the result that the market is *ahead* of events in the economy. The Dean of technical analysis, Charles Dow, based a series of market rules on this fact, but yet it is obvious that when the market occasionally explodes in panic, some other phenomenon must be at work.

The problem is that the market may be extremely well informed but it does not always base its behavior on this knowledge alone. There is a second element, the irrational, and sometimes, when amateurs go into the market, this element will dominate completely, while at other times it can be unimportant.

The Basic Rules of the Market

So let's try to summarize the basic rules for investors:

Rule 1: *The market is ahead.* The sum of the insight of all current and potential investors is normally more than one single human being can grasp. Perhaps "the others" know something we don't? We can never be sure. We have to agree that it is an impossible task to be ahead of the general market's knowledge and its early discounting of such knowledge in its prices.

Rule 2: *The market is irrational.* The market may react quickly to facts, but it can also be subjective, emotional and ruled by the whim of changing trends. In periods, prices can fluctuate in step with investors' financial situation and interests, shifting between mass hysteria and indifference rather than security values. Individual investors' attempts to be rational can therefore actually be irrational behavior.

Rule 3: *The environment is chaotic.* Macro-economic forecasts are normally too inexact to have any value for an investor. This especially as economic interrelations are constantly influenced by small, but crucial, details no-one could predict or gauge, but which can change everything. Even worse: The same applies to financial markets.

18

These three rules have existed for as long as the markets, although only very few people seem to understand what they mean.

But today there is a fourth rule, created by technical analysts who use graphic charts to analyze markets: The rule is that charts are self-fulfilling. If many people draw the same lines on the same charts and feed their computers with the same decision-making systems, the effects will be self-reinforcing.

So the rule is:

Rule 4: *Charts are self-fulfilling*. If many people use the same chart systems they may profit on their trades, regardless of whether they actually *are* right.

Making money in the markets is a game, and to play this game you have to understand these four rules. We will examinate these rules in more detail in Chapters 3–6, but before that, some practical terms need explaining. The next chapter is devoted to this groundwork.

2.

A Few Practical Terms

They told me to buy this stock for my old age. It worked wonderfully. Within a week I was an old man.

Eddie Cantor

Before continuing with the rules of the game let's consider a few basic terms.

Three Types of Chart

The price curves shown in this book are *charts*. When you have read the book they will give meaning to you and then, you can call yourself a *chartist*. Many of the charts shown are *bar charts*, each bar showing one day's price range. A week's trading can appear as follows:

The small horizontal lines on the bar show the day's listed *close price*. This will often be a good expression of the day's actual relation between supply and demand as it closes off all short-term speculation on that day. When drawing patterns and formations on charts it is best to concentrate on close prices, if known.

A simpler variation is so-called *line charts* which show only development in close prices:

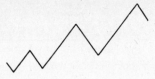

Line charts naturally tell us less than bar charts, but give a clearer picture.

Finally, there is a third type of chart (which we will not use in this book, however):

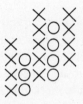

These are called *point-and-figure charts*. The idea here is to insert prices vertically, having defined a suitable minimum unit on the scale. When the price goes up a series of crosses are plotted as it rises. The first time it drops by a minimum unit we shift to the right and plot a zero. Then zeros are plotted one below the other for as long as the price drops, until it rises again by a minimum unit. Then we shift to the right again and plot a cross.

Point-and-figure charts thus have no time axis, giving the advantage that events over a long period can be compressed into limited space. Many use point-and-figure systems in combination with mechanical rules and thus study the market on a purely statistical basis, rather than behavioristic. The lack of a time axis makes the method less suitable for detailed study, which is why these charts are not used in this book.

Rising and Falling Markets

Markets go up and down, and there are special terms to describe this. A market with a rising trend over a long period is called a *bull market*. If the market is falling it is called a *bear market*. Anyone who thinks the market should rise is *bullish*, and those who believe it should drop are *bearish*. The origin of these expressions is unknown, but a popular explanation is that a bull keeps its head up (=rising) while a bear keeps its head down (= falling). In fact, a bull keeps its head down when it charges, which may add an extra symbolic twist.

When the market goes up a bullish dealer buys and his position is *long*. When it goes down he sells. If he is out of the market the slang term is that he is *on the sidelines*.

If an investor is very bearish he may go a step further by, in popular terms, selling his chicks before they are hatched. Imagine a wheat grower expecting a large wheat harvest in September. In February he has a very strong inkling that there will be a good wheat surplus in the next harvest and that wheat prices will drop. He therefore sells his wheat straightaway, but for delivery in September. So he has sold something he does not actually have but which he naturally expects to get. In stock exchange terms his wheat position is *short*, and he has taken cover against the coming price drop. If his only motive is to protect his position, he is a *hedger*. A hedger will take no further action before the wheat is safely harvested, after which he delivers the corn, fulfilling his contract by physical delivery.

But let us imagine that as early as March wheat prices have dropped more than our wheat farmer expected. He can then buy back the same quantity of wheat as he sold, for delivery on the same date. This will give him a speculative profit, so he is no longer a hedger but a *speculator*. This type of deal, aimed at profit from a price drop, is called a *short sale*.

An interesting element in selling short as a speculator is that sooner or later you have to buy back your contract in order to close the deal. But if nobody wants to sell at the time, you have to bid whatever prices are necessary to find a seller. Consequently, the price can go sky-high, and if that happens we refer to it as a *"corner"* or *"bear-squeeze"*. Those were very frequent in the middle of the 19th century when masterminding a corner was considered the ultimate test of a professional trader. As Commodore Vanderbilt said, once he was cornering Daniel Drew, who was begging for his mercy:

He that sells what isn't hisn, must buy it back or go to prisn.

Corners are more rare today, but they *do* exist. So: Beware!

On many markets special instruments are used, making it equally easy to be "long" or "short". These are called *futures* and *options*.

A *future* is a standardized stock-exchange listed contract for future delivery of a specific security or commodity on a fixed date and at a price fixed in advance. If Smith buys a futures contract for delivery of US T-bonds in March he will agree a fixed price now, but will not take delivery of the security before March, when he settles payment. At the same time Brown can sell the same contract short and buy it back later, possibly at a cheaper price, making a profit on the price difference. The good thing is that, as with traditional bull and bear trading, you can make the same profit regardless of whether the market is rising or falling, as long as you have predicted the movement and traded on it. In addition, only modest collateral is needed. At the outset you deposit only a small percentage of the contract amount.

A particularly interesting type of future is *index futures*, involving purchase or sale of a wide selection of one country's stock (described as the contract's "underlying securities"). If you think the stock index will drop, all you have to do is go short in its index futures and profit from the falling market. Many large stock markets have these contracts.

The instrument closest to futures is *options*. In principle, an option is a future where, at a modest risk premium, the loss risk is limited to a maximum amount, while the potential profit is unlimited. (If an option is sold instead of bought the reverse is naturally the case. A speculator will often find it most logical to sell options, as on average the risk premium exceeds the actual risk.) Options are terribly complicated and not of crucial importance to the professional speculator. Consequently we will not consider them in detail.

Futures and options can also be used in currency trading, although the most common instrument is *forward exchange contracts*, time-limited transactions where the investor is simultaneously long in one currency and short in another. When the position is closed a gain or loss is realized unless prices have not moved. The profit includes interest accrued on the long currency, less interest paid on the short currency. This can naturally also be a loss.

Sometimes an investor will be long in a traditionally weak currency and short in a traditionally strong currency. The argument is that the interest rate for the weak currency is so much higher than the interest rate for the strong currency that the profit on this interest differential will be higher than the potential loss on price movements. This is called *interest rate arbitrage*.

As a consequence of the widespread use of these flexible investment instruments, differences between rising and falling market patterns are sometimes not as high as they used to be. This reservation should be kept in mind in the discussion of bull or bear markets in this book.

Choice of Charts

Finally, there are the markets. The charts used as examples represent large liquid markets. These are the markets where understanding of the market dynamics is most important. The examples in this book include money rates, stocks, bonds, index futures, foreign currencies, precious metals and commodities.

It may be strange to see commodities included. What have coffee, copper or oil got to do with the stock exchange? Quite a lot. By far the greatest proportion of international commodities trading takes place via stock exchanges, based on pure speculation by investors who do not have the slightest intention of utilizing or delivering the physical commodity. (On the contrary, they would be quite horrified if they ever got a physical delivery of their commodities). Twenty-four hours a day people all over the world study detailed price charts for pork bellies, live cattle or copper bars, purely in the quest for the answer to the perennial question: "How is the market's sentiment?"

So much for the technical terms. Equipped with these, we can now move forward to our four basic rules of the game.

II

The Four Terrible
Truths About
Finance

Great God! This is an awful place!
Sir Robert Falcon Scott

3.

The First Rule: The Market is Ahead

Consciously or unconsciously, the movement of prices reflects not the past but the future. When coming events cast their shadows before, the shadow falls on the New York Stock Exchange.

W. P. Hamilton

Anybody trading on stock markets over a period will note how analysts, economists, investment advisors and journalists, who are expected to predict the financial markets, are always helplessly behind with their news, analyses and forecasts, which are mere post mortems of what the market worked out long ago. In other words, the market is ahead of the news.

In his book entitled *Das ist die Börse*, stock-exchange speculator Kostolany expresses this as follows:

> Generally the news does not create prices but prices create the news. This is true of Paris, London and New York. At the close of the day's trading everybody starts looking for arguments to explain a price deviation, or a trend alteration, and these are arguments of which he would never have dreamt two hours before.

One explanation is probably that nobody likes people who serve bad news and analyses to a rising market where everybody is happy. This is not what people want and if they hear it they won't believe it. More or less unconsciously, the information presented to the general public is sorted to confirm moods and markets, and there is an avid audience for economists in favor of the trend. When the market has just peaked and is starting to slide news and analyses are often at their most positive.

But there is another more obvious explanation: When the market is ahead of the news this quite simply reflects that it is *ahead of the economy*.

27

The first to draw the public's attention to this interesting fact was a highly remarkable American called Roger Ward Babson. Babson was born in Massachusetts in 1875, graduated as an engineer in 1898, and then went straight into stockbroking (for which stockbrokers never forgave him). A few years later he developed tuberculosis and was told to stay outdoors as much as possible. So he set up an open air office, in 1902 founding his own company, "Babson Statistical Organization", which performed financial analyses. (It was later said of him that he was the man in the USA to make the most money from statistics.) Wearing a special coat with an electrically heated pad in the back and assisted by a secretary obliged to wear mittens and use small rubber hammers to hit the typewriter keys, in the cold and fresh air Babson built up his company. A company which made him a public figure and even the personal friend of several US presidents.

In 1907 Babson, now restored to good health, was fascinated by a wave of panic on the stock exchange. Inspired by this he started up a special analysis service which he called "Babson Charts" and in which he compared the country's economic development with charts showing price movements on stock markets. In 1910 he published his first book, *Business Barometers Used in the Accumulation of Money*. In this early book, to be followed by an additional fifty, on the subjects of links between stock markets and economic trends, he concluded:

> In fact, if it were not for manipulation, merchants could almost rely on the stock market alone as a barometer, and let these large market operators stand the expense of collecting the data necessary for determining fundamental conditions.

Babson's hypothesis was not aimed at the micro-economy. He did not expect the price of a given, small stock to give efficient forecasts for this company. But if you added it all up, the total stock market should forecast the total economy. This macro-economic barometer would work, if it were not for some market dealers' success in manipulating it.

Twelve years after Babson's first book, the editor-in-chief of the *Wall Street Journal*, William Peter Hamilton, published a book with a related title, *The Stock Market Barometer*. Hamilton was partly inspired by Babson's theory (although primarily by Charles Dow). He described a classic example of the market's ability to discount the economy. This was after the 1907 panic when, as editor-in-chief in 1908–09, he was at the receiving end of a deluge of angry letters to the editor against stock trading on Wall Street. The reason was a rising bull market at a time when things were going very badly for the country's economy. Among the milder accusations were that "Wall Street was playing the violin while Rome burned".

Nonetheless, in this period Hamilton stuck to the view that the market was merely discounting an impending economic upturn. And this upturn did come. What the market had in fact predicted was the economic revival of the following years. So Hamilton agreed with Babson that the stock market acted as a barometer for the economy, but he did not share Babson's reservations concerning large market operators' ability to manipulate the market. In Hamilton's opinion they might be able to influence the market in the short term, in individual securities, but they had no possibility of controlling the large movements, and therefore the market was in fact a "unique barometer".

The Test of the Barometer

No-one could have dreamt up a better test of the barometer than the 1929 Wall Street crash. In the two years prior to this crash Babson's advisory service began to recommend that investors sell their stock. But the market continued to rise and Babson began to appear rather ridiculous in many people's eyes. This impression was strengthened by the fact that he was virtually alone in his pessimistic opinion. Almost all the experts, from economists to investment advisors, were extremely optimistic, recommending the purchase of more stocks, rather than the sale.

One of the people the market listened to was Professor Lawrence of Princeton University, who stated in 1929 that he could not see how stocks could be overvalued. A second expert, Professor Irving Fisher of Yale University (a leading theoretician in the field of fundamental analysis) declared that stocks appeared to have reached a permanent high. But the most striking example of this optimism was a newsletter published for a number of years by a group of leading Harvard economists, *Harvard*

Economic Society, to evaluate prospects for the economy. This authoritative organ predicted, from before the beginning of the crash in 1929 to the autumn of 1932, that the economy would go forward – while in the meantime the depression grew steadily worse. After three years of constantly wrong predictions, the society was finally dissolved.

Also President Hoover, leading bank presidents, the head of the New York Stock Exchange and a majority of the country's prominent financial periodicals kept their optimism until after the crash and a long way into the following Great Depression.

But Babson stuck to his guns. On 5 September 1929, when the market lay just below its "all time high", he gave a speech at the Annual National Business Conference in which he not only repeated his general advice to sell all stocks, but also predicted a "60–80 point" drop in the indices, to be followed by a depression in which factories would be closed and people evicted from their homes. This speech marked the start of the Wall Street crash and this crash signaled the beginning of the deep depression which would last for most of the following decade. Babson's barometer had passed its hardest test. (It appears likely that the crash in itself was a major reason for the following depression. This does not change the fact, however, that the market was ahead.)

The Negative Derivative of 1st Degree

In 1939, Joseph Schumpeter, in his book *Business Cycles*, made his bid to explain the early reaction of the stock market. Schumpeter found the main reasons to be that these markets were not susceptible to "friction", in contrast to industry. At a point where prospects were beginning to look brighter after the depression, many companies were, according to Schumpeter, so debilitated by the hard times that they nonetheless collapsed. This gave industry its delayed "friction". But there was no equivalent delay on the stock market.

> Hence, it is natural to expect that upward movements on the stock exchange will, in general and in the absence of unfavorable external factors, set in earlier and gather force more quickly than the corresponding upward movements in business.

For this reason a bear market on the stock exchange would end sooner than the corresponding depression in the economy. He also believed that the stock market reacted more quickly than the underlying economy during peaks in upswings:

> While general business may and often does settle down into recession in a perfectly orderly way, this is hardly imaginable in the case of the stock exchange. Recession means reduced profits and, for many concerns, more or less serious troubles. It gives scope to bear attacks. But even if nothing of this sort ever happened or were anticipated, the mere fact that there is no reason to expect, save in particular cases, any upward movement would suffice to make speculators lose interest in their holdings.

This argument is based on the premise that investors actually have some understanding of the future economy. The fact that for example stock prices have so excellently discounted future development must be due to individual investors' very early sense of what will happen. If a man notices that in his business a given auxiliary will be in less demand, he sells his stocks in the companies producing this auxiliary, perhaps even at a time when the management of these companies have no suspicion of the commercial danger. If he discovers that a subsupplier's delivery times are lengthening he may conclude that their order book must be full, and he buys their stock.

Such rapid insight on the part of market operators will often lie behind the market's ability to react quickly. But even more important – as Schumpeter expressed it – is the fact that as soon as investors stop seeing further reason to buy, they will sell. Or, in other words: The market price is not a direct expression of the general expectations, but rather the negative derivative of 1st degree of general expectations. This is a situation where, while the general atmosphere of the economy remains good, the lack of any *additional* good news will cause the selling of stock. Although this may sound like common sense, at times the market can have an inverse relationship to the general mood of the economy.

Later Surveys

In 1981 *The American Economic Review* published an article by Eugene F. Fama, who had undertaken a comprehensive survey of the links between stock yields, economic activity, inflation and money supply. This investigation was based on empirical material from the USA in the years since 1953. Fama concluded: "Stock returns lead all of the real variables, which suggests that the market makes rational forecasts of the real sector." This investigation led him to the following remark on the stock markets' treatment of information:

> The evidence suggests a "rational expectations" or "efficient markets" view in which the stock market is concerned with the capital investment process and uses the earliest information from the process to forecast its evolution.

In other words: The stock market is ahead of the economy – not very far ahead but further than any qualified economist can hope to be. This assumption is called the "Efficient Market Hypothesis". (It is remarkable that most investors take a different view. A questionnaire sent to 500 American stock investors after the 1987 crash (Barrons 9–11–87) showed that 45% believed that the stock market generally reflected the economy, 25% believed that it had very little connection with the economy at all, and only 17% believed it was generally ahead of the economy).

Because the stock market *is* ahead, this has been pursued to its logical conclusion in making it one of the official leading indicators for the American economy. According to analyses by the National Bureau of Economic Research in Cambridge, Massachusetts, it has proved to be the best of the 12 leading cyclical indicators (see appendix 2).

Bonds are Better

We can go one step further: Bonds appear to be even better economic forecast tools. On 28 September 1982 the *Wall Street Journal* published an article on the bond market's ability to discount events in the economy. The conclusion was as follows:

> The bond measure, which reflects the price average of 10 highly rated public-utility bonds and 10 highly rated industrial issues, has consistently reached a peak or a low point, as the case may be, months before the Commerce Department's leading-indicator index, for example, has similarly signaled a major turning point in the business cycle.

This is nothing new either. In his book *Business Barometers Used in the Accumulation of Money* from 1910 Babson used twelve leading indicators, including the money market interest rate, on which he wrote: *"Money* is the basis of all trade and is therefore probably the most sensitive of all barometers." Since bond and money market rates are such efficient indicators it may come as a surprise that the National Bureau of Economic Research does not use them as leading indicators today. The reason is that, quite correctly, rising interest rates are considered to be a "lagging indicator".

They function better than any of the other five lagging indicators. If you study the money rates in reverse, however, (this can be done by monitoring short bonds which rise as short rates drop), it will be seen that they act as excellent leading indicators (Moore, 1969).

The ability of finance markets to predict economic reversals is not particular to the USA. In 1984 Bruno Solnik published a survey in *Financial Analysts Journal* which confirmed stock market relations in nine different countries over the period 1971–82. He wrote: "According to one explanation of the observed negative relation between US stock returns and inflation, a drop in stock prices signals a drop in economic activity . . . evidence from nine major world stock markets seems to support this theory." On the basis of these and many other studies it is now generally acknowledged that stock markets can be used as leading economic indicators with a typical lead time from financial to economic trend reversals of 6–9 months, and interest rates with a typical lead time of 8–25 months. This does not mean that the market is always right. But it means that it is more likely to be right than any singular macro-economic indicator, science has yet found.

Beating the Market

The case is similar for isolated stocks, bonds, commodities, precious metals and currencies. The markets react before financial news is known and understood by most official experts, let alone the general public. Just as the birds stop singing right before the storm breaks, investors stop buying while the poor fundamentalists watch and wonder.

The consequence is obvious, although unpleasant to the fundamental analyst. Forecasting the economy alone is seldom enough to forecast the market. You have to *beat the market* at predicting what the economy will do, which means you have to be out *very* early indeed. But the chartist doesn't have to worry about this problem. He uses the market as its own barometer. Ironically enough, we shall see that this can make him the engineer of the best forecasts of the economy.

4.

The Second Rule: The Market is Irrational

> We find that whole communities suddenly fix their minds upon one object, and go mad in its pursuit; that millions of people become simultaneously impressed with one delusion, and run after it, till their attention is caught by some new folly more captivating than the first.
>
> *Charles Mackay*

We have seen that general market patterns are ahead of the economy. However, as the fun and games of 1929 so clearly illustrated, sometimes there is water in the barometer.

A Little Experiment

Here is a little experiment to illustrate one of the reasons that the markets can lose touch with reality so quickly. Choose the foreign currency market for this experiment and pick a day in European trading on which it is clear that Europeans do not intend to shift prices very much. Spend the whole morning studying all the financial news of the last twenty-four hours. Then try to guess what the Americans will do when they start up at 4–5 p.m. Will they *buy*, or *sell* dollars? Think through all the arguments for rises and drops and then decide whether to lie "long" or "short" in dollar against D-mark when the USA opens. Let's imagine that most arguments are that they will sell and that you choose to sell short.

Just after lunch you open a short dollar position so large that anything more than moderate movement in the wrong direction will be pretty serious. This makes sure that you are committed. Then sit down and stare intensely at the computer screen, monitoring the dollar second by second (it actually does change from second to second). The combination of a too exposed position and this intense monitoring will prepare your mind for the irrational feelings the experiment is designed to demonstrate.

When the Americans start dealing at 4–5 p.m. London time

the first random turbulence is about to appear. Then you will experience something very strange: As soon as the first marginal movement starts, in a remarkable way it will shed new light on the entire logical reasoning you had worked out, and the floodlights will be on the arguments in favor of the movement. If the dollar drops, as hoped, your victory will be supreme. "I knew it" you will think, surprised that you were in any doubt at all. "Any arguments to buy were silly." If the dollar starts to rise instead, suddenly all arguments to buy will gain weight. "What a fool I am, of course it's going up." There will be a violent urge to reverse the exposure positions, even though anybody knows that the first small movements in a market like this one are completely insignificant.

What you will discover is that the mood follows the price. If the price goes up the feeling is that it should keep going up. If it goes down people believe it should continue to do so. This is true of professionals and amateurs alike. The only difference is that experience has taught professionals to keep their cool. But sometimes a special mood will spread from a few investors to more and more, ending as a mass movement and, finally, mass hysteria. These phenomena reveal the weaknesses of the human mind in a way which is embarrassing, but very instructive. History has seen many examples of this. The world's first speculative stock exchange crash of any real dimension took place in France in 1557 when the Habsburg Empire stopped paying interest and installments on the glut of government bonds issued in previous years. Since then every century has seen major speculative stock exchange ventures, all ending with the inevitable crash (see appendix 4). Among the most instructive was the crash in Holland, 1636, the South Sea Bubble in England, 1711–20, and of course the 1929 Wall Street crash.

The Crash in Holland in 1636

The story of the crash in Holland in 1636, at a comfortable distance of over 350 years, is a fine example to us of investors' irrationality. The fantastic aspect of the crash (which was probably the largest in stock exchange history) is that although hysteria precipitated a wave of affluence throughout an entire nation, followed by bankruptcy and depression, the investment object was neither stocks, bonds nor commodities. It was tulip bulbs.

The first account of tulips in Europe is from 1559 when a collector of exotic flora, Councillor Herwart, received a consignment of tulip bulbs from a friend in Constantinople, which he planted in his garden in Augsburg, Germany. His tulips drew a good deal of attention and in following years this flower became more and more popular among the upper classes, particularly in Germany and Holland, where it became the custom to order bulbs at exorbitant prices direct from Constantinople. Up to 1634 this custom became increasingly common, and from that year affluent society in Holland considered lack of a tulip collection to be proof of poor taste.

Year by year tulip bulb prices rose, finally reaching astronomic heights. According to original accounts of the peak of the tulip mania, in one deal the following price was paid for one single tulip bulb of the rare Semper Augustus variety: 4,600 florins, a new carriage, two gray mares and a complete bridle and harness.

As a fatted ox at that time cost 120 florins, 4,600 florins was an awful lot of money! One single bulb of another rare variety, "Viceroy", was sold for: 24 carriage loads of grain, eight fat hogs, four cows, four barrels of ale, 1000 pounds of butter and a few tons of cheese.

In 1636 demand for tulip bulbs had risen so drastically that people started to trade them on exchanges in a number of Dutch towns. Tulips were no longer bought only by well-to-do collectors but also by agents and speculators. At the smallest price drop they bought up, to sell later at a profit. To facilitate trading on the margin tulip options were introduced, requiring a margin deposit of only 10–20%. Ordinary people in all business sectors started to sell off assets to invest in this attractive market.

The Dutch tulip boom also drew attention abroad and capital began to stream into the market. This capital jacked up prices for land, property and luxury goods, as well as tulips, to new record heights. Fortunes grew and a growing *nouveau riche* group was added to the old upper classes. This new affluent class had earned its money from, and reinvested in, tulip bulbs. The story is told of a brewer in Utrecht who went so far as to exchange his brewery for three valuable tulip bulbs.

Suppressed Mirth

In September and October a classical feeling started to spread:
The nagging feeling of doubt. How could one be *sure* that three
tulip bulbs were worth as much as a brewery? Suppressed mirth
began to be heard. Who said a tulip bulb was worth anything at
all? The market was seized by panic and prices began to plummet.

Many of the *nouveau riche* had to face the fact that they owned
a fortune consisting only of tulip bulbs which nobody wanted,
less broker cash loans which they could not repay. The government tried to find a compromise by declaring all tulip contracts
from before November 1636 invalid, while all subsequent contracts would be honored at 10% of original value. But prices
dropped below this 10% and the number of bankruptcies increased day by day. The Dutch tulip mania was followed by a depression from which it took the country many, many years to recover.

The South Sea Bubble

A second instructive example of the markets' irrationality is the
speculation in England at the beginning of the 18th century.
Events are described in the entertaining volume *Memoirs of
Extraordinary Popular Delusions and the Madness of Crowds*
from 1852 by Charles MacKay.

The company later known under the name "The South Sea
Bubble" started in 1711 when the Earl of Oxford founded the
South Sea Company, financed by a number of the merchants of
that time (the company's full name was "The Governor and
Company of the Merchants of Great Britain to the South Seas
and other parts of America for the encouragement of the Fishing"). The company acquired almost 10 million pounds of the
British national debt, against a guaranteed annuity of 6%, and
the monopoly on all trading with Latin America.

A short time after the company's founding rumors of incredible profits from this South Sea trading arose, where English
goods could be bartered for gold and silver from the "inexhaust-
ible" mines of Peru and Mexico. In fact, the Spanish colonial
power allowed only one English ship to call per year, against one
fourth of all profits and 5% of turnover. On the stock exchange

the South Sea stock led a quiet existence, the price often moving only two or three points over a month.

In 1717 the King of England recommended that the national debt be "privatized" once more. The country's two large financial institutions, the Bank of England and the South Sea Company, each submitted a proposed solution, and after heated parliamentary debate it was resolved to allow the South Sea Company to acquire a further debt liability at an interest rate of 5% per year.

But in 1719 an event took place in France which was to be of great significance for the English company. A well-to-do man named John Law had founded a company in Paris, "Compagnie d'Occident", to trade with, and colonize, the American state of Mississippi. By a series of manipulations John Law succeeded in starting a massive wave of speculation in this company's stock, the price rising from 466 francs on 9 August to 1705 on 2 December 1719. Buyers were French and foreigners alike, which caused the British Ambassador to request His Majesty's Government to do something to stop the massive flow of English capital to the "Mississippi Bubble" on the French stock exchange. The Mississippi Bubble culminated on 2 December 1719, and in the ensuing crash capital moved back from France to England in eternal pursuit of new investment openings.

This provided an interesting opportunity for the principle stockholders in the British South Sea Company, who now offered to take over the entire debt of the English State. On 22 January 1720 the House of Commons appointed a committee to consider the proposal. Despite many warnings, on 2 February the decision was taken to submit a bill to Parliament. Investors were delighted at this prospect of further capitalization of the company and over a few days the price rose to £176, supported by an inflow of funds from France. During further readings of the bill new rumors started to circulate on the unbelievable profits which could be made and stocks rose further to a price of £317. On the final passing of the Act on 7 April 1720, however, a wave of profit-taking (i.e. sale) pressed prices back to £307 and to £278 on the following day.

Even at this price the company's original founders and co-directors could reap a capital gain which was enormous by the standards of that time, and in a virtually inactive company. This whetted their appetites for more, and new positive rumors were circulated on 12 April and fresh stock was subscribed to for one million pounds at a price of £300. The issue was subscribed twice over and a few days later stock was traded at £340. The company then declared that a 10% dividend would be paid on all new and old stock and further new subscription was invited for one million pounds at a price of £400. This was also over-subscribed. The company was still almost inactive.

More Bubbles

This inspired many an entrepreneurial spirit and in the years 1717–20 a new phenomenon appeared on the stock market: There were more and more stock offerings in new "blind issues". These were companies which, like Compagnie d'Occident and the South Sea Company, sold nothing but plans, ideas and expectations. They were completely inactive on the subscription date, managed by novices in the planned commercial area. Stocks were bought up with great enthusiasm and quickly rose in price. Speculation in stocks was no more just a rich man's game – anybody and everybody, high or low, men or women, took part. These companies quickly acquired the popular name of "bubbles", because the original founders often sold their own stock at a profit a few days or weeks after the new issue, leaving other investors with an inactive company at an inflated price.

On 11 June 1720 the King proclaimed a number of these companies to be "public nuisances" and trading in their stocks was prohibited on penalty of a fine. A list of 104 prohibited companies included the following make-believe activities:

– For improving the art of making soap
– For extracting silver from lead
– For buying and fitting out ships to suppress pirates
– For the transmutation of quicksilver into a malleable fine metal

Despite the government's endeavors new bubbles appeared every single day and the speculation fever continued to rise. The first and largest bubble – the South Sea Company – was traded at a price of £550 on 28 May 1720. From this already impressive level, during June the price rose above £700. In this period price

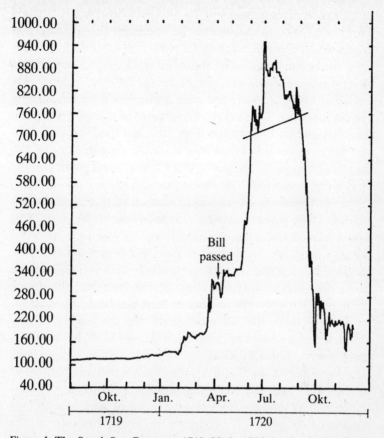

Figure 1. The South Sea Company 1719–20. In 1720 the South Sea Company was the largest security on the English exchange, but over its 140 years of existence it never fulfilled its original objects of fisheries and trading. The straight line drawn in below the stock's peak is called a "neck-line" in a "head and shoulders" formation. This is explained in Chapter 19. The arrow marks the date on which Parliament passed a bill for the company to take over the national debt.

movements were extremely nervous, with great periodic shifts. On a single day, 3 June the price thus dropped before noon to £650, to rise again in the afternoon to £750. Many large investors used the high summer level to take profits, which were reinvested in anything from land and commodities to real estate and other stocks. However, others bought the South Sea Company's stock, one of them the physicist, Isaac Newton. During the

41

stock's early rises he had sold all his South Sea stock, cashing a profit of £7,000. In midsummer he bought again, a transaction which would come to cost him £20,000.

At the beginning of June, South Sea stock rose again and for a short enchanted moment, on 24 June 1720, the security was traded at £1050. As only few were aware, the time was running out for investors. Those in the know were the company's original founders and its Board Chairman, who had used the high summer prices to get rid of their own stock. At the beginning of August this ominous fact began to leak to the general public and the stock price began to fall slowly and steadily.

On 31 August the Management announced that an annual dividend of 50% would be paid for the following twelve years. This would have drained the company completely and the news did not stop investors' increasing unease. On 1 September the stock continued to fall and when it reached £725 two days later, panic broke out. The security went through the floor over the rest of the month and when the company's bank was declared bankrupt on 24 September the fall accelerated. On the last day of the month the share could be bought at a price of £150. In only three months it had fallen by 85%.

In the wake of the South Sea Company's collapse banks and brokers were besieged. Many had raised large loans on portfolios of South Sea Company stock and the financial world was hit by a wave of bankruptcies. The company was finally dissolved in 1855 and its stock converted to bonds. In its 140 years of existence the company never succeeded in trading in the South Seas on any noteworthy scale.

The Wall Street Crash of 1929

The 1929 Wall Street Crash was the conclusion of one of history's largest episodes of mad speculation. For a number of years up to 1924 the American Dow Jones Industrial Index fluctuated within a relatively narrow price interval with strong selling pressure whenever it reached 110. At the end of 1924 stocks broke through this level, with massive rallies to over 150 throughout 1925. This rise in the stock index was a forewarning of a number of good years to come. From 1921, when the stock market was very depressed, to 1928, industrial output rose by 4% annually and by 15% from 1928 to 1929. Inflation was low and new industries sprouted forth everywhere.

This rising optimism, combined with easy access to cheap money, stimulated stock investors and after a temporary reversal in 1926 almost no month passed without a rise in stocks and a new generation of rich investors. This incited more and more to raise broker cash loans in order to invest more than they owned. Investment trusts increased in number as stock investments rose in popularity. From around 40 companies before 1921 the number rose to 160 at the beginning of 1927 and 300 at the end of the same year. From the beginning of 1927 to the autumn of 1929 the total assets of investment trusts increased more than tenfold and there was almost unlimited confidence in these companies.

The most remarkable of these companies was Goldman, Sachs & Company, founding Goldman Sachs Trading Corporation (GSTC) in 1928. Trading Corporation immediately issued stocks for 100 million dollars, sold to the parent company at par. The parent company resold the stock to the public at 104, keeping the profit of 4 million dollars. On 7 February 1929 these stocks were traded at 222.5. Among buyers were GSTC itself, which had bought 57 million dollars of its own stock on 14 March which naturally supported the price. Investors little suspected what was in store for them.

Panic Breaks Out

The crash did not come all at once. But when Babson foresaw a drop of 60 – 80 points in his famous speech of 5 September 1929, the market reacted to the warnings for the first time. The Times Industrial Index fell by 10 points on the same day, and soon there was talk of the "Babson break". After a few days buyers came back in, supported by positive statements from among others Professor Irving Fisher of Yale University, who stated that "Even in the present high markets, the prices of stock have not yet caught up with their real value". Many newspapers also published positive stock exchange comment to alleviate the minor crisis. The stock exchange magazine *Barron's* went as far as to poke fun at Babson in its leader of 9 September describing him as "the Seer from Wellesley Hills". No-one was to be in any doubt who was to blame for the crisis: Babson.

However, prices never reached the old peak and at the end of September there was a new strong drop, this time bringing prices down to the previous summer's peaks. The market once again recovered but without reaching its earlier high, and with trading far below that of the preceding decline. On 15 October Charles Mitchell, Director of National City Bank, stated that all over the country the stock market's health was good. Mitchell was quickly seconded by Professor Fisher, who made the following statement: "I expect to see the stock market a good deal higher than today, within a few months".

On 21 October 1929, however, *Barron's* subscribers could read an article by the chartist William Peter Hamilton in which he warned against the ominous index picture. Indices were breaking through their congestion areas. According to Hamilton, it would be a "strong bearish indication" if the industrial index penetrated below 325.17 and the railway index below 168.26. On the very same day the industrial index broke through the critical level and two days later the railway index followed. The market plummeted with the third highest trading in history of well over six million stocks, and the crash had started.

Shaken – Not Stirred

On 24 October trading reached twelve million stocks. People were gathering in the streets and panic was evident. As the situation was clearly getting out of hand, on 25 October President Hoover made the following statement: "The fundamental business of the country, that is, production and distribution of commodities, is on a sound and prosperous basis."

Hoover's declaration had the same reassuring effect as a pilot announcing that the engine was *not* on fire. Panic grew and in the next few days prices continued to plummet in what seemed to be an endless airpocket. This culminated on 29 October when, in a wave of enforced sales, sixteen million stocks were realized at any price going. The story goes that a messenger at the exchange got the idea of bidding a dollar per share for a lot without buyers – and got his deal. Prices did not start to stabilize until the index reached 224, on 13 November as shown in Figure 2. Those investors who took the risk of buying then because stocks appeared cheap made a grave error. Roosevelt tried to remedy the

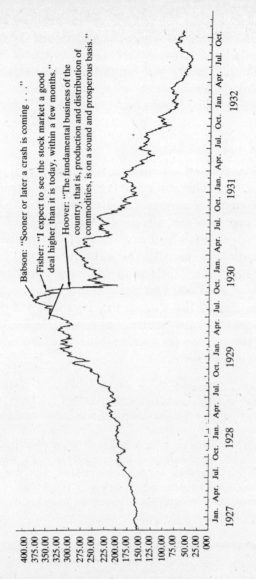

Figure 2. The 1929 crash. When Roger Ward Babson warned of an impending stock exchange crash on 5 September 1929 most people laughed at him. But the crash did come and it was even worse than Babson had predicted. The market dropped by almost 85% over three years. As in Figure 1, the straight line drawn in on the chart is the "neck-line" of a "head & shoulders" formation (cf. Chapter 19). This by and large corresponded to the level which Hamilton believed to be the "last line of defense".

crisis with his so-called "New Deal" policy, resulting in deterioration of the setback to large-scale depression. In 1930 prices started to fall once more, continuing to a bottom of 58 on 8 July 1932. Industrial stocks had lost 85% of their original market value, while Goldman Sachs' investment certificates were to be had for a price of just below two.

But What is the Conclusion?

The obvious conclusion from these three stories is of course, that the market from time to time gets completely dominated by such irrational emotions as hope, greed and fear. But while psychology may explain in part why people react as they do, it does not answer the question why they all react *at the same time*. To find the explantion for this collective aspect, we should instead consult someone with expertise in analyzing complicated movements. In other words, a mathematician.

Imagine that we had a mathematician friend and that we told him our tales and showed him our charts. He would probably consider these events for a while, study the charts carefully, and then look up and ask:

"The prices suddenly collapse, although no specific news has arrived, to explain it, is this correctly understood?"

"That's correct. It starts slowly, then suddenly accelerates and becomes completely hysterical."

"And, how many times have you seen this phenomena?"

"All in all, there have probably been 40 to 50 crashes during the last 500 years. But these are the major crashes, mind you. Apart from these, the events repeat themselves on a small scale. Of the small crashes we have probably seen thousands. In fact, they are a part of our daily life."

Our mathematician friend would then nod and examine the charts again. After a while, he would push down his glasses to the tip of his nose and look us directly in the eye. He would then say:

"The environment in which you operate is what we mathematicians call a dynamic system. I suppose you know that?"

"Yes",

we would answer:

". . . we are familiar with that expression."

"And I suppose we can agree that your dynamic system must have an in-built tendency to systematic instability since it behaves as you have just showed me?"

"That appears to be the conclusion, yes."

"Well, then, there is only one feasible explanation. That is, you have some frightfully strong positive feedback loops at force in your market. And they are possibly combined with the same kind of fractal behavior."

"Fractal behavior and positive feedback loops? What exactly does this mean?"

He would then push the charts over to our side of the table, point at them and say:

"It means that you can probably make short-term forecasts for these markets, if you understand the dynamics. But it also means, that it must be impossible to forecast their long-term behavior."

"Well, that is exactly what we have experienced. But is there a mathematical expression for such behavior?"

"There certainly is. In the mathematical world we call it chaos . . ."

5.

The Third Rule: Chaos Reigns

. . . there is a dramatic conceptual change in realizing that even without
shocks, controlled by its own locally rational logic, the development of a
social system can be completely unpredictable, and that the slightest change
in policy can produce a different type of behavior.

Mosekilde, Larsen & Sterman

It was a dark and stormy night. Thunderclouds loomed and
heavy downpours alternated with violent gusts of wind. The rain
sheeted down in torrents, covering the ground with streaming ri-
verlets of water. As the dawn broke, the icy air was shot by the
first pale rays of the new day and the seeping water began to
evaporate from the soil.

Edward Lorenz's meteorological computer model was a source
of great fascination. Since its completion in 1960 he had spent
many days in his laboratory at the Massachusetts Institute of
Technology, studying its artificial climate patterns. The principle
behind Lorenz's extensive model was actually quite simple:
Based on input values of a snapshot weather picture the computer could calculate a small projection. Data output from this
calculation was the basis for the next calculation, and so on.

The computer's chain calculations could simulate twenty-four
hours per minute. And when it did, Lorenz's computer screen
was the stage for a drama of future events: High pressure alternated with low pressure, hurricanes succeeded calm winds, and
dark and stormy nights followed quickly on lazy summer days.

Lorenz's model was more than just exciting. It was full of great
potential. Perhaps one day it would be able to forecast the
weather several months ahead?

However, on a winter day in 1961, Lorenz made an unusual
and very strange discovery. He had decided to examine a previous simulation, this time with a longer sequence. Instead of starting computation from the beginning he tried a short cut. He
typed in the values which had been printed out from a point in

the middle of his simulation sequence. Then he started up the machine and went down the corridor for a cup of coffee. Little did he know that meanwhile the computer's simulations were acting very strangely indeed.

The Butterfly Effect

When Lorenz returned he was taken by surprise. The computer's calculations, which should have been identical with the previous sequence, did not look right at all. Instead, they deviated more and more and by two months ahead had lost all resemblance to the first simulation.

Initially he attributed this to a fault in the computer but he soon perceived the real reason. His starting point for the chain calculations was a three-decimal printboard. However, the computer's calculator operated with six decimals, which proved to be of vital significance. His own intuition said it was reasonable to ignore the last three decimals in his data input, as these lay at the periphery of what meteorological measuring instruments could register: How important was 1/1000 or less of a degree? But in Lorenz's meteorological computer model these decimals proved to be of the very greatest importance.

Lorenz's discovery was not specific to meteorological projections. It was a general mathematical phenomenon which scientists had never noticed before. It was quickly named the "butterfly effect", as realistic simulations showed that the system's complicated calculations depended greatly on starting values, so greatly that the flap of a butterfly's wings in Brazil could be the factor releasing a tornado in Texas (Lorenz, 1979). Or, in financial terms: A little old lady selling a few bonds in Brussels could cause a crash in Japan! And it emerged that this dependence was not only true of complicated models; the butterfly effect could also be found in simple non-linear models showing instability.

Deterministic Chaos

The consequences of this discovery were revolutionary. Imagine that the earth's surface was covered with a three-dimensional network of weather stations only one foot apart, sending measurements to a central computer every minute. And suppose that

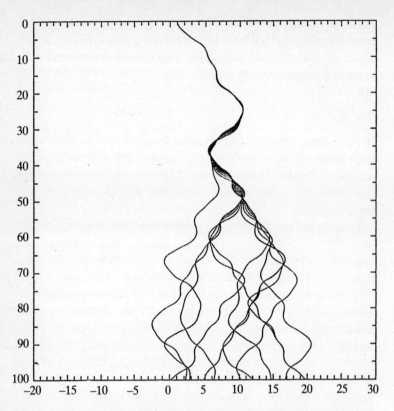

Figure 3. The Butterfly Effect. The graph shows a mathematical simulation of eleven objects sliding down an uneven slope with peaks and troughs arranged in a sinusoidal pattern. The slope is 100 meters long. In the simulation, the objects start with the same velocity of points separated horizontally by only 5 millimeters. After about 30 meters, the separation becomes visible in the graph and after 100 meters two of the objects are 20 meters apart. An interesting detail is the graph's resemblance to cigarette smoke, if you turn it upside down. (Source: Edward N. Lorenz, Center for Meteorology and Physical Oceanography, Cambridge, Massachusetts).

this computer was large enough to accommodate a completely correct model of global weather patterns. Even if that were the case, a reliable weather forecast one month ahead could not be made. Quite against his original intentions, and to everybody's general amazement, Lorenz could prove that it was not, and never would be, possible to make long-term weather forecasts.

The butterfly effect is one detail of a complex of mathematical phenomena, since termed "deterministic chaos". This phenomenon was defined by Chera L. Sayers as follows (1989): "A process is characterized by deterministic chaos if it is generated by a completely deterministic system, yet appears random by standard time series methods." We are surrounded by chaos. Consider the haze of cigarette smoke in a quiet room. Thousands of microscopic smoke particles rise in a tight column, borne by the hot air stream. Then suddenly the column is broken, replaced by turbulent, constantly shifting whirls of smoke. The linear current is transformed into chaos. And this will happen no matter where you are. Or consider a game of football. Not even the smartest expert can predict where the ball will be just ten seconds ahead.

Chaos primarily arises in relations with self-reinforcing mechanisms. Imagine a system where event A leads to event B and event B results in event C. If event C then stimulates event A there is a very simple positive feedback loop.

If we try to outline interrelations in a country's economy, as in meteorology, we will soon encounter complex versions of these mechanisms. Well-known examples are the so-called multiplier and accelerator effects, hoarding, self-enhancement of growth expectations ("keeping up with the Joneses"), the amplification of capital requirements due to labor/capital substitution, etc. Together these numerous feedback loops can mean that systems have no simple equilibrium but instead oscillate by themselves, or perform other complicated movements. Each of these positive feedback loops can contribute to an economic phenomenon's self-reinforcing nature, until it is finally braked by other mechanisms. To describe such systems correctly, one needs complicated non-linear mathematics.

Unpredictability as an Endogenous Property

Nonetheless, economic simulations have traditionally been built on linear models, based on equilibrium functions. These simulations show how all elements of the economy are continually adapting to all the others, but without correct reservations being made for the many positive feedbacks. When feedback loops have been incorporated these have generally been negative loops – those leading to stability – rather than the destabilizing, positive loops. These models have functioned very poorly in

51

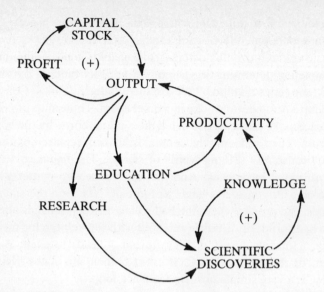

Figure 4. Feedback loop. Example of a double-loop structure of technological innovation in the economic system. Reading through the text we will find a number of similar feedback loops in the stock markets. See chapter 21 for summary. (Source: S. Rasmussen, E. Mosekilde & J. Holst).

practice, traditionally explained by "stochastic exogenous disturbances", as well as lack of accuracy in the models' details.

For this reason the results of the first non-linear computer simulations came as a considerable shock to the academic world. It was suddenly understood that linear models were not only incomplete but could be fundamentally wrong.

But more important was that even theoretically correct non-linear models could lead to total unpredictability even though they were deterministic and structured. This implied that the systems were not only disturbed by stochastic exogenous irregularities but that *unpredictability could be an element of macro-economic systems' own endogenous nature*. How this could be manifested appears for example from the phenomenon called "bifurcations".

Robert May's Mystery

One of the first to describe bifurcations was the Australian biologist Robert May (1976). At the beginning of the 1970s May had developed a mathematical model to simulate development in a fish population. When he entered a low value for one of the formula variables – the fish's reproductive trend – the model showed a specific ecological point of equilibrium for the size of the population. If the population lay outside this point of equilibrium from the outset, it would gradually revert to this point by "subdued oscillations". This result was what anyone could expect. However, if May entered a *high* value, the population size would instead fluctuate constantly up and down and never stabilize. So here the model was showing predictions of a completely different nature: It was showing chaos.

He found this to be something of a mystery and investigated the model's final result for all values of the reproductive trend. The result was remarkable. At the lowest values the fish population would naturally become extinct. If he raised the value of the

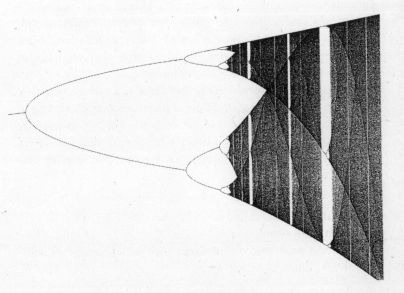

Figure 5. Feigenbaum cascade. The diagram shows how a simple equilibrium bifurcates into still more, finally resulting in chaotic behavior. The bifurcations are created by a simple equation ($X_n + 1 = r \cdot X_n \cdot (1 - X_n)$), where the parameter R (horizontal axis) is gradually increased from 1.68 to 4.00. (Source: E. Mosekilde & J.S. Thomsen, The Technical University of Denmark).

reproductive trend to a certain level the population could survive and a smooth curve showed its equilibrium levels: The higher the reproductive trend, the higher the equilibrium population.

But at a certain level the curve suddenly split into two halves. This meant that the population would oscillate between two *different* equilibrium levels. This phenomenon was called a "bifurcation" and was completely in conflict with traditional notions. If he further increased the reproductive trend the picture became even stranger: The two equilibrium levels became four, then 8, 16, 32 . . . and eventually chaos.

The bifurcation phenomena not only appeared in ecological models. In a 1964 article, "The Problem of Deducing the Climate from the Governing Equations", in *Tellus,* Lorenz introduced the theory that there might be more than one equilibrium climate for the earth. The fact was, and is, that meteorologists' simulation models have a recurring tendency, once in a while, to swing suddenly from the present climate to a global freeze, a state apparently as stable as the current state. Lorenz described such a system, with more than one stable state of equilibrium, as "intransitive". If he was right the known Ice Ages may have been consequences of bifurcations or intransitive characteristics in God's own formula. An interesting thought . . .

The reason for bifurcations is that there is a sudden dramatic change in the dominance of different positive loops. Reverting to economic systems, a theoretical framework was put forward by the researcher Ervin Laszlo (1987), who divided the parameters which can influence loop dominance in economic systems into three categories:

– Technological innovation
– Conflicts and conquests
– Social and economic disturbances such as a shortage of commodities, financial crises, etc.

On the basis of Laszlo's model an economic system can move from an uncomplicated state, e.g. simple cyclical fluctuations, to more complex oscillations between, say two equilibria. This takes place when a parameter is stimulated beyond a certain critical level. Imagine a cartel formed between commodity suppliers. On formation of a price cartel, price movements can shift from a traditional business cycle oscillation to shifting fluctuation between years with extremely high prices (price discipline) and years with extremely low prices (collapse and competition). Other alternative equilibria within one and the same system might be low inflation and hyperinflation or low taxation and high taxation.

The stronger the pressure on a critical parameter, the more bifurcations will arise. This process of staggered bifurcations is called a Feigenbaum cascade after the mathematician of that name. Ultimately such a process leads to chaos.

The Coast of Britain

One of the more peculiar elements in the study of messy systems was painted by the mathematician Benoit Mandelbrot, who was, incidentally, employed by IBM's Research and Development group to study whatever pleased him. Mandelbrot sought to discover pattern and structure in what were normally considered chaotic and irregular natural processes. This is, of course, what most scientists do, but what was fundamentally different about Mandelbrot was his approach to perspective and distance.

"What is the dimension of any object?" "That", Mandelbrot said, "depends upon how far away you are." From a great distance the object will occupy but a single point. From one meter away the object occupies an easily definable space. But as we move closer and closer to the object, the task of measuring the area becomes increasingly complex. Roughness, irregularities and brokenness are soon more evident on the object's surface.

This problem became evident to Mandelbrot when he felt inclined to check the length of border lines according to different maps. He asked a very simple question: "How Long is the Coast of Britain?" The standard response that the value could be checked in an encyclopedia was not acceptable to Mandelbrot. On the contrary, he argued that Britain's coast, or any coast for that matter, was infinitely long, the determining factor being how close you looked: Within the smallest bay you can always find one which is smaller, coves within coves, forever increasing the total coast length.

Mandelbrot thought about these recursive patterns, bays within bays, and termed the phenomenon "Fractals". What is interesting about fractals is that they show that a system can continually repeat its patterns in various scales. It can, in other words, be "self-simulating".

The coast of Britain should of course be considered a static phenomenon. But fractals can also be found in dynamic systems. A useful analogy is a string instrument such as the guitar. We strike the string and it produces a tone. But when we move our finger up the neck of the guitar the pitch rises and we will come to the twelfth fret where the tones begin to repeat themselves at a higher octave. We have a phenomenon where the harmonic system is in essence repeating itself on different scales. It is – in other words – self-simulating.

Or, consider the movements of the ocean. On the surface of the water we find tiny ripples, larger ripples and waves, with every seventh wave often being larger than the rest. If the friction of the wind on the water causes these phenomena, that is the ripples, waves, "superwaves", etc., then one may speak of these as fractal phenomena. But this term is justified only if their cause is, in fact, the wind and nothing else.

The unique element in Mandelbrot's method was that he did not seek to study just part of the phenomenon within well-defined limits (e.g. chemists are not allowed to dabble in the world of the nuclear physicist, even though the underlying phenomena are the same), but that he sought to understand the whole structure in terms of the branching it produced. In the same manner, we can choose to view ripples as "small waves" – given points in an overall recursive structure caused by the wind. But what about the ebb and flow of the tide? Is this also caused by the fractal phenomenon? While it would appear so on the surface, we know in actuality it is caused by the gravitational pull of the moon.

The important point is that we regularly find economic and financial phenomena which repeat themselves on different scales. We will see a number of such phenomena later in the book. But occasionally you will also find phenomena which may *appear* to be fractal, but are, in fact, just as independent as the tide and the waves in the sea. Among these are the various business cycles for example.

Economic and Financial Chaos

It appears intuitively correct that economic and financial equilibrium systems are subject to fractal phenomena, butterfly effects and bifurcations. Or, in other words: to chaos. Nonetheless, it took a very long time for theoretical economists to start to investigate chaos phenomena. But at the beginning of the 1980s researchers seriously became engaged in investigating economic chaos indicators and in the course of a few years a series of important observations were made (see Ploeg 1985, Chiarella 1986, Chen 1986, Lorenz 1987, Brock & Sayers 1987, Rasmussen & Mosekilde 1988). The further we dig, the more signs we find of patterns to indicate chaos phenomena in economic systems.

There is now every indication that systematic endogenous unpredictability exists in many economic and financial subsystems. Even where dampening mechanisms are strong or chaos does not appear in the current parameter interval, impulses from other chaotic subsystems will give rise to considerable uncertainty. In metaphorical terms the problem can be compared with a tree stump passing through the rapids. Even if we knew all there was to know about fluid dynamics, water and the shape of the riverbed, we could never calculate the trunk's path for more than a few meters at a time. It would be equally impossible to determine where it came from on the basis of its current position. A similar situation applies to the economy.

Therefore there is growing recognition that deterministic chaos can be an important reason for the abysmal value of long-term economic forecasts, and that linear models can give a poor image of reality. It is also clear that dynamic systems will often repeat the same phenomenon in different scales, thus adding further to the challenge of forecasting.

The Question of Dimension

An important aspect regarding chaos is the question of "dimension". This word is used by mathematicians to describe how complicated a dynamic system's behavior is. Although it is a purely mathematical expression, dimension can be explained (in popular terms) as indicating the number of past observations you need in order to predict the next movement.

If the system makes a simple, sinus-oscillation, prediction becomes a piece of cake and dimension will be zero. But if we have a very large number of interrelated, positive and negative feedbacks, the dimension rises sharply and you will need a lot of data to "decode" through mathematics where you are in the process. When dimension becomes very high, even a lot of back-data will not help you anymore; however, in that case it becomes impossible to prove through mathematical tests the presence of non-random dynamics. In the words of William A. Brock (1990): "In practise it is impossible to ever tell whether data is generated by a high-dimensional deterministic system or a stochastic system".

As science stands today, it is pretty clear that the financial markets are in fact dominated by strong loops generating a high-dimensional mathematically difficult-to-decode chaos. This is evidenced partly by mathematical tests showing that there is "something" which is not random – you just cannot nail down what it is. Partly it has been evidenced by our recurring crashes, which intuitively prove the presence of strong feedback loops. But what is very important to note is that even if a computer cannot set a finger on what the systematic dynamics is – we can. How? Simply by studying the loops separately and identifying in each case exactly what it will take to trigger them.

Economic Understanding Is Not Irrelevant

If high-dimensional chaos is what we have, analysts' attempts to calculate true value begins to look like attempted alchemy. Keeping in mind that a stock's true value is the discounted value of all future profits in the company, this definition becomes almost comical if we can actually foresee only a year, six months or less. Comical because it is generally accepted that price fluctuations unrelated to true value can be of considerably more importance over one year than for example the company's ability to pay dividends.

Perhaps we should recall Keynes's earlier cited description of the behavior of professional experts:

. . . most of these persons are, in fact, largely concerned, not with making superior long-term forecasts of the probable yield of an investment over its whole life, but with foreseeing changes in the conventional basis of valuation a short time ahead of the general public.

The successful speculator doesn't behave in this way because he has a profound knowledge of the economy's bifurcations, butterfly effects and intransitivities. It is acquired behavior selected by a survival of the fittest and learnt by trial and error. This behavior is based on the simple experience that short-term prediction is fairly easy, while fighting the dark forces of time and ignorance is often impossible.

The conclusion is *not* that economic insight is irrelevant for stock trading – by no means. As will be shown later, the identification of macro-economic cycles and the interpretation of delicate titbits of micro-economic information are indeed important instruments.

The essence of the chaos phenomenon is that attempts to predict long chains of events, to make long-term, quantitative prognoses or to calculate "true value" accurately are often close to absurd. Even though Keynes can hardly have been familiar with the deeper consequences of non-linear mathematics he was absolutely right to draw the following conclusion in his *General Theory*:

Investment based on genuine long-term expectation is so difficult today as to be scarcely practicable. He who attempts it must surely lead much more laborious days and run greater risks than he who tries to guess better than the crowd how the crowd will behave; and given equal intelligence he may make more disastrous mistakes.

6.

The Fourth Rule: Charts are Self-fulfilling

Never follow the crowd.

Bernard Baruch

. . . the fact is that it is really quite comfy to be part of the crowd.

"Adam Smith"

True or not, the story goes that John Mendelson, technical analyst at stockbrokers Dean Witter Reynolds, USA, came to the conclusion that the stock market would drop while he was out fishing with his son.

Irrespective of how he reached this conclusion it is a fact that at the company's strategy meeting the following Monday morning he convinced the company's sixty salesmen that the market had peaked. After the meeting everybody rushed to find a phone. Before the end of the day the message had spread to around 600 institutional investors and Dow Jones Industrials had dropped 62 points. In this way one man provoked one of these terrible "air pockets" in the market. This was on 7 July 1986.

After a month in a mild state of shock the market began to rise again. This climb continued to a level around the previous top and prices consolidated at this level. Nobody could know that a new and larger shock was on its way.

During trading in Europe on Thursday 11 September 1986 there was talk of rising inflation in the USA. Futures contracts on American government bonds (T-bond futures) dropped but this decline was not very strong compared to the previous seven days. However, on the stock market the barometer had moved to storm.

When the USA opened, considerable sales of Standard & Poor's 500 index futures contracts commenced, quickly bringing them two to four points below the price of the 500 underlying stocks. This drop activated a series of the common computer-based trading systems, ordering sale of stocks. However, sales

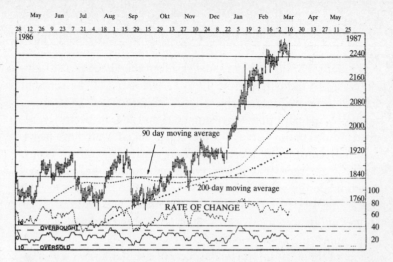

Figure 6. Dow Jones Industrials. The chart shows daily trading ranges and close prices for the Industrial Average May 1986 to March 1987, where the two major drops in 1986 should be noted. The chart also shows 90 and 200-day moving averages, rate of change and overbought/oversold. These indicators are explained later in the book. (Chart: Investment Research of Cambridge.)

pressure on the underlying stocks brought futures prices further down and a self-reinforcing trend continued until the industrial index had dropped 87 points at close of trading. The day after this "Black Thursday" the index fell by a further 34 points, and was then supported at the previous troughs.

In the chart in Figure 6 "Black Monday" and "Black Thursday" are not hard to spot.

Reasons for Buying and Selling

Shortly after Black Thursday US economist Robert J. Schiller (1986) sent out a questionnaire to 175 institutional investors and 125 large individual investors throughout the country, selected on a random basis. He put the question "what reasons to buy or sell did you have during this period?"

Out of the 113 replies he received, not one stated the economic news and rumors to which the press had attributed the market's drop. In fact only three of the 113 respondents referred to concrete financial news or rumors at all. What was emphasized most was something completely different: the market's

drop in itself. People were not selling due to fears of rising inflation. They were selling because the market was beginning to
drop.

Schiller (1987) found the same result in the October 1987 global crash. In the period from 19 to 23 October 1987 he sent out
2,000 questionnaires to private stock investors and 1,000 questionnaires to institutional investors; 605 and 284, respectively, replied. In this major survey Schiller again asked what news investors had considered most important during the price drops.
Again it emerged that it was not economic and political news
which made the greatest impression, but price movements. The
preceding drops in bonds and stock prices had exerted a far
greater influence on investors than any of the individual news
items appearing in the media.

One of the most interesting aspects of Schiller's survey was investors' views of "true value". He first asked whether they had
been net buyers or sellers (or neutral) from 12 September to 12
October, i.e. up to the crash. Then he asked whether in the same
period they had considered the market to be overvalued in relation to fundamental value. When the replies were assessed this
paradoxical picture emerged: No less than 68.1% of private investors and 93.1% of institutional investors buying up to the
crash had believed the market to be overvalued in the same period. *Sic transit* "true value". It was just as interesting that more
than 10% stated that in the period up to the crash they had followed a defined stop-loss policy (i.e. they sold if prices fell below
a certain level). Often the individual motive for this policy will be
that the investor cannot afford a loss, with the consequence that
critical price falls release sale orders.

Schiller also asked whether respondents had been personally
affected by the market's drop during its 200-day moving average,
or equivalent "long-term trendlines", up to the crash. To this
37.3% of private investors and 33.3% of professional investors
replied in the affirmative, again illustrating how price movements in themselves can motivate people to buy or sell.

Keynes and the Beauty Contest

This positive feedback loop, where everybody concentrates on
guessing what everybody else is going to do is best described in

Keynes' famous "Beauty Contest Metaphor". Here he compares the stock market with US newspaper competitions, where competitors try to choose the picture they believe most will prefer from among 100 female portraits:

> It is not a case of choosing those which, to the best of one's judgement, are really the prettiest, nor even those which average opinion genuinely thinks the prettiest. We have reached the third degree where we devote our intelligences to anticipating what average opinion expects the average opinion to be. And there are some, I believe, who practise the fourth, fifth and higher degrees.

We have not got there yet, but there is no doubt that on many of today's most speculative markets patterns can only be explained by the fact that thousands of market investors have drawn in the same lines on the same charts or shoved the same floppy-disk into their PCs. Some of the dealers see the patterns for which logical hypothesis can be formulated. Others understand nothing but look for patterns anyway. But even if a pattern is entirely co-

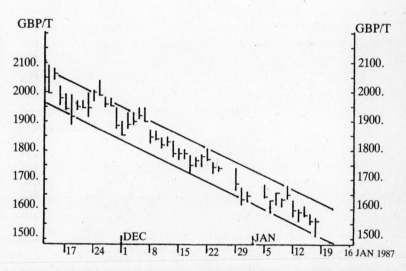

Figure 7. Coffee Futures Contracts. The figure shows the coffee futures price trend around 1986/87. As will be seen, the market is moving within a well-defined parallelogram, or "channel". When people discover this phenomenon on their charts it becomes self-fulfilling. Note that from the outset the channel is delineated only by market close prices.

incidal, it may start generating valid signals if enough dealers use it.

While the media will try to explain price movements with different political and economic events, the dealers' reasons will be very different: "We're trading in a channel", they will say or "we're testing a resistance line" or "we've just broken the 20-day moving average, but tomorrow we'll go out because Rate of Change will exceed 90." (These expressions will be explained later in Chapters 18 and 20.) Figures 7 and 8 show how the market looks.

Therefore part of the truth behind the widespread use of chart analysis is that it is not just a technique to read the mind of the market. Sometimes it is the analyses that create the psychology. It must be remembered that there is a coda to the rule, however, which is that if (almost) everybody has made the same analysis it will no longer be self-reinforcing, but self-destructive.

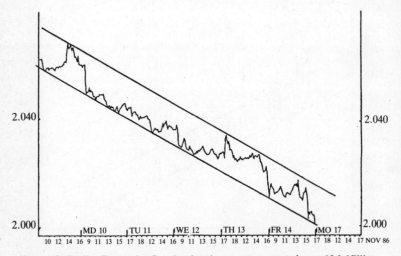

Figure 8. Dollar/D-mark. On the foreign currency market self-fulfilling formations are just as common as on futures markets. The figure shows how the price for dollar against D-mark moved in a well-defined channel over seven days in November 1986, when the bottom was tested thirteen times.

64

Self-Destructing Chart Signals

Imagine a market dominated by 1,000 well-funded investors, of whom 900 are chartists thinking synchronously. The last 100 are fundamentalists. All are bullish, all are buying and the market is rising steadily. But at a specific price, e.g. an old top, all 900 chartists intend to go out, i.e. sell. As this chartpoint is approached, more and more of the 900 chartists stop buying and finally only the 100 poor fundamentalists are still in. When the chartpoint is finally reached, 900 sale orders are given at one time and the price plummets. As there is a dearth of buyers, many sale orders are executed at a much lower point than they had intended.

The next time the market rises, the 100 fundamentalists have learnt their lesson and decided to go out if the old top is reached again. All 1,000 investors are chartists, all staring at exactly the same point. But two things have changed: Firstly, nobody wants to buy in the last section before the point, and secondly, many decide to go out earlier to be sure that their sale order is effected. So the point is never reached and the chart signal has destroyed itself.

In some cases charts can become self-destructive for a different reason. In "thin" markets one or several market operators use a massive order to deliberately trade the price through an important psychological level, to release an avalanche of limited stop-loss orders. If for example 160 is an important psychological price many investors will have instructed their brokers to sell immediately if the price falls below this level. In a thin market large investors press the price down below this level, effect all limited stop-loss sale orders and finally press the price back up above the critical point, all with the consequence of a Very Profitable Turnover. When all the other chartists report for work the next morning the market lies where they expected, but the little drama has thrust them out anyhow.

In practice chartists usually work with many individual methods and priorities, and often make up only a limited section of those involved in the market. As long as this is the case anonymous fraternities of chartists, who have never met, can nonetheless guess each other's thoughts and together control the market into wonderful patterns and formations. And each time the game will continue to the point where it gets obvious to everyone and patterns consequently dissolve of themselves. But meanwhile new fraternities will have begun to see new patterns developing and . . .

No wonder that many, finally realizing the true nature of the market, might agree with Sir Robert Falcon Scott's exclamation on finally reaching the South Pole: "Great God! This is an awful place!"

III

The Tree of
Knowledge

We want a few mad people now. See where the sane ones have landed us.
George Bernard Shaw

7.

An Investment Philosophy

One man's noise is another man's signal.

Preben Gudmandsen

As we have now studied the basic market essentials, it is time to systematize our thoughts a little. Let us begin with a loose definition of the problem.

Systems and Surprises

Regardless of philosophic orientation, most people will probably acknowledge a frame of reference where we distinguish between two dynamic systems: one economic, which is influenced by stochastic exogenous disturbances, and one financial:

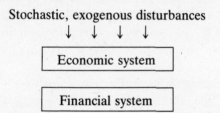

The exogenous disturbances are, for example, when Reagan is shot or the Berlin Wall is brought down. This includes all factors which cannot be predicted by the economic model. The more limited you have defined your economic system, the more of the daily events you will regard as exogenous disturbances. If you don't have any model at all, everything will be a disturbance.

As we have defined these disturbances as the unpredictable, let's leave them for the moment to concentrate on our two systems. How does one predict their interaction and their independent behavior, respectively?

Markets as Barometers

Let us start with the classic academic assumption which we dealt with in Chapter 3: "The Efficient Market Hypothesis" ("The Markets are Ahead"). One assumption here is that the markets are ahead of the economy and thus function as economic barometers:

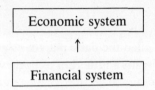

As described in Chapter 3, this point of view is justified on the large macro-economic systems. But although it is substantial, it is not omnipotent. Even where the markets are our best economic barometers (e.g. the stock market as a leading indicator), their efficiency is not very impressive. Because of chaos effects, exogenous shocks and the madness of crowds, speculators are only able to see some broad intervals of probability within which the prices should be. The only thing the Efficient Market Hypothesis guarantees us is consequently that the prices will fluctuate within these intervals with the possibility of a crash between top and bottom.

But what can we then use this point of view for?

"Nothing", would the cynic say. "That a market is efficient is only a complication." Here, however, the cynic is wrong, because if you think about it, you will realize that the hypothesis opens an interesting strategic possibility. Sure, like what?

Well, in the words of Hamilton, the efficient markets are an expression for coming events casting their shadows before. If we, in these coming events, are able to identify a substantial systematic and continuing sequence of events which are discounted by a corresponding substantial sequence of events in the financial barometers, then we have a usable tool. Here the conscious person will of course immediately think about the business cycle. This is actually reflected by a systematic phase shift in the financial markets: time shifts of bull and bear markets in money rates, bonds, stocks, commodities and precious metals. If we reduce our economic subsystem to a cyclical model (which is hereby done), we are able to base the strategic assumption of our investment model on this long-term but basic phenomenon.

The Assumption of Fundamental Analysis

Let us now move away from barometers. In opposition to the notion that the markets are ahead is the assumption of fundamental analysis. The point here is that it takes infinite energy to make the markets completely efficient. As the human race does not have infinite energy, there must be untapped arbitrage possibilities; you just need to look hard.

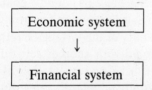

This is true, of course, but holds more for micro-economic issues than for the more actively traded. Fundamental analysis can be illuminating if you use it in an investment niche, but in the big liquid markets it is rather doubtful. We will therefore tip our hats and move on to the third assumption: The theory of deterministic chaos.

The Chaotic Angle

The third school is embodied in assumptions of systematic instability, of feedback loops and deterministic chaos. According to these assumptions, each subsystem is, in part, living its own messy life with myriads of feedback loops.

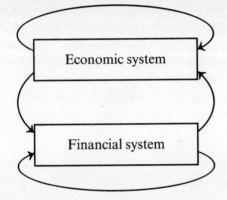

The economy's business cycles, together with the irrationality of the financial markets and numerous crashes, – as already stated in Chapter 5 – must be taken as strong indications of the dominant role played by feedback loops and chaos. Furthermore, it holds that feedback mechanisms not only dominate in each of the two subsystems (obviously they are far stronger in the financial system, i.e. the volatility of the system), but that the two systems are also interconnected with another set of feedback loops via the self-validating effect (e.g. revaluation of a currency at 5% leads to falling inflation and interest rates which perhaps, over a few years, will more than compensate for the initial drop in competitive situation). The more the investor believes in this point of view the more meaningless it becomes to squander time on economic analysis. Chaos is an invitation to a "beating the gun" tactic because it is infinitely easier to forecast a chaotic system in the short-term than in the long-term.

Strategy and Tactic

The consequences of our observations in Chapters 3–6 are thus that in large liquid markets you can operate exclusively by analysing the financial charts. Specifically, you can operate with an economic cycle diverted strategy, analyzed via the behavior of the financial system, combined with a non-economic "beating the gun" oriented tactic.

This is rather interesting because it forces us to renounce one of the most fundamental instincts of the classical economist: the desire to seek correct equilibriums. When the market is ahead of the economy on the one hand, and characterized by the ever-returning irrationality, deterministic chaos and the use of self-reenforcing charts on the other, the short-term dynamics become so important that they appear . . . well . . . most important.

Put in another way, our observation invites us to forget the equilibria and instead to use the instability as our analytical fundamental. Our analysis is hereby an exposure of those mechanisms which can initiate and suppress the movements in the market's endless fluctuations. The focus thus becomes the phenomena which are, in more traditional thinking, brushed aside as noise.

But How Do We Analyse the Noise?

Analyzing the noise can be tackled in many ways, but a natural approach is to split the analysis into three steps:

- First, we can analyse the *dispositions* which occur in the markets: how the money flows and how the financial prices move in comparison to each other. This we will do in Chapters 9–12.
- Secondly, we can analyse how bits of *information*, for instance investment recommendations, are disseminated in the market. Chapters 13–16 are devoted to those aspects.
- Finally, we can concentrate on investigating the investors' *decision-making process*, how they react in different situations and why. This aspect will be analyzed in Chapters 17–21.

But before we begin, in the next chapter we will consider where our analytical tools come from and who the first chartists were.

8.

The First Chartists

Can a surgeon write a few simple rules which would enable a banker to remove an appendix from a broker?

Robert Rhea

Today's knowledge of stock markets has developed in a curious way. While the academic world has been constantly searching for general theories that could be "proven", the practitioners of the marketplace have concentrated on sub-theories that are difficult to verify scientifically but easy to use. Contributors to this scientific "fall from grace" have been very different, but with one thing in common: They have all used charts as their most important analysis tool.

Whispering Candles

Nobody knows today when charts were first used to analyze financial markets. The oldest documentation we have goes back to the Japanese rice market, however.

In 1730 the Japanese introduced standardized trading in forward rice contracts. These contracts were identical with the commodities futures traded on many exchanges today, with one single exception: It was not possible to request physical delivery of the goods. A forward contract could be bought and it could be sold, but it could not be exchanged for a delivery of rice. However, a problem soon arose: While cash rice prices fluctuated only little, forward contracts began to show large fluctuation, which proved to be permanent. In 1869 this became too much for the government and the decision was taken to close the forward market.

But then something very interesting ensued: As soon as the forward market had been closed the *physical* market began to fluctuate violently. After two years total chaos reigned and the

74

government reopened forward trading. Now forward contracts were pegged to the underlying market by demand for physical delivery of each forward contract, after which the market became relatively stable.

What this taught Japanese speculators was that stock prices do not just express simple supply and demand equilibria. They also include a psychological element. The consequence was that dealers developed a number of methods for exploiting this psychology. They soon began to draw charts of price movements, creating rules for interpretation of market movements. These methods are still used in the Far East and the special symbols plotted on the graphs are called "whispering candles".

Meanwhile in the West

In the West charting first appeared in the USA in the 1880s in a form called the "book method". Only a minority used this instrument and there was no single explanation of how the diagrams

Figure 9. Charles Henry Dow (1850–1902). Charles Dow made the greatest contribution to understanding stock market movements. His primary interest was using stock market analyses to forecast the economy, but in practice stockdealers have used his theories far more than economists. His models gave clear warnings of both the 1929 and 1987 crashes. (Photo by kind permission of Dow Jones & Co., Inc.)

75

should be interpreted. However, in 1900–1902 the *Wall Street Journal* published a series of relatively unnoticed articles on mechanisms in stock price movements. The author was the newspaper's own founder and editor-in-chief, *Charles Henry Dow*, who in addition to this newspaper had founded the famous Dow Jones financial news service.

Dow's successor to the editorial post, William Peter Hamilton, described him as an "ultra-conservative", cool, competent and intelligent man who "knew his business" and never allowed anything at all to aggravate him. For a period of his life he had a seat on the New York Stock Exchange and therefore had a good practical insight into stock trading. Unfortunately, he died in 1902, only 52 years old, and therefore never published any other material on his observations than the aforementioned newspaper articles. However, these observations were later summarized into what we today call "Dow Theory", which must still be considered one of the most important contributions to our understanding of the markets.

What Dow Discovered

One of Dow's innovations was that he (in 1884) had begun drawing up an index of price development for a group of leading stocks. Later, in 1896, he amalgamated a number of industrial stocks to form "The Industrial Average", and a number of railway shares to form "The Rail Average" (later amended to the "Transportation Index"). This provided him with a valuable analysis tool in studying the idiosyncrasies of the market and formulating his rules.

Dow Theory comprises the following six observations:

1. *Stock indices discount everything in advance*. Together, market participants hold all information of importance for interpreting a stock value, and this knowledge is discounted in the market's price fluctuations. This "Efficient Market Hypothesis" was described in more detail in Chapter 3.
2. *The market has three movements*, described as "primary", "secondary" and "tertiary". Price fluctuations are always a

consequence of these three types of movement, which act simultaneously but not necessarily in the same direction.

The largest movements are *primary*, which are trends extending over several years. A primary bull market starts when all the worst information has been discounted in price formation and the first hopes for the future begin to germinate. This is called the "first phase" of the bull market. In the market's "second phase" these hopes are confirmed and the economy shows an actual improvement. The "third phase" of the primary trend reflects exaggerated optimism without any foundation in reality. A primary bear market has the same three phases, but vice versa.

A *secondary* movement lasts from three weeks to several months, often comprising a correction of one-third to two-thirds of the preceding primary phase.

A *tertiary* movement lasts for less than three weeks. It is relatively sensitive to stochastic exogenous disturbances and has little or no relevance to prediction of other movements. Considerations and applications for the markets' three movements are given in later chapters.

3. *Support and resistance areas give price signals*. When prices fluctuate in a narrow interval for two to three weeks or longer there can be an "accumulation" of securities among the few professionals (before an increase) or a "distribution" of securities to the many amateurs (before a drop). The concept of accumulation and distribution is discussed in Chapters 15, 16 and 21.

4. *Volume supports price*. The significance of a price movement as a signal is strengthened if it appears at high volume (turnover). Volume follows the trend direction and if volume is high when the market rises and poor when it drops this will indicate that the market will go up. We will deal further with volume in Chapters 18–21.

5. *A trend must be confirmed by peaks and troughs*. A rising trend is intact as long as all new peaks and troughs are rising. A falling trend is correspondingly intact for as long as all peaks and troughs are falling. This simple rule is illustrated and explained in Chapter 18.

6. *Both indices must confirm a stock trend*. An initial trend in a stock market does not become credible until both the Indu-

strials Index and Transportation Index have started the trend movement. Chapter 12 elaborates on this aspect.

One reason that Dow's theories were remembered by posterity is that an acquaintance, S. A. Nelson, in 1903 published *The ABC of Stock Market Speculation*, in which he gathered a number of Dow's theories and in which he was the first to introduce the concept of "Dow Theory".

In 1921 William Peter Hamilton further developed Dow's theory in *The Stock Market Barometer*, also inspired by Babson's "Babson chart" system. However, Hamilton's frequent articles in the *Wall Street Journal* and *Barron's* attracted more and more attention. With impressive accuracy, and using Dow's rules, he predicted market movements. Best-known of these articles was a series in which he analyzed speculator James R. Keenes's manipulation of US Steel stock. Hamilton revealed Keenes's tactics so accurately that Keenes was convinced that Hamilton was using a spy in his organization. But in *The Stock Market Barometer* Hamilton explained to an amazed public how his only tool had been his charts and Dow's six rules.

Hamilton's last articles were written for a panic-stricken market. On 21 October the day before the start of the major stock exchange crash in 1929, he wrote an article in *Barron's* in which he warned against the psychological situation. The stock index levels he stated as potential psychological reversal points were penetrated on the following days. Under the headline "A Turn in the Tide" he wrote four days later in the *Wall Street Journal*, (again referring to Dow's rules) that the bull market had come to a definitive end and that the stock market's trend reversal signaled an economic downturn. He was alone in this opinion but, as we know today, it proved to be startlingly true. His last article was written on 3 September of the same year, entitled "Coming to Rest". This heading was prophetic in more than one sense: Hamilton died six days later.

In 1932, thirty years after Dow's death, there followed a further reviewed, structured amplification of Dow's and Hamilton's methods and their application, in *Dow Theory* by Robert Rhea, who also published *The Story of the Averages*.

In 1851 the French economist Clement Juglar published investigations of a strange phenomenon he had analyzed. Marriages, births and deaths in France appeared to move in harmonious cycles. He became engrossed in this wave phenomenon and in the following years began to investigate whether similar observations could be made for the economy.

This proved to be the case, and in 1860 he published *Des Crises Commerciales et leur Retour Periodique en France, en Angleterre, et aux Etats-Units*. This rather off-putting title belonged to a work which was epoch-making in both form and conclusions. Previously historical crises and revivals had been explained solely by sets of specific economic events. However, Juglar attached less importance to these individual explanations and instead found that there appeared to be systematic waves in the economy, underlying all the sporadic events, expressing something very fundamental about the behavior of people and companies. According to his observations there was an average of 9.2 years between each peak and trough in the economic cycle. Juglar's theories won much support, but as the model details were considered further, more and more deviant patterns were found which weakened what originally appeared to be a clear pattern.

In 1923 another economist, Joseph Kitchin, published the article "Cycles and Trends in Economic Factors" in *Review of Economic Statistics*, with a description of short-term fluctuations in prices, interest rates and stock markets prevalent in the USA and Britain since 1871. These cycles had around 41 months between each top and bottom. Kitchin also noted that "two to three" of these cycles appeared to constitute elements of a larger cycle (corresponding to that of Juglar). Kitchin explained these cycles by for example fluctuations in companies' building up of inventories.

With the description of these patterns the road was paved for a new opinion: Juglar had been right that there were underlying cyclical movements in the economy (and as we will see later, in financial markets) but he had overlooked that at one and the same time there were several prevailing cycles overlapping each other.

Only two years after Kitchin had issued his famous article on short cycles, the Russian economist Nikolay D. Kondratieff published an article on long economic cycles in *Voprosy Konyunktury* (No. 1, 1925). In 1926 he published a second article under the title "Die Langen Wellen der Konjunktur" in *Arkiv für Sozialwissenschaft* in Germany.

The material submitted by Kondratieff in these two articles was based on surveys of long-term movements in commodity prices, interest rates, wages, foreign trade, coal production, oil consumption, savings and lead and pig iron production in the UK, France and the USA. From his time series, the oldest starting in 1780, Kondratieff had been able to read an apparent international economic cycle with a gap of 48–54 years between each peak and trough. Material for only 145 years gave him little empirical substantiation of his theory. However, events on financial markets and in the global economy since his article was published have in fact matched the pattern rather well, so the theory continues to be interesting for the investor. That his conclusions were not very popular in his home country is another matter. He died in a work camp in Siberia.

Best known, however, is the book *Business Cycles* (1939) by the Austrian Joseph Schumpeter. This weighty volume is a description of cyclical movements in the economy, interest rates and stock prices. Schumpeter was a professor at Harvard University and also Austria's Finance Minister for a period. When he published his book he had been working for thirty years on studies of cyclical movements in the economy. From the outset, like Juglar, he had believed in a simple cyclical movement but gradually he reached the conclusion that there were *three* prevailing cycles, which he termed Kitchin, Juglar and Kondratieff. These three cycles were not the only ones he identified, but he believed that three overlapping cycles in his model provided the best compromise between clarity and truth.

Schumpeter was no great mathematician, for which reason his models have since been further developed by a number of mathematicians and physicists. (As physicists are generally very good at maths, they often clean up where economists fail). The most important addition to the findings of Schumpeter is probably the concept of deterministic chaos, which means that when several of Schumpeter's cycles are in action at the same time, the resulting movement gets rather complicated.

After the first well-known theories had found their disciples, an ever-increasing volume of books and articles on capital market analysis began to appear. Some of these developed logical hypotheses and then illustrated whether they were substantiated empirically, and others endeavored to rationalize after the fact, with different degrees of mysticism and superstition.

A "Hemline indicator" was invented, relating the stock market to the length of women's dresses (buy when they are long, sell when they are short). Books were written such as *An Inquiry into the Effect of Sunspot Activity on the Stock Market* (the market swings depending on magnetic radiation from sunspots). A veritable deluge of automatic trading systems was developed, matched by an equivalent flood of scientific reports to prove the inapplicability of these systems.

But in 1948 *Technical Analysis of Stock Trends* was published in the USA. This added an important element to market analysis. Its authors, R. D. Edwards & J. Magee had studied innumerable individual stock charts over many years and found a number of characteristic patterns (or what we call "formations") which recurred over and over and turned out to have prognosis value. All these phenomena were carefully described and classified, and the methods are still essential reading for anybody trading on charts.

In connection with the study of isolated price movements operators made a series of giant leaps forward with the introduction of personal computers in the 1970s. In this period British financial advisor Brian Marber launched the concepts "golden cross" and "death cross" for computer-based "moving averages"-analyses of price series.

On the subject of computer graphics, J.W. Wilder should also be mentioned. In his book *New Concepts in Technical Trading Systems* from 1978, Wilder described a formula he called the "Relative Strength Index" which was an efficient reflection of the oscillation of the market mood between exaggerated optimism and extreme pessimism. One of the most interesting aspects of Wilder's formula is that even though it is very new and is intended for use in computers it also functions excellently when used to analyze charts from around the turn of the century or earlier.

A peculiar curiosity of price graphics is that it was not before the 1980s, after anybody and everybody had learned graphic price analysis, that somebody actually sat down to explain its actual background. One pioneer was American economist Robert Schiller, who was the first to draw attention to the link between market phenomena and the special psychological/sociological complex of theories concerning human attitudes.

Dissemination of Information

Another important tool is interpretation of the dissemination of information and attitudes. The principle behind this is Charles Dow's thoughts on "distribution" and "accumulation" (cf. his third rule). In practice, distribution and accumulation processes had to be a consequence of the way information and attitudes were disseminated from the large expert operators to the small amateurs.

A basic tenet was laid down by Garfield A. Drew, who in the 1940s investigated publicly accessible stock trading statistics comprising under 100 securities, i.c. what were described as "odd-lotters". Drew found that odd-lotters, typically small, less professional market operators, were generally very unlucky, so often you could be successful simply by doing the opposite of what they did. In 1959 Drew published a collection of diagrams showing these odd-lotters' market behavior, which documented his theory (*Drew Odd Lot Indexes Daily 1936–1958 Inclusive, Monthly 1920–1958 Inclusive*).

However, H. B. Neill was better known than Drew. In 1954, in *The Art of Contrary Opinion*, Neill introduced the Contrary Opinion concept, which is the special art of consistently trying to think the opposite of the majority. Neill apparently did not understand his own theory and gave no quantitative methods for putting his ideas into practice. It was not before 1963, when A.W. Cohen began to compile statistics of different newsletters'

Figure 10. Sources of the financial market analysis practiced today. One ▶ simple theory is not enough for an understanding of the capital market. Many different factors are involved, so a number of subtheories must be combined.

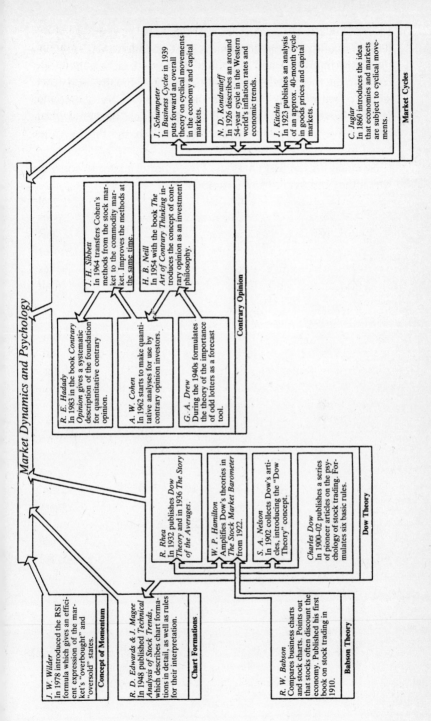

Market Dynamics and Psychology

Market Cycles

J. Schumpeter
In *Business Cycles* in 1939 puts forward an overall theory on cyclical movements in the economy and capital markets.

N. D. Kondratieff
In 1926 describes an around 54-year cycle in the Western world's inflation rates and economic trends.

J. Kitchin
In 1923 publishes an analysis of an approx. 40-month cycle in goods prices and capital markets.

C. Juglar
In 1860 introduces the idea that economies and markets are subject to cyclical movements.

Contrary Opinion

J. H. Sibbett
In 1964 transfers Cohen's methods from the stock market to the commodity market. Improves the methods at the same time.

H. B. Neill
In 1954 with the book *The Art of Contrary Thinking* introduces the concept of contrary opinion as an investment philosophy.

R. E. Hadady
In 1983 in the book *Contrary Opinion* gives a systematic description of the foundation for quantitative contrary opinion.

A. W. Cohen
In 1962 starts to make quantitative analyses for use by contrary opinion investors.

G. A. Drew
During the 1940s formulates the theory of the importance of odd lotters as a forecast tool.

Concept of Momentum

J. W. Wilder
In 1978 introduced the RSI formula which gives an efficient expression of the market's "overbought" and "oversold" states.

Chart Formations

R. D. Edwards & J. Magee
In 1948 published *Technical Analysis of Stock Trends*, which describes chart formations in detail, as well as rules for their interpretation.

Dow Theory

R. Rhea
In 1932 publishes *Dow Theory* and in 1936 *The Story of the Averages*.

W. P. Hamilton
Amplifies Dow's theories in *The Stock Market Barometer* from 1922.

S. A. Nelson
In 1902 collects Dow's articles, introducing the "Dow Theory" concept.

Charles Dow
In 1900–02 publishes a series of pioneer articles on the psychology of stock trading. Formulates six basic rules.

Babson Theory

R. W. Babson
Compares business charts and stock charts. Points out that stocks often discount the economy. Published his first book on stock trading in 1910.

recommendations to the stock market, that the foundation was laid for quantitative application. After Cohen followed J. H. Sibbet, who improved and simplified Cohen's practical methods, transferring them to the commodities market. Finally, as a provisional conclusion, in 1983 came the book *Contrary Opinion* by R. E. Hadady which stipulated the theoretical background for quantitative and qualitative work methods based on the Contrary Opinion concept.

So much for the first chartists. We will return later to concepts which they discovered and described.

IV

Cross-Talk

Listen to the bloodless verdict of the market place!
Senator Spooner

9.

International Investment: Three-Dimensional Chess?

Business is a game – the greatest game in the world,
if you know how to play it.

Thomas J. Watson Jr.

As we saw in "Chaos Reigns" the realistic forecast timespan in chaotic systems is relatively short. In the classical problem of forecasting the weather it was very difficult to see more than one week ahead. Even with the best possible meteorological simulation tool available and an infinite number of continual measurements, the picture will be blurred by butterfly effects, bifurcations and hyper-chaos. (Whatever that may be. Mathematicians claim it exists.)

In the same way – and for similar reasons – the use of information flows and psychological indicators to forecast financial markets gives very short visibility, often only a few weeks (see Chapters 13 to 21).

To see *longer* than a few weeks ahead these methods are of little use. Instead, the markets should here be considered on the basis of an economic-cycle model, which is best for more far sighted evaluations.

The Joseph Effect

Mathematicians call long-term fluctuations – seasonal weather changes, or long-term shifts in economic trends – "the Joseph effect" ("There came seven years of great plenty throughout the land of Egypt. And there shall arise after them seven years of famine"). Long-term fluctuations are endogenic oscillations which occur as a predictable element in an otherwise chaotic environment.

Present-day economic cycle models are still primarily inspired

87

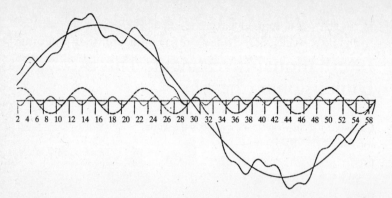

Figure 11. Cyclical movement in inflation. Superimposing three different cyclical movements on top of each other, a fourth appears, which is an irregular cycle. On interest rate and stock markets this phenomenon appears to exist where bull and bear markets' three phases otherwise correspond to the Dow model. (Chart after *Business Cycles* by Joseph Schumpeter (1939) by kind permission of the McGraw-Hill Book Company.)

by the economist Joseph Schumpeter. Considering Schumpeter's model from his book *Business Cycles* (Figure 11) we will see four cycles. He outlines three of these as stylized harmonious curves, symbolizing "Kitchin", "Juglar" and "Kondratieff", respectively. The fourth very irregular curve is the resulting curve, i.e. the sum of the other three.

But the real world is far more complicated than in Schumpeter's stylized model. There are two reasons for this:

1. *Each single cyclical phenomenon does not result in a pure sinus curve effect.* The fact that cyclical fluctuations can be observed proves a non-linear dynamic: It is the result of positive feedback loops in the economic system. However, it is extremely unrealistic to imagine that non-linear influences will result in completely harmonious oscillating effects. It is reasonable that each single underlying cycle phenomenon describes a more complicated oscillatory movement.

2. *Synchronization between cycles will be inaccurate at best.* In Schumpeter's stylized drawing the Kitchin and Juglar cycles are completely synchronized. It *is* in fact a well-known phenomenon that cyclical fluctuations tend to show mutual synch-

ronization, described as "mode-locking". If you hang two mechanical clocks close to each other on a wall they will often synchronize completely. But in the economy it is difficult to imagine perfect synchronization. And this just needs to be a little inexact to make the resulting curve very complicated.

Cyclical phenomena are complex and can never be forecast using just a ruler and chart. Nonetheless, they are important tools in predicting markets, for reasons we will return to later.

So let us take a look at how the two most important – Kondratieff and Kitchin – work.

Kondratieff's Cycle

When Kondratieff in 1925 described the phenomenon that over a survey period economic trends had moved in 48–54 year cycles, he observed this with the help of a three-stage method:

1. First he calculated the long-term trend curve in one of his time series (commodities, interest rates, commodity production and foreign trade, etc.) with a 1° or 2° line of regression.
2. Then he straightened out the trend curve to a pure "line of reference" and calculated the cyclical oscillations around this line.
3. Finally, he drew a nine-year moving average of these deviations to eliminate general turbulence and shorter cycles, primarily the eighteen-year Juglar cycle.

The curves he arrived at showed a long-term cyclical movement which was very clear, particularly on commodity and interest-rate charts. His explanation of this phenomenon was that investments in long-term capital goods showed cyclical oscillation in the same way as short-term economic cycles, although over a considerably longer period.

During long-term trend rises there is exaggerated investment in new capital apparatus, leading to increases in affluence, commodity production, inflation and interest rates. The accumulation of capital requires in itself a lot of capital, however, giving a positive feedback loop, which ultimately leads to excess capacity.

When this excess capacity is later acknowledged it leads to a painful dampening of the economy (cf. the laying up of tankers in the 1980s). During this slowdown first economic growth and commodity prices drop, and somewhat later (typically around ten years later) inflation likewise. Considering English, French and American commodity charts from 1780 to date, it will be seen that on average they peaked in 1812, 1866, 1920 and 1974, i.e. at exactly 54-year intervals (this accuracy is naturally coincidental).

Every drop in commodity prices signals an initial drop in global new investments in long-term capital goods and thereby later long-term economic slowdown. When this underlying recession starts demand for investment capital falls, and thereby also inflation and interest rates.

However, things are more complicated than this. When the cycle is in the middle of its declining phase with falling commodity prices, inflation and interest rates (rising bond prices), central bank directors can be tempted to postpone the downturn by increasing money stock, as this does not immediately result in price inflation. Money supply in the USA thus rose by 45% between 1921 and 1929, while wholesale prices dropped by 46%. Global money stock likewise rose strongly in the first half of the 1980s, when Kondratieff was also in the middle of its downturn phase. But rising liquidity gives a very unexpected effect: Instead of generating economic activity it leads to "financial inflation", i.e. roaring financial bull markets (we will return to this in Chapter 11).

There are a large number of surveys of the Kondratieff cycle in different countries. A 1984 analysis by Bieshaar and Kleinknecht concludes that from 1890 the Kondratieff cycle was present in a number of survey economies, with the exception of Great Britain. In time series *before* 1890 the picture was more doubtful for England, France and Germany, while a clear Kondratieff cycle was apparent in Belgium, Italy and Sweden. A survey by Rasmussen, Mosekilde and Holst from 1989 showed strong indications that the Kondratieff phenomenon had also been present in Denmark from 1818 to 1983.

In all circumstances it is plain that if an endogeneous structure exists in the economic systems which can stimulate a Kondratieff wave, it will have an impact. In Mosekilde and Rasmussen's words, if a single beer more than what is produced is purchased on a hot summer's day, it could trigger a latent Kondratieff cycle . . .

Kitchin's Cycle

The best known of the cycles in Schumpeter's original cyclical movement theories is probably Kitchin's "business cycle". In Kitchin's first article on this subject from 1923 he compared figures for money supply, interest rates and inflation in the USA and UK over 31 years and found a recurring 40-month cycle which he explained as "the result of rythmic movement due to psychological factors". At times the cycles deviated from the forty months, but if one was longer the next one was often equivalently shorter, so that the model kept its credibility.

Reference material in the Kitchin survey was very modest but in 1977 researchers Robert Schiller and Jeremy Siegel published an equivalent analysis of short-term cyclical phenomena in England from 1730 to 1973. In this they concluded that a short-term cyclical phenomenon in the money-market rate of interest, which they described as the "Kitchin cycle", in fact existed over this 243-year period. They found no equivalent short cycle for long-term interest rates (long-term bonds), but a longer cycle corresponding to the long-term cycles in the economy.

Just as interesting, a Kitchin cycle can also be observed for the American stock market throughout this century, interrupted only by a two-year displacement in 1946 and 1947, which reversed the cycle, after which it functioned to the mid-1980s when it was again interrupted. Today the Kitchin cycle is primarily explained as a consequence of systematic oscillations in the business sector's build-up of stocks.

During cyclical upturns business enterprises build up increasing stocks to meet demand, which they believe will continue to rise. This is a positive feedback loop in the economy. At some point, however, demand will peak and start to drop. Sales outlets react with alarm and reduce stocks before goods are re-ordered. This new loop gives a sudden lack of new orders in the producing sector, thus contributing to the cyclical downturn and thereby to upholding oscillations.

91

A Self-Simulating System?

As there seems to be not one but many business cycles, it could be assumed that a fractal phenomenon is in effect. Like the wind causes the ripples, waves and superwaves in the sea, a single force *could* appear to create all the business cycles. But when looking at the economic covariance, this does not seem to be the case. On the contrary, at least three independent oscillations seem to be in force: capital investment (Kondratieff), credit expansion (Juglar) and business inventory (Kitchin). For this reason, examining the business cycles with economic time series is far from simple.

Cross-Talk

If the frequencies of cyclical movements were very certain we could invest as the calendar dictates. But this is not true in the real world – trying it would be a sure road to ruin. Knowledge of a typical cyclical duration is useful background knowledge, but to identify trend shifts the picture requires a much more detailed analysis.

A key to this analysis is the "leading", "coincident" and "lagging" indicators used by economists to evaluate the state of the economy. As we saw in Chapter 3, the best of these barometers are the financial components – i.e. money and stock markets. As the stock index is an efficient "leader" and the money market an efficient "lagger", *these two markets can obviously forecast each other*: When interest rates climb this forewarns a drop in stock prices, and vice versa.

In reality, chartists have not only these two barometers but an entire weather station at their disposal. All the different markets – money markets, bonds, stocks, commodities and precious metals – oscillate asynchronously, since they forecast different phases in the economic cycle. When bottlenecks in the economy are expected it rains on the bond market, while the sun shines on gold. When an economic upturn is expected stocks will typically rise while the commodities' barometer will be at storm. By studying the market's "cross-talk" you can become an efficient market meteorologist. However, use of this weather station has to be made with care and sophistication.

Understanding the Game

The art is to understand what each individual market is signaling about the whole. This is one of the most fascinating aspects of international investment and also the reason that investment is sometimes compared to playing a game of three-dimensional chess.

To understand the game, we have to consider its three dimensions. The first dimension is the markets' shifting phases, each phase of the economic cycle with its own characteristic bull and bear markets. The following chapter will describe how these cycles appear in practice.

The second dimension is the most abstract. It is the market's liquidity. In many ways its functioning is as big a mystery as electrical current to a little child putting a finger in a socket to see where "it" went. Liquidity only has an impact when its current is active, and even then we can wonder how much liquidity really exists and how much is illusion. This aspect is discussed in Chapter 11.

The third dimension is the analogy between markets which *should* follow each other but which at times refrain from doing so, in a most alarming fashion. This dimension will be considered in Chapter 12.

10.

Rhythm and Swing

Models of economic and social systems should portray the process by which
disequilibrium conditions are created and dissipated, not assume that the
economy is always at or near equilibrium, or that a stable equilibrium exists
at all.

E. Mosekilde, E. R. Larsen & J. D. Sterman

The joke goes that after his death Einstein was shown to a four-
bed dormitory in Heaven. Worried about how he would pass the
time in his new surroundings he asked his first roommate what
his IQ was. "160" was the reply, to which Einstein said in relief:
"Good, so we can discuss some key aspects of my theories I
didn't get to finish on Earth." He asked his second roommate the
same question. He replied "120". Einstein retorted happily that
if all else failed they could discuss a few mathematical details of
his earthly works. The third roommate stated his IQ to be a modest 80.

Einstein thought for a while with a worried look on his face.
But suddenly he cheered up and asked him: "So how are things
on the stock exchange?"

Everything is Relative

In the financial markets everything is relative. As in ecological
systems, changes within any micro-economy will manifest themselves throughout the greater macro-system. To understand exactly how, is essential to all investment. The starting-point is the
model in Figure 12, which shows the traditional rhythm of the
business cycle:

1. *Short bonds* can be viewed as the market's locomotive and
   earliest indicator. Here money rates should also be followed,
   where 90-day deposit rates in particular are indicative (re-

membering that interest rates show reciprocal movement in relation to short bonds).

2. *Long bonds* react somewhat later. The decline of long bonds indicates fears of inflation.
3. *The stock market* is the train's third car, peaking when there is no prospect of any more good news and interest rate hikes make stock-purchase financing a costly affair.
4. *Commodities* peak after economic cycles primarily due to the positive feedback loop, called the "accelerator effect". This effect is the situation where bottlenecks during the late phases of an upturn lead to a badly-timed expansion of the capital apparatus. Capital augmentation in itself requires capital, leading to excess investment and a substantial increase in commodities consumption.
5. *Precious metals* rise latest, at a time when both stocks and long bonds are falling and inflation rising. In this situation precious metals are a safe haven.

After precious metals come short bonds again, thus closing the circle.

Market Rotation and the Financial Seasons

Keeping this pocket relativity model in mind, let us consider each of the financial seasons in more detail.

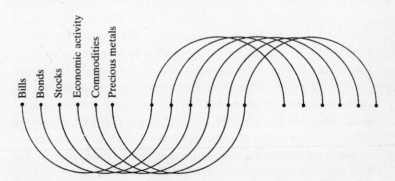

Figure 12. The business cycle and the financial markets. Traditionally, financial markets and economic activity will fluctuate in the sequence illustrated in the diagram.

1. Slump

The economy is poor, investments low, and unemployment is rising. The property market is depressed. Earnings are bad, bankers are scared, and nobody is in a position to help anybody.

Financial liquidity is good and rising. Time saving deposits and brokers' cash accounts are high. Short-term interest rates are falling. (Financial liquidity is described in more detail in the next chapter. In brief, this is the liquidity available for stock and bond investments.)

The media focus is primarily on the negative elements of the economy, even though first bonds and then stocks have already started to climb.

Bonds are in a clear rising trend, after the drop in short interest rates.

Stocks have started to rise some time after bonds. In the start phase-consumption-oriented paper such as building stocks, retail chains and manufacturers of short-term consumables in particular are rising strongly. Financial institutions providing consumer credit facilities are also among the good securities. In bottom position are mining stocks and manufacturers of capital goods. Stock rises provoke astonishment as earnings are still falling.

Commodities are falling strongly, and the same applies to

Gold which peaked some time before the actual slump.

2. Economic Expansion

The first upturn in the *economy* is due to an increase in consumer demand. Newbuilds and purchases of consumer goods soar and demand for consumer credit increases. Industry and retail links start with relatively high stocks, which are gradually reduced. In the mature phase of the upturn industry seriously starts to register a rising order intake. Money supply exceeds targets and the prime rate may be raised for the first time, after earlier reductions. Inflation has reached bottom. Property prices for private homes rise, while the professional property market stagnates.

Financial liquidiy has stopped rising. Time saving deposits and brokers' cash accounts are falling and mutual funds are increasingly tied up in investments. Brokers' security loans are accelerating. Short interest rates begin to nudge upwards. Leveraged buy-outs may contribute to increasing the liquidity impact.

At the start of the upturn *the media* are still pessimistic, only turning to optimism after midway in the upturn. Adverts for new mutual funds are still few and far between.

Bonds have been rising for a long period. Some months after short interest rates began to climb bonds go into a culmination phase.

Stocks have also been rising for some time, possibly 6–9 months, before the economic upturn began. In the upturn phase industrial stocks in particular are rising strongly. Considerable takeover activity contributes to the rises.

Commodities have bottomed at a low level, and there is no indication of increases in the first phases of the upturn. Later on more and more commodities start to rise.

Gold enters a bottom formation after falling over a long period.

3. Boom

The economy is booming and industry's capacity utilization is high, but there are more and more bottlenecks. Inflation and short-term interest rates are rising. Industry has started to expand capacity, and demand for labor, capital and commodities is rising. More and more enterprises start to sell out bond portfolios to raise liquidity for this capacity expansion.

Financial liquidity has long been falling and "liquidity reserves" are now low. (Liquidity reserves could be likened to a charging battery. This will be explained in the next chapter.) The primary source of liquidity expansion is equity price increases, converted to security capital as positions are traded. There are many new issues and accelerating rises in money market rates.

The media are positive and a lot of column inches are devoted to stock investments. There are a multitude of advertisements for investment offers, some for borrowed funds. New mutual funds appear and more or less "blind" issues are not unusual.

Bonds go into a falling trend after breaking out from a large top formation.

Stocks start to drop some months before the climax in the economy. The drop starts with consumer stocks, hitting them hardest, and affects commodities, mining, chemical and drug industries last. Internationally the drop will probably start in leading markets such as the UK, the USA and West Germany, and last in commodity producers such as Australia, Canada and South Africa. This tendency is amplified because many institutional investors, instead of abandoning the stock markets altogether, will move into defensive, commodity related stocks.

Commodities are now in a clear rising trend, also including Dry Cargo Freight Futures.

Gold breaks up from its bottom formation and starts a rising trend.

4. Economic Decline

The economy is now marked by drastic reductions in private consumption. Industry faces rising excess capacity, partly due to recent ill-timed investments. Inflation rises for a period, but peaks in the middle of the decline. In this period many interest-rate sensitive sectors are hit by bankruptcies and enforced sales are common on the property market.

Financial liquidity stabilizes and liquidity reserves gradually start to rise. However, owing to price drops many market operators face margin calls, as paper liquidity quickly shrinks. Compulsory liquidations are frequent.

The media are pessimistic. Higher interest rates are prophesied and capital intensive industries are caught in credit squeezes. There are more and more adverts for investments in precious metals and stones. Silver is bought up for smelting.

Bonds reach bottom before the end of the economic decline. Because of margin calls, many of the last sales are forced.

Stocks also fall, reversing later than bonds.

Figure 13. Economic Cycle in Stocks, Commodities and Short Bonds. ▶ The figure shows fluctuations in US stocks, commodity prices and money-market interest rates in 1897 up to 1923 (the year Kitchin's theory was published). This is interesting because it illustrates two cyclical phenomena. Firstly, the sequence at every economic boom is that stocks peak first, then commodities and finally money market interest rates. This corresponds to the model in Figure 12, with the modification that money-market rates correspond to the inverse of "bills". Secondly, it shows a clear Kitchin cycle, easiest to see in the black curve (commodities). (*Source: The Review of Economic Statistics and Supplements*, Harvard University Press, 1923.)

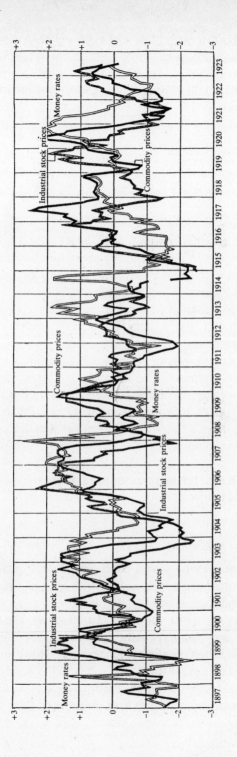

99

Commodities peak before inflation and have now started to drop.

Gold is beginning to fall simultaneously with, or shortly after, commodities. Gold price drops start six to nine months before inflation peaks.

An Important Reservation

It should be said that the above scenarios are naturally simplifications. Events never keep strictly to the model, for three reasons:

1. In small economies with a large international sphere of contact, the pattern is disturbed by exogenous factors. The model is increasingly accurate the larger the subjects described. It is most easily interpreted globally.
2. Sometimes isolated political or technological events will seriously distort the pattern ("stochastic exogenous disturbances").
3. If stocks crash instead of undergoing a gradual bull-trend reversal, the system can be disturbed by the shock waves, promoting strong federal bank intervention. In this instance, the federal bank's activities can be so extreme that the markets are no longer a barometer, but rather a major cause of economic movements.

Having said this, the markets should always be considered on the basis of this model.

Structure of Subordinate Markets

The aforementioned model concerned overall phase shifts between key markets, but there is also an internal market rotation for bond and stock markets.

As to interest rates, the short rates fluctuate the most. When short rates are close to peaking the shortest will often be considerably higher than the slightly longer rates. However, short-term bond prices do not fall most, due solely to the purely mathematical/technical factor that short securities are less sensitive to interest rates than long ones. For long-term bonds there is a different market rotation. Junk bonds are the market leader, with RJR Nabisco considered the benchmark of American junk bonds. A bear market for long bonds thus begins in the least secure papers. But the most interesting leaders/laggers phenomenon is shown by stocks. The sequence through the three phases of a bull market is as follows:

First Phase: In the bull market's first hesitant phase, the greatest increase is in stocks related to households' consumption and investments:

– utilities
– small loan institutes
– consumer goods, drugs
– food chains
– foodstuffs
– packaging materials
– finance companies
– retail stores
– banks
– insurance

Second Phase: In the middle of the upturn many companies' and stores' inventories are being pressed far down due to rising demand. New industrial orders rise even more significantly than consumption and this makes *industrials* the best shares in this phase. Often this phase is where the market begins to develop a penchant for companies with less financial clout but more innovative ideas. Sometimes the number of mutual trusts will increase strongly and bubbles – more or less blind issues – will begin to appear. Industrials peak about the same time or shortly after the total index. Important industrials can include:

– energy
– firms of contractors
– paper
– textiles
– consumer durables (e.g. automobiles)

Third Phase: While consumer stocks function as leaders and industrial stocks generally peak simultaneously with the total index, stocks related to *fixed investments* and *commodities* are typical laggers. Examples are:

– machine plants
– chemicals
– transport stock (including aviation)
– metalworking
– mines

The reason is that in the final phase of the boom the industry will suffer a dearth of capacity so (inadvisable) investments are made in new capital.

Stocks which are very sensitive to economic trends are described, not surprisingly, as "cyclicals". The most business-cycle sensitive sectors among those mentioned are automobiles (and tyre manufacturers), chemicals, airlines and metalworking. The easiest way to get an overview of leaders/laggers' performance is to study the stocks subindex. In the USA the utilities index is a slight leader, the industrials index a weak lagger and the transportation index a definite lagger. In a number of other countries similar leading and lagging sub-indices are computed, e.g. F.T. Stores in the UK (leader) or Metals and Mining in Australia (lagger).

11.

The Importance of Money

As a student of human nature, I always have felt that a good speculator
should be able to tell what a man will do with his money before he does
it.

Bernard Baruch

The second dimension of our three-dimensional chess game is
money. Few factors in the economy cause so much disagreement
among economists as the importance of liquidity and money.
Watching present-day "Keynesians" and "Monetarists" discuss
money is like witnessing the parting of the Red Sea. Opinion is
always divided, since each debater has his own tailormade view
not only of what money does, but also (much worse) of what it
is.

A Simple View of Liquidity

To understand what money is, and what it generates, you have to
simplify your thinking. A good starting-point is to lean back, put
your feet up and remember your schoolday theory of electromagnetics. The problem with electromagnetics was that while it
was possible to measure "amperage", "impedance", "capaci-
tance" and "inductance", you could never actually, well, you
could never really *see* the current.

The same goes for liquidity. If there is money in Mr. Smith's
account, it's hard to say whether it's Mr. Smith's money or it
really belongs to Mr. Jones (because the bank has lent it to him),
or somebody else completely. If both Smith and Jones *believe* the
money is theirs, isn't it most correct to say they both have it?

This is why the discussion always returns to the definition of
money. According to temperament, people swear by "M1", or
"M2", right up to "M7" as definitions.

"M2" is generally considered to be the most sober choice. M2 is notes and coinage, checking accounts of private persons and companies (but not banks' accounts with the central bank) and other accounts, including small-time saving deposits. In other words, it is the immediate purchasing power private citizens and companies believe they have.

A flow of money, returning to the physics lesson, is best compared with an electric circuit where a lamp is made to light up as a function of amperage and impedance, where amperage corresponds to the money flow and impedance to the induced activity. (The economy's tendency to develop self-reinforcing activity is called the "multiplier" in economic terminology.) In economic life a money flow can radiate pleasant economic vibrations in the form of goods produced and jobs created.

"All right then", more than one government leader has said, "so we have to create more liquidity!"

But more liquidity is not necessarily a good thing.

Effects of Rising Liquidity

Liquidity can be created in many ways but the most important source is the central bank. (To isolate this powerful tool from the irresponsible hands of governments, most central banks are independent institutions which both buy and sell bonds and fix daily interest rates at which private banks can borrow or deposit.) In the short term the central government is also important, as its accounts are held with the central bank. When central government pays out funds, they are drawn on the central bank and released into circulation.

But let's get back to electromagnetics. When national liquidity rises, e.g. by the central bank's lowering of interest rates or purchase of bonds, in our school experiment this corresponds to an increase in amperage. In popular terms this can have three different consequences:

– an increase in economic activity
– price inflation
– financial inflation

It is essential that these three alternatives exist, as their individual impacts on the markets are very different.

Criteria for the Three Effects

First imagine what happens if money flows to private consumers. When loans are cheaper, and the bank advisor more understanding, consumption rises. People buy automobiles, washing machines and homes, and money flows to the business sector which manufactures the purchased goods. In business, money will pass through the financial food chain from the grocer on the corner to the wholesaler, to the finished goods manufacturer, and finally to the machine manufacturer and raw materials producer who note the impact last but strongest (the phenomenon called the "accelerator effect"). In other words, liquidity produces *rising economic activity*.

The stimulating impact of liquidity on the commercial economy is only relative, however, and if underlying economic trends are poor it is very possible that rising liquidity will succeed only in dampening further economic decline and will only be absorbed by the economy to a limited extent. Even in a boom, more liquidity may be injected than can be absorbed immediately. If bottlenecks arise non-absorbed liquidity gives general *price inflation*. (Our bulb becomes overheated). This inflation does not arise immediately but can be the consequence of the accumulated sins of many years, surfacing sometimes, in fact, so late that it can be likened with smoke from a fire almost extinguished. Finally, if there are *no* bottlenecks and the economy still cannot absorb the rising liquidity, we will see the third consequence of money: *financial inflation*.

Financial inflation is a swear word for bull markets, caused by mobile cash funds rather than economic expectations. This hot money is often called "financial liquidity", and if you want to play the market game, you'd do best to familiarize yourself with it.

How Is Financial Liquidity Measured?

Our school electrophysics experiment illustrated how the current could pass through the three parallel circuits – private, commercial and financial – and how the consequence of expansion in liquidity can be growth, price inflation or financial inflation. Concentrating on the financial liquidity flow we need to use our imagination again. Close your eyes and think of financial liqui-

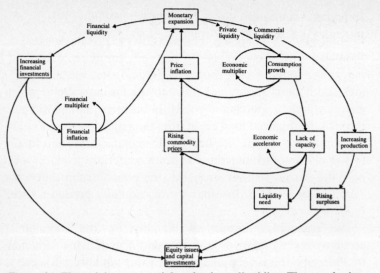

Figure 14. Financial, commercial and private liquidity. The graph gives a simplified picture of how a liquidity expansion can influence different sectors. Such a system is of course very difficult to fine-tune, which is one of the reasons for the popularity of "monetarism" – the principle of fixing total money supply instead of using it as a business cycle smoothing instrument.

dity as a wire with a bulb representing financial heat (price rises). The filament's thickness represents the number of securities on the market.

If this picture is to be accurate we must connect a battery where financial liquidity can be recharged, and a coil for inductance (false current). In other words a situation with:

1. "Financial amperage"
2. "Financial filament"
3. "Financial battery"
4. "Financial inductance"

The whole picture will fit together if we define these phenomena.

Financial Amperage

Amperage is the *total financial liquidity*, defined as follows:

> Total financial liquidity is the difference between the liquidity created by the banking system and the liquidity absorbed by the commercial, private and public economy.

106

In practice there is no direct gauge of this liquidity. Instead it is measured indirectly via the following four indicators:

– velocity of money
– debit/loan ratio
– bank investments
– net free reserves

1. *Velocity of money.* Velocity of money in commercial and private cycles is measured indicatively by dividing GDP by M2. When velocity rises this indicates that the commercial economy is forcing the liquidity flow to make ends meet. Rising velocity indicates a credit squeeze and typically coincides with rising interest rates and falling stock prices. A decline in the velocity of money indicates that financial liquidity can be increased. Therefore, in general, a falling velocity of money has forewarned or coincided with rising stock prices. M2 is currently published in the Market Laboratory section of *Barron's*.
2. *Debit/loan ratio.* The total level of private and commercial bank deposits compared to the total level of short-term and commercial bank loans. This difference is a direct expression of the private sector's liquidity surplus. A rising debit/loan ratio is thus a bullish indicator for stock and bond markets. Figures can be obtained weekly from *Barron's* and the *Wall Street Journal*.
3. *Bank investments.* The banks' overall investments in securities. These reflect a lack of private and commercial liquidity absorption and thus express the liquidity released to the financial market. The indicator is published in *Barron's* and the *Wall Street Journal*.
4. *Net free reserves.* This is the excess reserves less discount window borrowings other than extended credits to banks. The trend indicates the central bank's willingness to inject liquidity into the financial system. A rising trend is bullish. Net free reserves are published in the "Fed Report" in the *Wall Street Journal* every second Thursday and in *Barron's Market Laboratory* every week.

Common for all indicators, and for the financial liquidity as a whole, is that rates of increase or decrease often culminate one

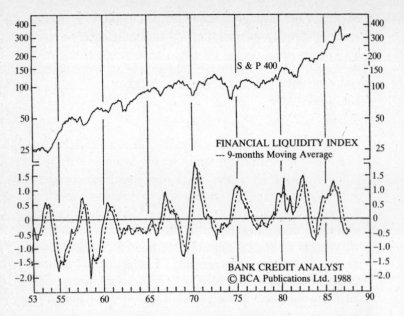

Figure 15. Financial liquidity index and the stock market. The chart demonstrates how a strong rise in financial liquidity precedes each major bull market in stocks. (*Source*: The Bank Credit Analyst.)

to three years before stock markets' peaks and troughs. Furthermore, what is important is the *change* in financial liquidity, not the absolute level. Like an electric current, liquidity has no effect without movement or change. Unless money circulates, it does little good for anyone. Historical data for the mentioned time series can be obtained from the Federal Reserve Library in New York.

Financial Filament

The filament is our expression of the financial market's supply of securities through which liquidity passes. The fewer securities available, the greater the impact of liquidity changes. There are two important phenomena:

1. *Issues*. Large waves of new stock or bond issues mean transfer of financial liquidity to the business sector and thereby a drain on markets. Issues are therefore a bearish factor.

2. *Buy-outs*. When publicly listed stock is bought up and enca-
shed by private individuals and cancelled from stock market
lists the market supply is reduced. The filament becomes
finer, so to speak, and sensitivity greater, so buy-outs press
the general price level upwards.

The aforementioned phenomena are important only when appearing on an unusual scale.

Financial Battery

A key rule for financial markets is that money does not flow into
them, but flows right through them, as every buy is set off by a
sale. There are two exceptions to this key rule, however: the "inductance" (which we will consider later) and the "financial battery". The financial battery is the liquidity dedicated to purchase
of securities but not yet allocated, i.e. the money on "the sidelines" which on placement will directly raise prices in the market.
This money is registered by four indicators:

1. *Total Time Saving Deposits*. Short-term saving deposits are
the simplest placement for cash funds which are available for
a few days to a few months. If saving deposits start to rise
strongly this indicates that large investors, otherwise buyers of
stocks or bonds, now fear price drops, so they accumulate
liquidity for later use: The battery is being charged. Time saving deposits in the USA are sometimes published in *Barron's*
and the *Wall Street Journal* and always in *Survey of Current
Business* and *Business Conditions Digest* from the US Department of Commerce.
2. *Brokers Cash Accounts*. When large cash deposits are held by
brokers there is naturally ample liquidity in the market, which
must be placed sooner or later (if the intention were not to
place funds, they would not stay in these accounts for very
long). The indication is positive when these accounts increase
and negative when they decrease. US brokers cash accounts
are published in *Barron's* and in *Survey of Current Business*,
the latter with a certain time lag.
3. *Brokers' Security Loans*. A broker's security loan is a loan
raised by a broker for a customer speculating on the margin.

These are funds drawn from the overall M2 pool to the financial battery. A rise in security loans is a bullish indicator because the battery is being charged and also because it shows that the smartest investors (the margin speculators) have confidence in the market. United States figures are published, occasionally in *Barron's* and the *Wall Street Journal* and systematically in *Survey of Current Business*.
4. *Mutual Funds Cash/Assets Ratio*. When mutual funds report large unplaced cash holdings this naturally indicates recharging of the financial battery. As funds are usually placed on time deposits they may also be registered there. The cash/assets ratio has been published since 1954 and can be obtained on a continual basis from *The Investment Company Institute, Washington DC*.

The four aforementioned indicators thus all show the state of the financial battery. Often this will gradually change when the economy is on the decline. When the battery starts discharging we are in the middle of a slump and when equity prices consequently start rising, this will usually be to the great surprise of economists: "Everything looks bad. Buying stocks is pure speculation with no basis in reality."

Financial Inductance

Anybody who has owned an old-fashioned tapedeck may have experienced a remarkable phenomenon: Sometimes the deck will be able to play for a few seconds even though the current has been disconnected for several minutes. The reason is *inductance*, a self-induced false current, which pulses away in a coil long after the primary current source has been disconnected.

In the same way financial markets have their own false current of liquidity. Let's imagine an example: A bullish market has started and Mr. Smith places 100,000 dollars as collateral for a stock purchase of 300,000 dollars. The stocks' price doubles, after which he sells, leaving him with 400,000 in his account. This serves as collateral for a new and larger stock buy, this time for 1.2 million dollars. These stocks also double in price, after which he sells and increases the account balance to 1.6 million dollars.

110

He then decides to stop and buy a new home for the money. The bull market has made money for Mr. Smith.

But let's imagine that Jones (Smith's new neighbor), encouraged by Smith's success lodges 1 million as collateral for a stock buy of 3 million, after which stocks drop 50% to a value of 1.5 million. He has now lost more than he pledged as security, so the bank forces him to deposit a further 1 million. He is forced to sell his home to get the money. The bear market has absorbed Mr. Smith's money.

So the *bull market creates liquidity, while the bear market absorbs liquidity*. This is an important observation, even though in total terms this liquidity is a fictitious entity. (This observation is not specific to trading on the margin. A bull market also generates liquidity for conservative placements.)

The "false" liquidity created by the bull markets contributes to stimulating further price rises long after the "genuine" financial liquidity flow has started to decline. As price gains are converted to real money only on profit-taking, high volume is a criterion for the generation of this financial inductance. Furthermore, rapid price rises are obviously important. So, strangely enough, financial markets react just like the commercial economy in a "credit squeeze": by increasing the velocity of money.

Liquidity and Cross-Talk

As funds can flow in many directions it is a waste of time to use development in overall money stock as an indicator for anything at all. Rising liquidity can be bullish, bearish or indifferent, depending on where the money flows. If liquidity is to be watched, it must be done with care and understanding. This can be done by two methods: the hardworking method and the simple one.

The Hardworking Method

The hardworking method consists of setting up a measuring apparatus wherever possible to register liquidity movements and accumulation. Forewarnings of price inflation are recorded for example by wage inflation, producer prices, capacity utilization and import prices. Liquidity absorption for production purposes can be measured by industry's investments and new orders, building permits, etc. Financial liquidity is measured by the methods described in this chapter and summarized at the end.

And, finally, if you are *very* hardworking, you make daily prognoses of central government deposits and withdrawals in the hope that the central bank and the large banks will not do the same with even greater accuracy, thus eliminating potential day-to-day market fluctuations.

The Simple Method

If you are lazy you use the simple method. Like all use of charts, this is based on the markets as economic barometers. The lazy investor will concentrate on interest rates, yield curves and the gold price. He also checks out our specific indicators of financial liquidity where he can see them.

Lazy Indicator No. 1: The Short Interest Rates

Short interest rates are the best overall indicator of national liquidity and have an element of both cause and effect for financial markets. Short rates are usually measured as the three-month deposit rate, i.e. the annualized interest rate on three-month money-market deposits. (Registered by LIBOR, London Inter Bank Offered Rate.) If interest rates are rising this is a bearish signal to the stock market. If they fall, it is a bullish signal. There are four reasons for this, two financial and two concerning the investors' situation. The financial reasons are as follows:

– If interest rates are rising this is often related to an economic upturn, where the productive economy absorbs liquidity. As the stock market is also ahead of the economy it will often peak out while the interest rate is rising.
– A rising interest rate is bad news for companies, so stock yields and prices drop with rising interest rates.

The other two reasons concern the situation of investors:

– If the interest rate is low, loans for speculation on stock markets will be cheaper, thus increasing financial liquidity.

– If yields are high on bond placements or time deposits, stock yield must increase correspondingly to compete. Everything being equal, this can only happen through lower stock prices.

It should be noted that the absolute interest rate level is less important than its trend.

Lazy Indicator No. 2: The Yield Curve

The yield curve is a separate story. This concept refers to a curve drawn of the relation between bond maturities and interest rate yields. In a typical situation the yield is highest on long-term issues, as there is a premium on time-risk. In later phases of a boom price inflation will start to occur, so central banks often

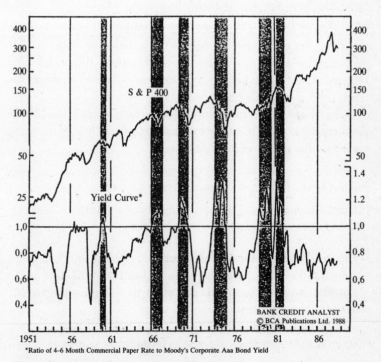

Figure 16. Stock prices and the yield curve. The shaded areas represent periods with an inverted yield curve. In most cases this has signaled major stock bear markets. (*Source*: The Bank Credit Analyst.)

113

raise short rates above long rates. In such cases an "inverted" yield curve is involved.

Traditionally these are bad times for the stock market because high interest rates give a financial credit squeeze and because we are seeing the late phases of the boom. Times are also bad for bond markets, as both short and long securities are falling.

This is assuming that central bank directors are respectable citizens who shave twice a day, wear ties and only react to inflation when they see it. But just suppose they wear cowboy boots, drink whiskey and reach for their guns as soon as they *hear* the word inflation? In that case short interest rates can rise without long rates moving at all, or even falling. This signals that the market thinks that early aggressive combating of inflation will be successful and in such cases an inverted yield curve is a signal to *buy* stocks and long bonds rather than to sell.

Lazy Indicator No. 3: The Gold Price

The price of gold is a very efficient barometer of price inflation and poor stock markets. If the gold price is rising, markets expect price inflation, low real interest rates and a financial credit squeeze, and if it is falling they expect low inflation, high real interest rates and ample financial liquidity.

Using these three indicators for the lazy (which should be monitored globally) it is easy to draw a rough outline of the market's liquidity status and expectations.

What About Trading of Commodities or Currencies?

Financial liquidity is of limited roundabout interest for commodity and currency dealers, for two reasons:

- The commodities market is a full-scale global market. Currency markets can be called national but their investors trade globally. National money is therefore in a sense unimportant from the market view.
- It is virtually meaningless to talk about bull and bear markets here, as short positions are just as frequent as long ones.

Commodity dealers' primary interest is not financial liquidity but commercial and private liquidity, which influence demand for

114

commodities via the multiplier and accelerator effects. Currency dealers' key interest is the money market interest rate where a rising interest rate is an argument for buying a currency, cashing in the interest. The currency dealer is most of all on the lookout for a country where the central bank director has developed a liking for cowboy boots. Learning from experience the dealer will know that this often occurs in the late phases of a boom where interest rates are rising, the balance of payments is close to its low point, and export sector bottlenecks make devaluation unlikely. In this, cyclical, respect, it can be said that a country's currency has a slight tendency towards being a financial lagger.

Let's close by summarizing methods for covering development in financial liquidity and thereby in one of the security dealer's most important control areas:

Key Rules for Market Liquidity

The Total Financial Liquidity Flow (the "amperage")
1. *The commercial velocity of money.* Bearish if it is rising and bullish if it is falling. The absolute level is unimportant.
2. *Debit/loan ratio.* A rising ratio is bullish and a falling ratio is bearish. The absolute level is unimportant.
3. *Bank investments.* Bullish if they are rising and bearish if they are falling. The absolute level is unimportant.
4. *Net free reserves.* Bullish if they are rising and bearish if they are falling. The absolute level is unimportant.

Financial Supply (the "filament")
1. *Issues.* Bearish if there is a strong rise in the number of issues.
2. *Buy-outs.* Bullish if there are many buy-outs.

Financial Liquidity Reserves (the "battery")
1. *Time saving deposits.* Bullish when time deposits are high and bearish when they are low.
2. *Brokers' cash accounts.* Bullish when liquidity is high and bearish when it is low.
3. *Brokers' security loans.* Bullish when they are rising and bearish when they are falling. The absolute level is less important.
4. *Mutual funds cash/assets ratio.* Bullish if they are large and bearish if they are small.

115

False Liquidity ("inductance")
1. *Volume*. Bullish if the volume is high when the market is rising and bearish if it is high when the market is falling.

General
1. *Short-term interest rates*. A bullish sign for stocks is when short-term rates are falling and a bearish sign when they are rising.
2. *Yield curve*. Bearish if it is leveling out and possibly becoming inverse, but only if long-term interest rates rise simultaneously.
3. *Gold price*. Bullish for securities markets if the gold price has been falling for some time and bearish if it has been rising for some time.

12.

Harmony and Resonance

It's a house of cards no matter how you stack it. They stand together and fall together.

Harry D. Schultz

The starting-point for the cyclical approach is that the observed movements within a market sector actually reflect rational expectations. To evaluate whether a market is acting as an economic barometer, or is simply a game of musical chairs, we must study whether movements are in harmony and resonance. This chapter considers this third dimension of our financial game of chess.

If the Mood is Bullish

In 1901 Charles Dow wrote an interesting paragraph in an article in the *Wall Street Journal* on the market's response to increases in individual securities:

> A method employed by some operators of large experience is that of responses. The theory involved is this: The market is always under more or less manipulation. A large operator who is seeking to advance the market does not buy everything on the list, but puts up two or three leading stocks either by legitimate buying or by manipulation. He then watches the effect on the other stocks. If sentiment is bullish, and people are disposed to take hold, those who see this rise in two or three stocks immediately begin to buy other stocks and the market rises to a higher level. This is the public response, and is an indication that the leading stocks will be given another lift and that the general market will follow.

As expressed by Charles Dow at the beginning of this century, market movements in isolated securities must be confirmed by a broader movement involving many securities. Only then will the trend be credible. This phenomenon is sometimes described as

117

market breadth. Dow also formulated the rule that an increase in industrials, not confirmed by a rise in transport stock, would be untenable. The reason could be explained as follows:

> If industrials rise it must be because rising growth in industry is expected. As manufactured industrial goods do not move of themselves, there must also be growth in the transport sector, so transportation stock should also rise. If this doesn't happen, something is wrong.

In other words: If the markets do not confirm each other, their movements are due to irrational speculation rather than to the discounting of future economic trends in current financial prices.

Later the idea of harmony and resonance has been developed further in many areas. Let us consider each market separately.

Stocks

Many stock analysts recommending purchase of a specific stock refer to its being "cheaper" than others on the market, but the problem is that if the whole market starts to drop it takes everything with it, "cheap" or "expensive". People sell all the securities they can find a market for, to make money to keep the securities they cannot get rid of.

Securities influence each other and so it is not always enough to be interested in a single stock's chart. We must consider the market in a broader context. The first thing to look for is what we call the market analogy or "breadth".

Breadth

To look for simple analogies between different charts the stock market can be divided into six different levels (Figure 17).

First an individual paper's price development can be compared to development in its "family". For example, a specific insurance stock can be compared with other insurance paper. If the general trend is falling we keep our hands off or sell short. It is even more important to look at the overall national index. Charts of national stock indices usually tell a fairly clear message. Comparison of individual stocks with the total index is by two methods. Firstly, the total index's chart is used as an indicator in itself: We

118

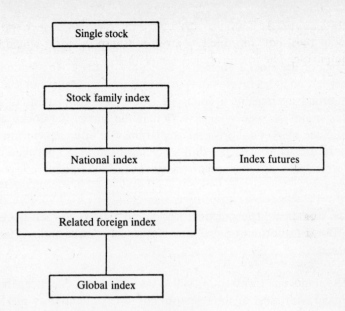

Figure 17. Market analogy on stock markets.

postpone individual stock buys if the total index shows a dangerous pattern.

Secondly, we can use what is termed the *relative to total index*
as a separate screening tool. The method is to calculate an isolated issue's price development as an index value *in relation to*
development in the total index. If this specific stock and the total
index are completely level, the "relative to total index" will be a
constant 100. But if the paper is stronger than the average the
value rises to over 100.

This indicator will often be an easy way to identify securities
facing atypical development, up or down, when monitoring
many different stocks. If the indicator suddenly starts to rise this
will be a promising sign and if it starts to drop it will signal danger. But the scenario where a small double top arises on the individual paper's chart, with a lower top on the "relative to total
index", is the most alarming. In this case it will almost always be
a good idea to sell the stock.

Cash and Carry

Today the vogue is more for comparing stock prices with the price of the stock's corresponding index futures. As mentioned earlier, an index future is a contract for future purchase or sale of a broad average of a country's stocks. Futures contracts are easier and cheaper to juggle with than the underlying stocks, and thus the market's short-term oscillations will often appear fastest in futures contracts. If a difference has been found between the futures price and the underlying stocks the conditional reflex will be:

– If futures are cheaper than stocks, buy futures and sell stocks.
– But if futures cost more than stocks, buy stocks and sell futures.

This innocent transaction, called *cash & carry*, has been burdened with most of the responsibility for contemporary market calamities, particularly the recurring nosedives in the USA and Japan. Typically the "index arbitrageur" speculating in these market imperfections will have his computer calculate the price disparity between the stock index and the future index every few minutes. As the futures owner also earns interest on his colateral, he will code this interest rate into the system. Then, whenever a worthwhile discrepancy occurs, he will have his system do the cash and carry trade. Before placing responsibility for such price drops on this so-called computer trading, one detail should be remembered, however: When futures contracts drop, there must be a reason.

While dealing with index futures contracts it should also be stated that futures contracts of different maturities will not necessarily react in the same way. When they don't, it is an indication of the market's long-term, versus short-term, expectations. The last market analogies when trading stocks are the analogies to the related foreign index and the global stock index (the latter calculated for example by *Capital International*). This relative effect has become more and more important because today we invest globally.

In addition to the market analogy, there are three different indicators used as special stock-market tools to tell us the market's breadth – how many securities help to carry a bull or bear trend.

The main argument is that the more stocks follow a trend movement, the more credible a financial barometer will be. The indicators used are the following:

– advance/decline line
– new highs/new lows
– diffusion

Advance/Decline Line

This indicator is the best known of the three. Its principle is to identify the ratio between the number of rising and falling stocks. The A/D line, as it is also called, was introduced in the USA at the beginning of this century. At that point there was only one industrial index based on twelve industrial stocks and a railway index based on twenty railway stocks. If you were interested in the broad market's "response", then you needed a figure to tell you how the market's up to 1,500 other securities were faring. Were they following the leading issues, or was there no response in the market?

As there were no computers at that time brokers counted each day how many securities rose and fell respectively and then plotted the relation between them on a chart. (One man making these computations was the famous speculator Jesse Livermoore, who hired 40 "statisticians" as personal assistants. Shortly before the 1929 crash they presented him with a report which showed that while the industrial index's leading stocks had risen significantly since the beginning of the year, 614 out of a broader selection of 1,002 stocks had actually fallen in the same period. Only 338 had risen. Thus, the indices were rising but the advance/decline line was falling, and the use of this observation helped Livermoore to survive the ensuing panic).

Today two different formulae are primarily used. The first is extremely simple, as a random figure is selected as the starting value, then adjusted daily, according to the following calculation:

A/D line = number rising – number falling

Alternatively, the calculation can include the number of unchanged securities, in which case this formula should be used:

$$A/D \text{ line } = \sqrt{\frac{\text{number rising}}{\text{number unchanged}} - \frac{\text{number falling}}{\text{number unchanged}}}$$

If the square root figure is negative we just change it to positive, (i.e. we use the absolute value). The advance/decline indicator naturally rises when the index starts to climb, but it has a practical tendency to turn at the top of a primary bull market before the narrow stock index. This is because many securities which are very sensitive to economic trends or interest rates stop rising before leading stocks.

The 1987 crash was no exception. In the weeks up to the drama of Black Monday the indicator showed that more and more stocks were beginning to lag behind the leading securities, see Table 3. While the index, comprising the 30 leading industrials, moved through a sideways consolidation, the advance/decline indicator released a very strong warning signal: The bull market lost breadth.

New Highs/New Lows

This indicator also expresses the market's breadth, its name almost speaking for itself. The principle is that we monitor how many stocks reach new highs or lows in terms of for example the

Table 3. Weekly fluctuations on the New York Stock Exchange, autumn 1987.

Week	Number rising	Number falling	Number unchanged
35	709	1,274	215
36	544	1,445	199
37	917	1,006	250
38	626	1,333	229
39	1,064	849	263
40	1,274	699	215
41	400	1,608	158
42	143	1,944	101

Stock Exchange crash. While the Advance/decline line thus drops before a primary bull market top, the signal on a bear market low is more surprising. Here the A/D line will often continue to drop without being confirmed by new lows in the narrow index.

last fifty-two weeks. As a break-out from an old top is very bullish (and a break-out from an old low is bearish), this indicates the market's strength rather differently to the A/D line.

In practice, experience tells us that a rising market does not need to have an increasing number of new highs, but if new highs drop while the market is rising there can be grounds for concern. In all cases, in a rising market there should be more new highs than new lows. The usual formula for this indicator is:

New highs/new lows = Number of stocks currently with the last year's so far highest level, less the number currently with the last year's so far lowest level.

Diffusion

The third indicator of breadth in the stock market's trend movement is called *diffusion*. The scale for this indicator is 0–100 and the calculation is as follows:

Diffusion = Percentage of stocks lying above their own 200-day moving average.

The basis for this indicator is that very often an intact rising trend for a stock is "carried" by its 200-day moving average, (the reason will be explained in Chapter 18). When the paper drops back due for example to profit-taking, it is thus very common that buyers return to around the 200-day average. This gives the general rule that a bull trend on the stock market will generally be most credible if a large proportion of individual papers are above their 200-day moving average. If diffusion starts to decline while the index is rising or unchanged, this will signal danger.

Bonds

Bond markets are generally more closely interrelated than stock markets and the individual market is much more homogeneous. To analyze links and reiterations we exclusively consider the simple market analogy between related securities and markets (Figure 18).

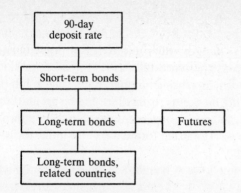

Figure 18. Market analogy on bond markets.

Again charts are compared to find consistency in what they tell us. Internationally, bond markets appear to converge even more than stock markets. While in stock analysis the starting-point is an overview of the picture shown by the total index, in bond markets the money-market interest rates should be the foundation. With a little practice it is easy to form a picture of their trend patterns and get ahead of the majority of bond market operators. The most important interest rates are yields on 1, 3, 6 and 12-month deposits, where the 3-month rate (London fixing) gives the best signal. The chart will give the best picture if the 50-day moving average is plotted (see Chapter 18).

In addition to short money market rates there is a second bond market indicator, resembling the stock market's leader/lagger indicator, and this is the *yield curve*. As touched on in Chapter 11 the yield curve expresses the relation between short-term and long-term yields. (In Chicago the interest differential between 10-year T-notes and 20-year T-bonds can be traded as a futures contract called "Notes over Bonds" or "NOB spread".) When the market starts to become overheated in the later phases of an economic upturn, short-term yields are almost always the first to start to rise (bonds with short maturities start to drop) while long-term yields follow suit with some delay (long bonds start to drop). As a general rule if short-term yields fall far below long-term yields this is a bullish sign for long bonds, and a bearish sign if the short yield approaches the long yield. Exceptions to this rule were described in Chapter 11.

Currencies

The fact that international investment at times most resembles three-dimensional chess is not least due to the currencies. When we buy stocks or bonds we pay for them in a given currency. If we are not spending our own currency we incur a double risk as the security as well as the currency can fluctuate. Currencies add an extra dimension to investing, which some investors could do very well without.

But others rejoice in this dimension. Typical currency market investors are elated when markets fluctuate, participating in trading to profit from market movements. These investors "swap" money. In forward contracts – the dominant element of the currency market – they always stay exposed in at least two currencies at a time: short in one and long in the other. As they do not actually buy anything in the traditional sense, a forward contract is self-financing and practically nothing more than a wager. Over time it will give price losses or gains, as well as interest gains or losses, in accordance with which of the currencies has the highest money-market rate.

When trading on the currency market, two different types of chart are compared, those showing development in spot currency rates against each other, and those showing development in their interest rates (where the 90-day rate is considered). Figure 19 shows how dominant currency combinations and money-market rates are related to each other, and which charts should be compared to evaluate one of these markets.

This may seem very complicated, but if you are a habitual currency market player you will soon find your way around and get used to not going into the market before all relevant charts, long-term and short-term, have been studied and interpreted.

One of the most important tools for evaluation of currency trends is "effective exchange rate" charts, a currency's index value in relation to a weighted basket of trading currencies. Very often a buy or sell signal for a major currency will appear on the effective exchange rate chart before the ordinary charts, particularly if central banks try to break a potential trend by intervention. This phenomenon corresponds to the market breadth indicators on the stock market.

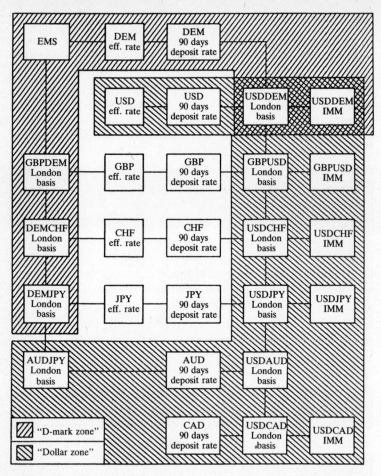

Figure 19. Market analogy between major currencies. The figure includes four concepts which require further explanation. "Effective Exchange Rate" is a currency's index value vis-à-vis a weighted basket of mutual trading currencies. Effective Exchange Rate for major currencies is calculated daily by the Bank of England and published in among others the *Financial Times*. "IMM" stands for "International Monetary Market", Chicago's extremely popular exchange. This is where many currency futures are traded, whose signals sometimes deviate from those arising in Europe. The European charts are based on "London basis", i.e. spot prices during British banks' trading hours, official close 5.00 p.m. GMT. Finally, "EMS" naturally stands for the European currency snake.

In addition to cross-trading of major currencies many concentrate on interest rate arbitrage between high and low interest currencies. Typically they will follow the links shown in Figure 20. Sometimes, in analyses on currency markets, people will draw conclusions from currency combination charts which are completely irrelevant as they describe combinations with insignificant turnover. It is a waste of time to chart the Swedish krone against

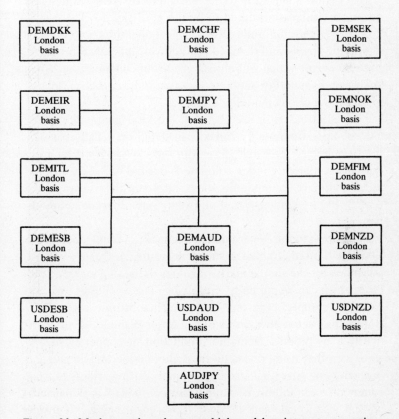

Figure 20. Market analogy between high and low-interest currencies. For three of the high-interest currencies the charts should be followed against USD, because they are traded strongly against the dollar. These are pesetas (ESB), Australian dollars (AUD) and New Zealand dollars (NZD). For others, as a main rule the technical strength should be evaluated by charting them against the D-mark (DEM) and then analysing the D-mark against the yen (JPY) and the Swiss franc (CHF) to select the weakest of these three currencies for sale.

any other currency than the D-mark as this is the dominant relation for the krone. And to discover the dollar's strength against the lira you should look at the lira against the D-mark and then the D-mark against the dollar. It is no good studying a chart for dollars against lira.

Commodities

Commodity markets are generally the most volatile and psychological of the financial markets, such that surviving commodity dealers are often considered to be the most skillful. These markets' movements naturally reflect market operators' expectations of specific supply and demand relations for individual products, but also events which will impact groups of commodities. When analysing commodity markets we not only consider isolated products but also commodity sectors.

The senior indicator used by most is a total commodity index, C.R.B. Spot Commodity Index, calculated on a daily basis by the Commodity Research Bureau in the USA. This is far from the only commodity index computed, but the only one with parallel trading of a commodity index future on the exchange, the C.R.B. Futures Index, based on twenty-one different commodities.

In addition to this general index a number of family indices are calculated, often grouped as shown in Figure 21. Dealers will use this index for the simple market analogy of looking for trend pictures which can be mutually reinforcing. This applies to corn and oats for example, both feedstuffs which substitute each other. But the link is not always so simple. As an example, silver is primarily a by-product from the production of copper, lead and zinc, such that rising prices on these three minerals will give *falling* prices on silver, all else being equal. But regardless of what commodity you follow, it is important not to stick to dollar indices but also to calculate in Swiss francs for example, to ensure that you are not in fact staring away at a currency movement on your chart.

Precious Metals

There are four precious metals: gold, silver, platinum and palladium (palladium is insignificant). Gold is naturally the best

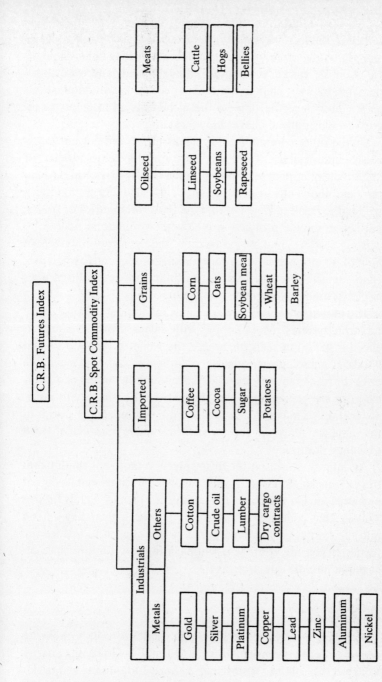

Figure 21. Market analogy on commodity markets.

known and most important, despite the fact that all the gold mined in the history of mankind (around 400,000 tons) could be stored in three ordinary detached homes. As long as new gold offered on the market continues to flow smoothly and commercial demand does not change radically, speculation will dominate its price. And since the time of the alchemists all attempts to increase yields radically have shipwrecked.

Unlike other commodities, precious metals are not put to exclusive industrial use. Gold and silver are collected as jewelry, or hidden away in people's bottom drawers – in France in particular – and the vaults of central banks (in 1968 there was so much gold in the Bank of England that the floor collapsed). For gold in particular, annual production is extremely minute in relation to existing stocks – making production and consumption levels of limited importance to price formation. Consequently, when precious metals are pushed up to exorbitant prices this often does not correspond to any industrial factors.

The motive is a simple cover against inflation or collapse of the financial systems. Most people with savings will have experienced a period in their life where the value of their stocks and bonds crumbles away because of inflation and the inevitable price drops. As soon as they see that commodity prices and interest rates are beginning to rise they switch their money to precious metals (usually gold) to shelter from the impending storm. In the same way they will run for cover if they fear a wave of stock exchange crashes.

An important reason for this protection motive is that in contrast to stocks, bonds and bank deposits, precious metals do not pay interest. On the contrary, traders of precious metals futures will see that contracts increase in price the longer they extend into the future, as you have to pay dollar interest to finance the metal. If you are short you will earn interest and are thus engaged in interest rate arbitrage.

Price Fixing

Every day, shortly before 10.30 a.m. and 3.00 p.m. Greenwich Mean Time, five gentlemen from Mocatta & Goldsmit, Sharps, Pixley & Co., N.M. Rothschild & Sons Ltd., Johnson Mattley and Samuel Montagu meet at Rothschild's offices in London to

130

agree on the morning and afternoon gold fixings. All five are in telephone contact with their dealers, in turn linked up to thousands of customers. As soon as the "correct" price has been agreed it is published on telephone lines and information systems all over the world, and can be read in hundreds of financial papers on the next day. This price, called the *fixing*, is an indicative price for the so-called OTC or "spot market" in physical metals, which is the dominant market.

Nobody knows exactly what proportion of precious metals are traded on the OTC market but it is known that this is the largest precious metals market. The price-fixing on this market is a bid for the "right" price on each day, but in practice trading prices fluctuate considerably around this price. As the OTC market is larger than the futures market, fixing or close prices on this market should guide the level for futures trading. In practice, the reverse is the case, however. On futures markets exact information is available of all contracts and prices entered. So normally futures charts with day-to-day high, low and close prices will be considered most important, while charts based on spot prices are used as a supplementary indicator.

On futures markets the most traded contracts are followed on the US COMEX gold and silver exchange and the New York NYMEX platinum and palladium exchange. To supplement

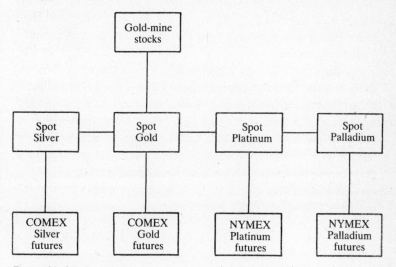

Figure 22. Market analogy on precious metal markets.

evaluation with spot prices, typically the London Metals Exchange afternoon fixings or close prices are used. Figure 22 shows the charts usually compared to find parallel patterns.

The earliest indication of an impending movement in precious metals will often be seen in gold-mine stocks, which are relatively efficient discounters of gold price movements. To catch these signals you should follow a gold-mine index, the most important being the following:

– Financial Times Gold Mines Index (F.T. Gold Mines)
– Australian Gold Index
– Toronto Stock Exchange Gold Share Index
– Standard & Poors Gold Mines Index

The first index is the one most commonly followed. F.T. Gold Mines is based on the indexed value of twenty-four South African gold mines calculated in pounds sterling. The index is monitored by many professional speculators, clearly used to trading on charts: The chart signals are highly self-reinforcing.

After studying gold-mine charts we go on to gold itself and gold futures, in daily trading the latter tending to be half a neck ahead (the contract most followed is the so-called CMX Gold Futures). Gold is traded primarily in dollars, so it is important to chart the metal in this currency. For a complete picture we should look at gold charts in Australian dollars, pounds sterling, Swiss francs and especially yen, the other four most commonly traded currencies.

For the other three precious metals it might be reasonable to think that the relevant mine stock would be a good forecast tool, but in practice it is difficult to find a representative mine index for silver, platinum and palladium (many silver mines are in Peru). So we have to make do with futures contracts as a short-term timing instrument for the physical metal. In addition, to a great extent interrelations between metals are used as an indication. If a clear buy signal on gold contracts arises, others will probably follow.

The Most Important Links

Before we move on to the third section of the book, let us try to summarize the key rules for how the picture shown by the different markets can be used to confirm a trend.

Key Rules for Market Relations

Stocks
1. *Market analogy*. Look for mutual confirmation between related charts, including stock families, national total index, index futures and international stock index.
2. *Advance/decline line*. This expresses the ratio between the number of rising, falling and unchanged stocks respectively, indicating a trend's sustainability.
3. *New highs/new lows*. Look for confirmation of a trend in the total index using this indicator, which expresses how many stocks lie at new highs or lows.
4. *Diffusion*. Look for confirmation of a trend in a total index by its expression of what percentage of stocks lies above its own 200-day average.

Bonds
1. Look for confirmation by comparing national and international charts and comparing short and long-term yields. Start with the assumption that short interest rates are normally ahead of long rates.

Currencies
Compare all relevant charts for the most traded currency combinations and key currencies' effective exchange rates and 90-day yields.

Commodities
The starting point is C.R.B. Commodity in dollars, Deutschmarks, yen, and Swiss francs and the equivalent futures contract. Also compare individual commodity charts with the related commodities within the same family.

Precious Metals

Look for confirmations of all isolated signals by considering three types of market analogy:

– analogy between gold-mine charts and gold
– analogy between the four precious metals
– analogy between each precious metal cash price and its futures.

The starting point is that mines and futures tend to be ahead of the physical metal.

IV

Information:
The Quest of
the Holy Grail

Know all ye men, that the wisest amongst you has recognized like Socrates,
that in the honest light of the truth his wisdom is worthless.

Socrates

13.

The Fastest Game in Town?

Knowledge – Zzzzzp! Money – Zzzzzzp! – Power! That's the cycle democracy is built on!

Tennessee Williams

On Wednesday, 21 June 1815, at 11.00 p.m. Lord Bathurst of the London War Office received a very tired man. His guest was Major The Hon. Henry Percy, who had been en route from Belgium for two days and eighteen hours. Percy had hurried to bring the British Government great tidings: A battle had been fought at Waterloo and Napoleon's troops had been beaten.

Together, Bathurst and Percy sped to the Chancellor of the Exchequer, impatiently awaiting news of the battle. Percy was besieged with questions before falling asleep in his chair, completely exhausted by his journey. But this was of no import: The information had been relayed and the next day Percy was promoted to lieutenant-colonel for his dedicated efforts.

Heavy Buying

But twenty-four hours before the ministers were told the news, one man in England was already in the know. A little fat man with blue eyes, red hair and a thick German accent. His name was Nathan Mayer Rothschild.

Nathan Rothschild emigrated to England at the age of 21 and within a short time became one of London's leading financiers. As well as being a gifted dealer and tactician, Rothschild was known for another special characteristic: He was always extremely well-informed. On the morning of Tuesday 20, the day before Henry Percy reached London, Rothschild made massive buy-ups on the stock exchange, scoring a considerable fortune. How did he know about the victory so long before his country's own war office?

We actually still do not know, but there are two probable hypotheses.

One is that he used his own courier service, which he had developed over the years. This was known for its unique speed. A source tells us that his employee John Roworth spent the night before the great battle on the battlefield at Waterloo (*Notes and Queries*, 1868). On 18 June at 7.00 p.m., i.e. as soon as Napoleon's defeat was a certainty, Roworth hurried to Calais on horseback and crossed to Dover in an open boat, despite the stormy weather. His speed can thus be explained by the well-oiled relay transportation methods of the courier service. This explanation is supported by an apparent statement by Roworth and an existing letter from Roworth to Rothschild. The letter was written on 27 July 1815 and includes the following remark: "I am informed by Commissionary White you have done well by the early information which you had of the victory gained of Waterloo."

The second theory is that Rothschild got the news of the battle via homing pigeons. It was generally well known that he often used homing pigeons to get quick information from the Continent. It is not known for sure where the pigeons were based, but as he had bought a farm in Kent for GBP 8,750 it is likely that the pigeons were kept there. Using homing pigeons it would not have been difficult for him to get the news by Tuesday morning, far earlier than the War Office.

His colleagues on the stock exchange assumed that pigeons were normally Rothschild's principal messengers. In fact they became so vexed by this that in 1836, according to the newspapers, they stationed a number of eagles and hawks on the Kent coastline to catch and eat up Rothschild's infernal pigeons when they flew in from the Continent. But the messenger traffic did not stop for this. When Nathan Rothschild died in Frankfurt on 28 July of the same year, the news first arrived via his own system: A huntsman shot down an exhausted pigeon in Kent and found a little slip of paper tied to the poor bird's legs (*The Times*, 3 August 1836). There stood three words: "Il est mort".

Rothschild's systems showed us the crucial importance of information. Nathan Rothschild's information network made a major contribution to his unbelievable success, because the most important parameter was no more than the ability to *get* information. Fundamental knowledge was a very scarce commodity in his day.

A New Situation

Today, information is still crucial, but the environment has changed. Present-day dealers are all armed with a battery of on-line information systems every day disseminating thousands and thousands of items of information in real time. Via electronic systems, decision-makers all over the world are equipped with one single artificial brain, covering the surface of our earth with a fine-meshed network, so that everybody knows the most important news at one and the same time. On top of this come myriads of telephone calls, where rumors and hunches are constantly being exchanged across every national and institutional boundary. In this situation the main problem is no longer how quickly we can get information, but of *interpreting* the news from the battlefield. As Prussian military theoretician Carl von Clausewitz wrote in *Vom Kriege*:

> Difficulties are already extreme on the first reconnaisance outside the actual war zone. But they are infinitely greater in the tumult of the battlefield and its constant flow of new information. Chance smiles on the receiver of contradictory information, who can reach his decisions after due evaluation and criticism. But far worse it is when one message supports, confirms and reinforces the last – adding more and more color to the picture, until finally forcing a new decision. Such decisions soon turn out to be foolish, and all information lies and delusion. Most information is misleading and men's fears a fertile breeding ground for lies and untruths.

What Clausewitz noted was that most of the news flowing in without abatement is false. But what concerned him more was that it is extremely difficult to hold on to one's original strategy or to see how it should be altered when our nerves are wracked by uncertainty in a never-ending stream of new information:

> Ordinary people, easily influenced, are usually indecisive when action is required. They find things different to what they expected – and even more so if they are influenced by others. Even he who has laid his own plans and now sees them in a new light will soon grow uncertain of his former judgement. His own firm self-assurance must arm him against the pressure of the moment.

The actual situation in the financial battlefield reminds one of the old story of the man who was preparing for a duel. Before the duel, his second asked him worriedly:

"Are you a good shot?"

The duelist answered:

"Sure, I can snap the stem of a wineglass at twenty paces!"

But then the second asked:

"That's all very well. But can you snap the stem of the wineglass while the wineglass is pointing a loaded pistol straight at your heart?"

Dealing in real life puts pressure on our nerves and then we easily make the mistake described by Clausewitz: *Exposed to the front line information fire we suddenly believe conditions are different to the original forecast.* If we are not used to tackling information and separating the important from the unimportant, the abundance of unimportant information and rumors will soon destroy our world view.

Marvin in the Jungle

Although the great amount of information was a problem for Clausewitz he nonetheless placed great emphasis on using spies. Although a thousand items of news were available, one might be absent, and this could be crucial. To procure this information spies had to be sent out. The same problem can also arise in the world of finance. In the classic *The Money Game* by "Adam Smith", a fine story is told about this very subject.

The characters in the story are the following:

1. Adam Smith, speculator and author of the book.
2. Great Winfield, the author's friend, a daily trader in stocks.
3. Marvin, a bankrupt cocoa speculator.
4. A cocoa dealer from the firm Hershey (anonymous).
5. A species of lice which may or may not infest cocoa plants in Ghana.
6. An African tribe.

140

It all starts when Great Winfield one day has a good idea. A close friend has told him that the Ghanian government "fix" their cocoa statistics. The statistics foresee a good harvest, but the fact is it will be miserable. The plan is obvious: When people discover the harvest is bad, cocoa prices will rise. Adam Smith and Winfield therefore invest 5,000 and 200,000 dollars respectively in cocoa at a 3% margin. (If the cocoa price goes up by for example 9% they will triple their money. If it drops by 3% they will lose it all). Then they start to wait for the price to rise.

The first two weeks are without event, but then something happens suddenly: revolution in Ghana. Adam Smith naturally has no idea what this means but he makes a few calls in the middle of the night to find out. He gets hold of a CBS correspondent. "Who is in power . . . are they pro cocoa?" he asks. Nobody knows, but contracts rise from 23 to 25 cents, and Adam Smith immediately ploughs back all his profits in more cocoa futures. So things are doing fine.

Some time later, a lecture is given on the subject of the cocoa market, which Adam Smith naturally attends. The lecturer, an expert from the cocoa firm Hershey, says there is plenty of cocoa for everybody. The day after contracts drop to 22 cents and this man starts to buy up. "Strange", thinks Adam Smith, "why is he buying now if there is plenty of cocoa?" Perhaps there is not really plenty of cocoa, because prices start to rise again and one day the news comes that riots have broken out in Nigeria, another major cocoa producing country. "Civil war!" Winfield shouts in delight, "civil war! The Hausas are murdering the Ibos. Tragedy! I don't see how they can get the crop in, do you?" Adam Smith agrees: Contracts continue up to 27 cents.

But despite false production statistics, revolution and civil war, contracts later start to drop and as time goes by Adam Smith begins to lose faith. But Winfield does not give up. "All we need", he says, "is heavy rain and the harvest will be devoured by lice." So lice in the harvest is their last hope, and so they contact Marvin, the bankrupt cocoa speculator. Marvin will be their spy and investigate whether lice are thriving down there. They outfit him with a bush suit, jungle pharmacy, compass and cocktail chilling equipment. (They draw the line when he asks for an elephant gun.)

Marvin's first telegrams report that the rain is moderate and that the people at the hotel think the harvest will be normal. Contracts drop to 24.5 cents. Adam Smith and Great Winfield are naturally not satisfied with what "people at the hotel" think. "Marvin must hire a car and go out into the jungle to have a look." And this is what Marvin does.

Marvin is never heard of again. The car gets stuck in the mud and Marvin wanders helplessly around in the jungle until finally, devoured by leeches, he ends up in a village where they tear his clothes off and put him in a pot of hot oil. Meanwhile contracts in the USA drop to 20 cents, and the two unfortunate speculators sell contracts at a heavy loss (Marvin survived since it turned out that the hot oil was to salve his wounds). But Adam Smith has lost a fortune and decides that he will stop trading in markets where he does not have the relevant information.

Stimulating and Resulting Factors

There is a moral to this tale. It tells us it is not always easy to find out whether or not there are lice in the cocoa plants. Initially, this kind of information will be known by local harvest workers far earlier than stock market speculators in a country far away. Then, like rings in water, the information will spread in wider and wider circles, first to the Marvins, then to the Great Winfields, then to stock analysts and economists and finally to the general public in a more or less reworked form.

In other words, information flows through different strata, of which those furthest away from the investor and speculator are the fundamental primary events such as lice infesting cocoa plants, loss of a company's export orders or the discovery of a new gold seam in a mine. These can be called the *stimulating factors*. By snapping up this information straightaway we can get ahead of other market operators, but to do this we really do have to send spies out into the jungle. This also requires a market which is not so large that 500 Marvins have already been sent out on field work.

All information on stimulating factors is gradually collected in a clearer, more presentable form. It is turned into statistics, budgets, account analyses and prognoses. These can be called *resulting factors*. Interpretation of resulting factors takes place in numerous economic secretariats, busily analysing the same figures

142

and writing identical reports (all things they could buy cheaply from a competent analysis institute). The resulting factors explain what all the small events are expected to signify for the value of the security/commodity, but often at a time where the market has already smelled danger and reacted.

Adam Smith and Great Winfield were smart enough to know that you cannot make do with looking for the information on resulting factors (the market is ahead). They had to know something about the stimulating factors, before the others in the market. The problems this strategy involved were something Marvin had a lot to tell about.

What About the Noah Effect?

If publicly available analyses and prognoses are unusable and the stimulating information is hard to get hold of, why not just trade quickly on all news? Why not trade on what mathematicians call the "Noah Effect"? The Noah Effect is loosely defined as an immediate response to any external shock – in contrast to the previ-

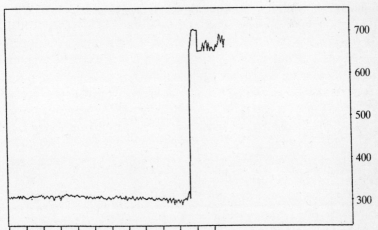

Figure 23. The Noah Effect. When the market is caught by surprise by a news story, it is impossible to benefit from the movement because it is instantaneous. The chart shows the intra-day movements of USD/DEM as trade figures were released.

ously mentioned Joseph Effect. Most new dealers try this. The situation is a bit like Pavlov's dogs and their conditional reflexes. When the green lamp lights up the dog rushes to its bowl and munches away at its meatballs. When the red lamp lights up it tries again, but gets a punch on its nose. After this has been repeated a few times the dog is either stubbornly refusing to do anything at all or has started to work it out. "Got it", it thinks, "green = meatballs, red = punch on the nose".

The problem with the Noah effect is that the market reacts immediately to any new market insight. In many cases it even over-reacts, so the best strategy is to sell on good news and buy on bad. So this is why we should (as described in Chapter 7) ignore these exogenous disturbances and define them as our noise.

The Real Problem

We know that a lot of information, in the honest light of the truth, is often worth zilch in the financial markets. If a piece of information is to be any good to us we must make sure that nobody else knows it. So we have reached a higher level, a second degree, where what is important is the *interpretation* of information rather than actually having it. But as we shall see in the next chapter, interpreting information is not always easy.

14.

The Second Degree: Interpreting Information

It does not help one's account to feel sure one is short theoretically
overvalued stocks that are currently rising or long those theoretically
undervalued but actually sinking in price.

Gerald M. Loeb

Most stock market trading takes place because the different market operators disagree on forecasts of the future. Buyers think prices will rise, and sellers think they will drop. This disagreement arises because people interpret their information differently. Although investors are different, we can identify six distinctive types:

- the fundamentalist
- the alchemist
- the random walker
- the puritan
- the tape-watcher
- the trader

The Fundamentalist

The fundamentalist carefully gathers economic statistics, interprets and evaluates political scenarios and calculates the true value of investment objects. If he is clever, he does not make do with the resulting information. Instead he dives deeper to find the stimulating information: He tests important details, lurks, watches and spies.

The fundamentalist can be extremely successful if he understands the limitations of his methods. The successful fundamentalist concentrates on smaller securities and illiquid markets where he knows not many Marvins are out. Often he trades in stocks and in most cases invests in relatively few securities at a

145

time, at times so heavily that he manipulates the market rather than follows. He has to concentrate his resources because his information search is very time-consuming. But in practice most fundamentalists are a fiasco on large liquid markets. After trying to predict price movements for a number of years they start to concentrate on post mortem rationalizations.

The Alchemist

Like the alchemists of old, trying to make gold with their flasks and test tubes, present-day alchemists are continually hunting for the secret formula of the stock exchange, with statistics and computers as the tools of their trade. The alchemist's problem is that he always thinks that *he has got it*. He does not have to study his historical material for very long before he finds the magical solution: If he had bought consistently for the last 50 years when price/earnings was X, when free reserves were Y, or "relative strength index" was Z, he would have profited every single time.

In secret he begins to trade according to his method, but alas and alack! At that very moment it stops working. "There must be a mistake", he thinks, and concludes after closer investigation that the indicator has to be combined with another before it can work. Everything goes wrong again, and as time passes he has to add more and more exceptions and extras until his original simple formula is so long that only a mainframe computer can handle it. And yet it doesn't work. The alchemist is the market's pathetic figure, for although like Elmer Fudd chasing Bugs Bunny he vainly follows one mirage after the other, he never realizes that the market does not adhere to linear mathematics and that no few simple market rules exist.

The Random Walker

The random walker has typically attended an institute of higher education. He has an impressive knowledge but one thought keeps nagging him: If he is so smart, how come he is not rich? His answer is that all knowledge (thanks to the fundamentalists) is discounted in prices and that all fluctuations around true value are random and unpredictable. He does not believe that cycles, liquidity, breadth and psychology can be used in market forecasts. His argument is that by a simple mathematical test the markets live up to the criteria for random fluctuations. He ignores the fact that this is a characteristic of deterministic chaos, where short-term forecasts are nonetheless possible.

If the random walker is confronted with stock market speculators who consistently, over a large number of years, have made exorbitant profits, he rejects this as a statistical coincidence. The random walker does not concentrate on buying or selling at the right time but on spreading his risk on the basis of a mathematical model. If everybody followed this principle the market would be reduced to a casino. For obvious reasons this is not the case.

The Puritan

In just the same way as the clever fundamentalist uses his ears, the puritan uses his eyes: He studies charts. The puritan believes that the absolutely only useful investment instrument is price charts. Armed with these he believes that he can see not only into the next month, but also into the next year. The axiom that the market is ahead has become a religion for the puritan: The markets are right. Always. If the puritan knows what he is doing he can earn a lot of money, and into the bargain with minimum effort, since studying charts does not take much time. He has just one problem. Once in a while the markets fail as barometers and then he is wrong. Dead wrong.

The Tape-Watcher

The classical market operator is the tape-watcher or, as his colleagues may call him, the "tape worm" or the "ticker hound". This animal is the prototype of the neurotic stockbroker of the comic cartoons. Chronically suffering from high blood pressure, with red eyes he follows the price trend minute by minute. For hours the tape-watcher stares at his screen like a hare dazzled by a car's headlights. Meanwhile he has a mental chart stored in his brain, remembering old price intervals he uses as hold points in his dealing. He also keeps an eye on turnover and who is buying and selling when.

The tape-watcher does not call himself a chartist, but his method is basically the same, although he replaces charts with memory. Bearing in mind what a chart looks like, a tape-watcher can be described as a person who intensely monitors the formation of every point on the graph over the six to ten hours this takes, but who attaches less importance to overview. The skilfull tape-watcher gets ahead in the market. But not for long: After five years he has so many prices in his head that they are coming out of his ears: He is burnt out and has to stop.

The Trader

The trader was bad at mathematics in school but good at getting new ideas. The trader does not believe in absolutes and is neither an alchemist nor a random walker. His method is a combination of fundamental economic espionage and interpretation of charts. If the trader knows himself and his methods he can be among the largest winners in the market. But if he cannot combine the different information he can inadvertently become a victim of his own psychology and end in ruin.

So Who Is Right?

Before identifying the winners it must be stated that most are losers. In 1927 Babson wrote that 98% of finance market operators in his experience were poorer on leaving the market than when they started. In his book *You Can't Win in Wall Street* of the same year, E. E. Hooker Jr. wrote about a broker's bookkeeper who found only one account showing a profit among 5,000. And this was written two years before the Wall Street crash, not after!

The classic for anybody who has lost money on the stock market is *A Random Walk Down Wall Street*, written in 1973 by speculator and economics professor Burton G. Malkiel, with the following thought-provoking conclusion: "No scientific evidence has yet been assembled to indicate that the investment performance of professionally managed portfolios as a group has been any better than that of randomly selected portfolios."

The conclusion is based on statistical surveys at for example Princeton University. Here it was found that most mutual trusts did poorer than in a hypothetical strategy in which the securities bought were selected on a completely random basis.

Actually it was not Malkiel who first drew the public's attention to this thought-provoking fact, but Nobel prize-winner Paul Samuelson, who introduced an interesting experiment at a senate committee hearing. He put a stock list up on a dart board and then got Senator Thomas McIntyre of New Hampshire to throw darts at it. The senator missed a number of times but finally "selected" a portfolio which it was agreed to evaluate after ten years. And quite right: After this period had passed the investor who had bought and then kept these random securities would have done better than most American "growth funds", despite their impressive arsenals of analysts and information systems. The same phenomenon can be observed for professional "money managers". In the USA they can voluntarily report their investment results to an organization called SEI Funds Evaluation Services.

Funds Evaluation Services frequently publish statistics of money managers' investment results. A survey of these statistics in *Business Week* (1985) showed the distribution given in Table 4. An increasing majority fared worse than the overall stock index and thereby more poorly than the expected yield based on hypothetical random selection with for example darts or by flipping a coin.

Table 4. American money managers' investment yields compared to development in the stock index.

Time interval	Better than the index	Poorer than the index
1984	26%	74%
1982–84	32%	68%
1980–84	45%	55%
1975–84	44%	56%

This conclusion is not limited to stocks. In 1949 the Commodity Exchange Authority in the USA published an analysis of a good 9,000 market operators' activities in trading in futures contracts on the commodity market over eight years. In this period, over 400,000 deals took place and the result was that speculators among the 9,000 had built up losses over *six times higher than their total profits*.

Somebody Has to Make a Profit?

But money can't just disappear, can it? Surely, somebody has to make a profit? Many believe the intelligent ones win. Some even think that if they are intelligent this should be enough to get success, irrespective of how they interpret their information.

Winston Churchill, undeniably a very intelligent man, in 1929 visited his friend, the financier Bernard Baruch, in New York. Churchill was fascinated by the hectic market atmosphere and decided to take part for a day. His transactions quickly went awry and when he tried to recover his losses with new speculation things got even worse. His deals became more and more frenzied and at the end of the day he had lost everything and was prepared to sell all his assets and give up his political career.

But things were not all that bad. Baruch had foreseen the catastrophe and asked one of his people to shadow Churchill and cover all his deals, each time doing the opposite on Churchill's account. So he was not poorer, but a good deal wiser. Intelligence is not enough. But who of our characteristic types will make any money?

The Catbird's Seat

Almost all real performers can be allocated to two categories of information strategy. One concentrates on the market dynamics and the other on stimulating economic factors.

Let's start with the man who takes the markets as his starting-point. He realizes that you can never get a global overview by investigating stimulating and resulting factors. Instead he makes financial barometers his starting-point: money rates, short bonds, long bonds, stock markets, commodities, precious metals, currencies and financial liquidity. By studying his charts with a trained financial ball-eye he can watch the scenario "top-down", first identifying the global scenario and then zooming down on the best short-term trends.

This method is very demanding intellectually because one must be very familiar with business cycles, human behavior, and distribution and accumulation phenomena (see later). On the other hand, for the professional it is very safe and not very time consuming. Half a day a week to consider the global scenario, supplemented with half an hour per day (in bed?) in control of all market information is sufficient. This method can give lasting success.

The second method is where, like Nathan Rothschild and Great Winfield, we dig stimulating information out of the wilderness of reality. If one is of a relaxed nature, a surveillance system can be used like Nathan Rothschild's: not using homing pigeons, but by cultivating a social network of intelligent, well-informed people. This will ensure a continuing flow of delicate and inspiring information, sometimes leading to new insight.

If we are more hardworking, we operate like Great Winfield, using systematic tests: hire a few Marvins and send them out into the field to check the well-founded hypotheses. If we are sensible, we do both. Anyone choosing this information strategy can have just as much success as someone using the first-mentioned. But for lasting success he will be well-advised to take time out to study national insider trading legislation.

15.

Smoke Without Fire?

What the superior man seeks is in himself; what the small man seeks is in others.

Confucius

In 1891 a 14-year-old boy by the name of Jesse Lausten Livermoore signed up for a job as quotation-board boy in a New York brokerage office. Jesse had an excellent memory and soon began to notice that some peculiar price movements tended to precede every major rise or decline in the market. As this caught his interest, he began taking regular notes of it in a little book. Every day he would write down what he expected the prices to do the day after. Later, he would check up his predictions with the actual transcripts. After a while he realized, that he was able to make fairly good predictions.

The Boy Plunger

One day one of the older office boys told Jesse that he had received a dandy tip on the Burlinton stock. Jesse checked the stock's preceding price movements and agreed that the stock was poised for an immediate advance. Together they agreed to "play the stock". The only thing they needed was five dollars if they played on margin in one of the numerous bucket shops. So they began trading as planned and after two days they cashed in their profit. Jesse made $3.12 dollars.

This was the beginning of one of the most remarkable speculative careers the world has ever seen. Soon Jesse Livermoore started betting regularly in the bucket shops all over New York. With his extraordinary talent for interpreting the minute by minute price fluctuations he earned a good deal of money.

After some years, however, his genius became so well known throughout the city that no bucket shop would let him play. For a while he tried to play under false names but finally had to move to St. Louis where he could play for only a brief period before the same problem caught up with him again. By that time he was known and feared among bucket shop owners throughout the country as the "boy plunger". After betting in the bucket shops for a number of years, Jesse was able to move into the real market. Although his trading career was very unstable at first, he ended up accumulating more than 30 million dollars on his own deals.

A Secret Tip

One evening, Jesse was in Palm Beach with his wife. During dinner she sat next to a Mr. Wisenstein, who was president of the Borneo Tin Company and at the same time manager of an insider pool manipulating the very same stock. Mr. Wisenstein, who had deliberately manouvered to be seated next to Mrs. Livermoore, was extremely friendly to her during dinner. Finally, he told her in a low voice:

> It has been a very great pleasure to meet you and your husband, and I want to prove that I am sincere in saying this because I hope to see a great deal of both of you. I am sure I don't have to tell you that what I am going to say is strictly confidential.

Then he whispered: "If you will buy som Borneo Tin you will make a great deal of money." It so happened that Mrs. Livermoore had received 500 dollars from her husband the same day. She therefore expressed some interest in the matter.

Mr. Wisentstein sensed this and continued:

> Just before I left the hotel, I received some cables with news that won't be known to the public for several days at least. I am going to gather in as much of the stock as I can. If you get some at the opening tomorrow you will be buying it at the same time and at the same price as I. I give you my word that Borneo Tin will surely advance. You are the only person that I have told this to. Absolutely the only one!

Mr. Wisenstein's hope was of course that Mrs. Livermoore would pass the tip to her husband who could then buy in the market – enabling the insider pool to sell. But she didn't. Instead, she decided for the first time in her life to trade a stock on her own. After all, she had the 500 dollars . . .

The next morning she went to Jesse's broker and opened her own account. She also instructed the broker not to let Jesse know about her activities. From the opening of the market she then bought as much on margin as possible. Her average price was 108.

When Mrs. Livermoore had left, her husband arrived. He was very bearish on the whole market and had picked a suitable stock for his bear-raids. It was a stock which behaved as if it was being distributed by insiders: Borneo Tin. Jesse sold short 10,000 Borneo Tin and 4,000 the next day.

The third morning, Mrs. Livermoore strolled by the broker office at around eleven. When the manager saw her, he took her aside and told her that Borneo Tin was trading at par and that her account consequently showed a substantial loss. More margin was needed. As he couldn't tell her that Jesse was short on the same stock, he simply advised her to consult her husband about the problem. Detailed records of the ensuing conversation do not exist.

When the Tough Gets Going . . .

What Mrs. Livermoore learned that day was that it is not very wise to trade against the most skilled operators. These operators can be divided into four major groups:

1. Insiders (owning over 5% of a company's share capital)
2. Stock Exchange members
3. Major hedgers
4. Major speculators

In the USA, the stock market trading of these important market operators is currently tracked and published by the authorities. And the study of these statistics is highly recommendable.

Insiders

Insiders are directors, officers or people owning over 5% of the capital of a listed company. The rules say that corporate insiders must file a Form 4 report when trading stocks in their own company. If insiders are behind massive stock sales, it could be assumed that they are selling because they are short of cash. But the second and more obvious possibility is that they have spotted bad news. So this is a warning signal. If insiders are buying there is not much doubt: They have positive information via their close knowledge of the company. Consequently, one glance at insiders' transactions can give more information than 1,000 earnings forecasts. Insiders' transactions are regularly reported in *Vicker's Weekly Insider Report* and *Barron's* and the *Wall Street Journal*.

Stock Exchange Members

In the 1940 book *Where are the Customers' Yachts?* Fred Schwed tells the story of a visitor to New York who was shown around Manhattan's Wall Street area. In the harbor the guide first pointed one way saying: "There are the bankers' yachts," and then the other: "and there are the brokers' ". The naive visitor asked the all-important question, the title of Schwed's book: "So where are the customers' yachts?" What Schwed meant was naturally that, in contrast to brokers, customers' deals do not earn them the kind of money that buys yachts. As he stated: Every day at closing time, brokers throw the day's profits up in the air. What gets stuck on the ceiling trickles down to the customers.

But the professionals do earn money. Studying mandatory trading reports it will be seen that this group systematically does better than the majority of market operators. So following their deals can improve our headway. The following indication can be used in particular:

- If the majority of short sales are by stock exchange members, this indicates that the market is going down.
- If, on the other hand, they are responsible for a small proportion of short sales, it is on its way up.

Statistics like these are available in no other country than the USA, but it can be confidently stated that the situation is the same almost everywhere.

Hedgers and Major Speculators

Midway through each month on the US futures market the Commodity Futures Trading Commission (CFTC) publishes a list, *Traders Report*, showing how open interests (see p. 161) are distributed between three groups described as "large hedgers", "large speculators" and "small market participants". Like the aforementioned groups, these statistics are based on mandatory reports.

The category which has proved to do best is hedgers. As mentioned, a hedger is a person who tries to cover a risk with a set-off financial deal, e.g. like our wheat producer who sold wheat for future delivery. These people can be assumed to have very good market insight, as they are commercially active in the market. This insight is naturally reflected in their financial hedges. It is therefore not surprising that hedgers do best among the aforementioned groups. "Large speculators" do next best – they are also smarter than the average, which is natural: If they were not relatively smart they would not be so large.

Musical Chairs

It's easy to imagine that somebody will protest: "Isn't it absurd to keep staring at each other instead of the economy and the markets?" The best answer is in Keynes's descriptions of the market in *The General Theory of Employment, Interest and Money*.

> For it is, so to speak, a game of Snap, of Old Maid, of Musical Chairs – a pastime in which he is victor who says *Snap* neither too soon nor too late, who passed the Old Maid to his neighbour before the game is over, who secures a chair for himself when the music stops. These games can be played with zest and enjoyment, though all the players know that it is the Old Maid which is circulating, or that when the music stops some of the players will find themselves unseated.

And further:

> It needs *more* intelligence to defeat the dark forces of time and our ignorance of the future than to beat the gun. Moreover, life is not long enough; – human nature desires quick results, there is a peculiar zest in making money quickly, and remoter gains are discounted by the average man at a very high rate. The game of professional invest-

ment is intolerably boring and over-exacting to anyone who is entirely exempt from the gambling instinct; whilst he who has it must pay to this propensity the appropriate toll.

As he himself documented, beating the gun was the most efficient way to earn money. And to do this, he said, we have to work with higher degrees of information strategy: "We have reached the third degree where we devote our intelligences to anticipating what average opinion expects the average opinion to be. And there are some, I believe, who practise the fourth, fifth and higher degrees." Studying insiders, members, hedgers and speculators is this third degree, because insiders, members, hedgers and speculators do this too. Even if we are among the smartest we cannot ignore this degree, because if the others don't do as we expect, we'll be the ones without seats when the music stops. But let's not spend too much time on the third degree. The fourth awaits us.

16.

Little and Big Fish

Master, I marvel how the fishes live in the sea.
– Why, as men do a-land – the great ones eat up the little ones.

Shakespeare

The fourth degree is naturally to keep an eye on the least smart and do the opposite of what they do. This is called "contrary opinion".

Traditionally, least smart has been synonymous with small. On the stock market these are often referred to as "odd lotters". Odd lotters are investors trading small portions of stocks (under one hundred at a time). Originally it was Garfield Albee Drew who studied trading statistics for these odd lotters and formulated the first rules. The picture he found was in fact not completely homogeneous. Odd lotters steadily sold when the market went up and steadily bought when the market went down. Not exactly smart, but not completely hopeless either.

Drew also found that odd lotters' net buys were very low in periods where a large bear market bottomed out, and their net sales were very small when the market peaked. So, as could be expected, small market operators were willing to take on the role of the famous "Bigger Fool", from whom stocks could always be bought at bargain price when the bear market was close to bottoming, and who were happy to buy yours when the bull market topped. Today this concept is less viable because small operators now mostly trade via mutual funds, and an increasing proportion of odd lot trades are generated by computers. While odd lotters were responsible for around 15% of stock trading on the New York Stock Exchange in Drew's time, today they account for less than 1%. So odd lotter statistics give only one single viable signal:

158

– If odd lotters' short sales rise strongly this indicates that the market is close to bottoming.

Odd lotters' transactions are published in among others *Barron's*.

The Bullish Consensus

As odd lotters' transactions have become an uncertain indicator, contrary opinion is now practised in a far more sophisticated way. One example is found in an American consulting firm which makes its living by making fools of the professionals. The company is the Hadady Corporation and its product *The Bullish Consensus*. (It should be mentioned that the Bullish Consensus is not the only contrary opinion statistic. One of the others is called Dick Davis Digest. This consensus found that among 350 newsletters monitored only 5% correctly predicted the 1987 crash.) Every week Hadady publishes statistics of how many professional newsletters recommend buying or selling different securities, currencies, precious metals and commodities on the futures market. By following them it is possible to "invest with the professionals".

Doing this would quickly ruin us. Practice shows that these advisors are usually mistaken. So much so, in fact, that generally we can earn money by doing the opposite of what they recommend if a large majority of them agree on the same. The main rule is to sell if the majority recommend buying, and to buy if a large majority recommend selling. Figure 24 shows how professional buy recommendations harmonize with the market's movements.

In practice, the Bullish Consensus is drawn up by the company's weekly reading of buy and sell recommendations in all of the country's leading newletters, and then evaluating their degree of optimism on a scale from −3 to +3, where −3 is used for an extreme bearish view, zero for a neutral standpoint, and +3 for a strongly bullish viewpoint (something on the lines of "We recommend buying aggressively at current market prices").

Then figures are weighted according to the newsletter's circulation. If it is a commercial newsletter, circulation is immediately available and if it is a customer newsletter reader statistics are

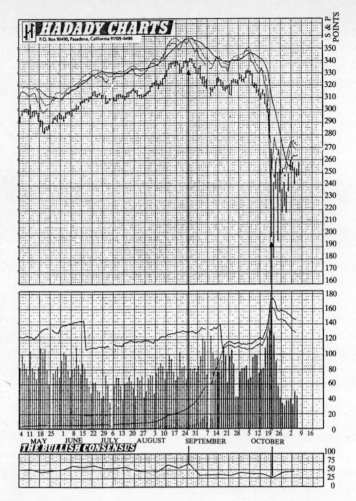

Figure 24. Standard & Poors Index Futures and the Bullish Consensus. The figure is divided into three sections, the top one showing American index futures before and during the crash in 1987. The middle section shows daily turnover in the period (columns) and open interests (curves) for contracts expiring in December 1987 and all contracts, respectively. Finally, the bottom section shows development in the "Bullish Consensus". On Tuesday 25 August the Bullish Consensus reached the critical optimistic level of 70 for the first time in 1987. As the indicator's value had dropped in the following week this indicated that bear trading was the order of the day (confirmed by the fact that open interests did not rise). On 20 October the indicator showed critical pessimism at value 25, and when the indicator lay higher in the following week simultaneously with a drop in open interests, a "contrary opinion buy signal" was released. (Chart: The Bullish Consensus. Hadady Corporation.)

based on the number of dealers employed by the publisher. Finally, the average of the scaled recommendations is converted to an index for each security, extending from 0 to 100. Here the figure 0 indicates that all newsletters are extremely negative and 100 that they are all extremely positive. This index is published every Tuesday after the US exchange has closed.

The most important key rule for use of this indicator is as follows:

> Don't buy on a market where the bullish consensus is 70 or over, and don't sell on a market where the bullish consensus is 30 or under.

However, it should be mentioned that the indicator reacts slightly differently for the different markets: On some markets greater consensus is required among the indicator's investment consultants than on others before the market can be described as "overbought" or "oversold".

Open Interests

To get away with trading on the above we must get to grips with an extra finesse called "open interests". Open interests tell us how much is invested in a market at a given point in time. On an ordinary bond or stock market there is no problem as no more papers have been bought than issued (disregarding bear trading). On futures, options and forward deals the situation is different. Here there is the special phenomenon that there is no limit to how many buy and sell contracts can exist at a given point in time, other than that there must be an equal quantity of both. Consequently, the number of open interests depends exclusively on people's interest in the market.

On futures markets, daily statistics are kept of the number of outstanding contracts or open interests (as each deal constitutes a buyer and seller of a contract, and thus one open interest). With this indicator in the picture we can refine the contrary opinion rules a little:

1. As long as the bullish consensus is moving without reaching overbought or oversold territory, as a general rule the indicator's trend must be followed.

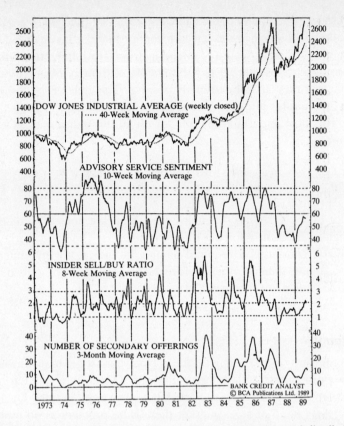

Figure 25. This chart illustrates the classical accumulation and distribution processes on the New York Stock Exchange. The upper graph shows Dow Jones Industrials through 1973–89. The second graph is a measurement of advisory sentiment comparable to the Bullish Consensus. A high level (75 and above) indicates distribution. A low level (35 and below) indicates accumulation. The third graph shows the insider sell/buy ratio where a high level (above 3) indicates distribution while a low level (below 1) indicates accumulation. The last graph shows the number of secondary offers, which are redistributions of stock some time after they have been brought to the market by a firm or a group of brokers. An increase in secondary offers is a direct measure of distribution. Insider sell-buy activity is reported by SEC in their "Official Summary of Insider Trading Activities that Relate to forms 3 & 4". Secondary offerings are also measured by SEC. When the three indicators are compared, a clear picture is drawn of major distributions in 1976, 1983 and 1986 and of accumulations in 1974, 1984 and – especially – postcrash 1988. (*Source*: The International Bank Credit Analyst in cooperation with Investors Intelligence Inc., Larchmant and Stock Research Corporation, New York.)

2. This is especially true if open interests rise together with development in the price trend.
3. If the bullish consensus shows an overbought or oversold market and open interests are rising simultaneously, the signal is eliminated.
4. If open interests fall, this indicates that trading is due to profit-taking or stop-losses. This weakens the trend movement's credibility.
5. If open interests drop simultaneously with the bullish consensus reaching an extreme and then moving into a neutral area, this indicates a very large trend reversal.

Finally, there is the special feature that if a trend has clearly reversed and very large open interests have been built up shortly before, the new trend can be further reinforced when all those holding losses need cover.

But Why Do These Rules Function?

Nobody wants to look into their mirror and say without faultering that he is looking at a genuine odd lotter, a typical "Little Guy", who always misreads the market, buying at the top and selling at the bottom, and who steadily loses on everything he does. However, this could be an excellent starting-point for success on the stock exchange. If we were quite certain of our own inadequacy we could just instruct our brokers to consistently do the opposite of what we suggest. As Baruch's people did for Churchill, the broker would short the stocks we suggest buying and double our bond portfolio if we suggest selling. In reality this is exactly what Contrary Opinion practitioners do. The logic is as follows:

> Most active investors subscribe to some form of newsletter with recommendations to buy or sell based on fundamental or market analysis. In general investors follow the advice they read in these newsletters. If a very large proportion of newsletters recommend buying it can be assumed that a very large proportion of investors will actually buy.

So far this logic is obvious. But it continues:

163

There will always be bought and sold equal volumes in the market. If most have bought, sellers must on average be larger fish than buyers. If 90% are bullish the average seller will be ten times as large as the average buyer. If 95% are bullish, he is twenty times larger. In other words, a large bullish majority indicates an end to the classical distribution process, so that the market should soon reverse.

The Bullish Consensus is thus the practical analysis of the phenomenon described by Charles Dow in 1902 as "accumulation" and "distribution": the big fish eating up the little ones.

We can vividly imagine how Dow would have smirked and Keynes laughed out loud if they had seen the Bullish Consensus statistics and their rules. While taking out subscriptions with great delight they would have speculated on when the fifth degree would be reached: everyone practicing contrary opinion, so that turning up on the stock market with the Bullish Consensus under your arm would be as great a catastrophe as arriving at a party in the same dress as your hostess. When this day arrived, you would have to be contrary/contrary to be really contrary and then . . .

But let's forget this mind-boggling prospect and instead look at other contrary opinion indicators. Let's study the media.

"When It's Obvious to the Public . . ."

The media are an excellent indicator for the retrothinking individual. What we should look for in the media is indications that things have begun to appear completely obvious and that everybody seems to agree. This situation is, as Joseph Granville expressed it in *A Strategy for Daily Stock Market Timing* from 1960: "When it's obvious to the public, it's obviously wrong." In this book he refers to newspaper stories on 14 August 1937, a day when things appeared really bright for the economy:

- Suspensions of payments had reached the lowest level since 1919.
- Further economic growth was expected during the autumn.
- Rising credit demand was expected, due to an increase in commercial activity.
- The depression was considered to be finally over.
- Building activity reached new heights.

164

– Canada's industrial production rose 20% in one year.
– Major department stores reported rising turnover.
– Record-high artificial silk production.
– Steel production rose 9% in one month.

The day after the stock market started to drop, and after seven months it had lost half its value.

The situation is not very different today. On 8 October 1984 the front page of *Business Week* showed a rocket-driven dollar accompanied by a very eloquent headline. "SUPERDOLLAR", it said, the headline inside the magazine amplifying this with: "It's reshaping the world economy – and could last a decade." Five months later the dollar peaked and started one of its fastest and longest drops ever.

It is hard to say for sure when something becomes obvious to everybody, but the market is close to reversal when the media start to predict that rises or drops will continue for years. On 13 August 1979 the front page of the same magazine proclaimed: "THE DEATH OF EQUITIES – How inflation is destroying the stock market." In the following two years the stock market treaded water, in 1982 beginning a 300% rise.

On 28 May 1984 the headline was: "TROUBLE IN THE GOVERNMENT BOND MARKETS", and the spread article in the middle of the magazine closed: ". . . investors can do little but brace for further depression of the prices of their bonds – posing even greater tests for already strained government bond markets." Immediately thereafter an aggressively bullish bond market started.

And so it continued. The heading "ARE UTILITIES OBSO-LETE?" on 21 May 1984 hit the magazine only nineteen days before the bottom of the Dow Jones Utility Average.

Likewise the magazine's heading: "THE DEATH OF MIN-ING" on the front page on 17 December 1984 acted as a good timing signal to go into mining stock.

In 1987, just before the global bull-market peaked, the senti-ment in *Business Week* had changed totally. In the 6 July issue 1987, the front-page displayed the following headline: "STOCKS ARE STILL THE BEST BET". An article on page 40 started with the headline: "The good times roll on for investors. On the tap of 1987; Lower inflation, stable interest rates and plenty of

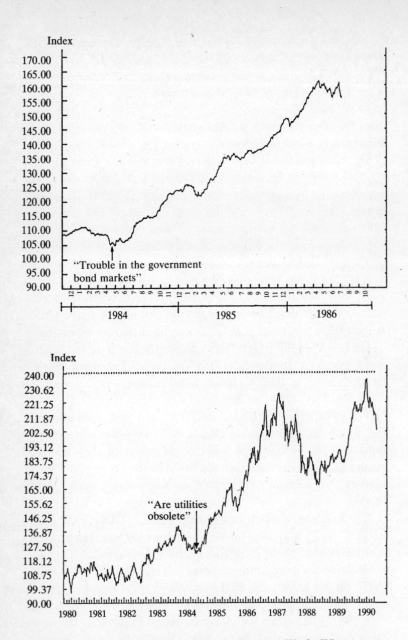

Figure 26. Two unfortunate headlines in *Business Week*. When everybody on the finance market believes the same it does not take long for the market to reverse.

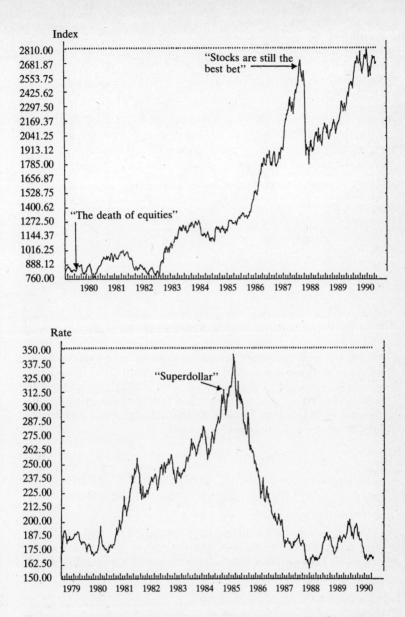

Figure 27. The first graph shows that while *Business Week* was very bearish in 1984, the magazine was bullish on stocks in its 1987 semi-annual investment survey. The second graph shows the unfortunate timing of the "Superdollar" analysis.

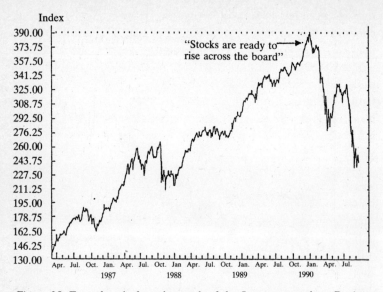

Index

Figure 28. Four days before the crash of the Japanese market, *Business Week* ran its own analysis. "Japan's investors say the best may be yet to come", the title ran. Three experts were cited in the article. The first was the President of Nomura Securities: "There may be some volatility, but prices will keep climbing." The second, Richard Greer from Baring Securities, claimed that increased takeover activity will continue to press the market up. And the third expert opinion, from an assistant investment manager from Dai-Ichi Mutual Life Insurance proclaimed: "Stocks are ready to rise across the board."

money-making opportunities". And on page 43: "What's propelling the market? Big, fat earnings". This article concluded:

> Even if the market's valuation level remains on the high side, that's no reason to sell, either. High valuations are the hall-mark of a bull-market. They can persist for years in an economy with steady growth and low inflation.

Seven weeks later, the market started to slide and in October made its fastest crash ever.

A similar case was seen prior to the Japanese crash in 1990. On 25 December 1989, *Business Week* contained an article with the following heading: "JAPAN'S INVESTORS SAY THE BEST MAY BE YET TO COME". The article's concluding remarks: "As it has so many times before, Tokyo could be about to confound the sceptics once again." Four days later the market peaked and in February 1990 it crashed.

But even though contrary opinion investing is fun, it must be practised with great care. If the Bullish Consensus or similar statistics are used to time investments, as mentioned we should not be afraid to buy when the Bullish Consensus is rising – in fact this is a good signal for as long as we have not approached the critical value of 70%.

Similarly, there are seldom grounds for unease if the media, weak voiced and in small type, point out that the market is in a rising (or falling) trend. The danger signal arises the day we read that market increases "can last for years", or a security is nominated as "a good investment paper" after significant rises. (A significant example most will remember is the global commodities shortage hysteria at the start of the 70s, in 1972 peaking with the bestseller *Limits to Growth* by Meadows. The book forewarned a catastrophic shortage of commodities all over the globe. Its publication coincided with the Kondratieff cycle's peaking, since when there has been a steadily rising commodities surplus.) On the other hand, the time when "it would be pure speculation to buy now" is often close to the optimal buying opportunity.

Is the Reverse Never the Case?

It's fun to think contrarily. It gives a feeling of superiority. But this way of thinking is not always healthy, so it is good that the rules do not always work. Sometimes the reverse is the case. The typical exception is a situation where a large market operator tries to manipulate a large market. In most cases this ends in disaster. In the final analysis the large market operator is the loser, while many small ones win.

A classic example of this was Bunker Hunt and his family's massive silver buy-ups in 1979. From the summer of 1979 to the beginning of 1980 they bought up silver in quantities estimated at around one sixth of all silver stocks in the entire Western world. Prices increased fivefold (from 10 to 50 dollars per ounce), and incredible as it may seem, it looked as though they were trying to annex a deliberate corner of this enormous market. This did not work. Many will probably remember the small ads which turned

169

up in newspapers: "Silver bought for resmelting. Good prices offered."

At that kind of price many European silver turines and many small Indian anklets found their way to the marketplace. And when finally the stock market enforced a small unobserved rule called: "Liquidations only, no new positions", the market collapsed with a thud. Shortly after it was all over. The brothers were left with a loss of around a billion dollars.

Losing so much money shows style, but it's hardly fun. It is almost impossible to dominate a very liquid market, and this is not just true of speculators eager for adventure. If a central bank tries to dam a currency's movements things usually go wrong. When the bank starts its intervention it can stop the trend, but like a dam stopping a gushing river, only for a period. As days and weeks pass the pressure builds up and finally the supported currency breaks through its chart points against one small currency after the other, until the inevitable breakthrough against one of the key currencies finally triggers off mass fluctuation which no government authority can prevent. And when that happens, it is, as "Adam Smith" wrote, "really quite comfy to be part of the crowd".

VI

The Madness of Crowds

Men, it has been well said, think in herds; it will be seen that they go mad in herds while they only recover their senses slowly and one by one.

Charles MacKay

17.

Tracing the Monster's Tracks

There is a great deal of unmapped country within us which would have to be taken into account in an exploration of our gusts and storms.

George Eliot

Like every good horror story, finance markets have their monster of the deep. This monster seldom appears in the light of day. Instead it hides away under the markets' calm surface of cycles, waves and ripples. Buried deep down in the mud, far away on the bottom of the sea, the monster lies watching, waiting and biding its time.

Although nobody can say for sure that they really know this monster, most people are aware of its existence. Because, like all other monsters, from time to time it rises from the dim and murky depths in pursuit of its prey. Sometimes the monster picks out a few titbits, a finger here and an arm there. At others its appetite is voracious, swallowing its victims whole and leaving survivors quaking and shaking in fear. And at other times again it goes completely berserk, trailing an unbelievable bloodbath in its wake. Bellowing with rage it tears its victims apart, spurting blood and intestines in a frenzied orgy, leaving no one in any doubt that it is the real ruler of the markets.

One of these bloodbaths, the worst ever, started on Monday 19 October 1987.

The End of the World

On this historic morning many dealers reported for work with an uncanny feeling of unease, because on the preceding Friday Dow Jones Industrials had dropped 108.35 points. A full 60 points had been seen before, and in 1986 the market had even dropped 87 on one day. But 108.35!

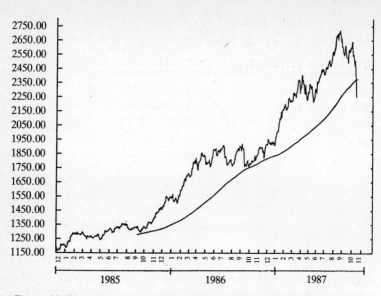

Figure 29. The Dow Jones Industrial Average on 16 October 1987. On the Friday before the 1987 crash, for the first time in over three years the index penetrated below the average of the last 200 days' prices. This 200-day moving average is drawn in on the chart.

The first market to open after the weekend was the exchange in Melbourne, Australia. Prices reflected uneasiness from the outset, with huge losses. In Tokyo the exchange also opened lower, however, closing with a moderate drop of 2.5%. But in Hong Kong there was no moderation. In hectic trading the stock index fell by 11%, at which the exchange management suspended all further trading for the rest of the week. The scenario was the same in Singapore.

In view of these events European markets opened under a cloud. In London and Zürich stocks dropped a record 11%, in Frankfurt 7%, and Paris, Stockholm and Copenhagen each fell by 6%, with heavy trading on all exchanges and in an atmosphere best described as varying degrees of collective panic. Even before European exchanges closed, the major American finance houses had started early morning briefings. One was Merrill Lynch, whose Chief Analyst, Robert J. Farrell, announced that he was extremely pessimistic. "A 200 point drop" would not be unrealistic. Also the President of Kidder, Peabody & Co., Max C. Chapman Jr., had become more and more concerned over the weekend. On this Monday morning he warned his people that they were in for a tough day. And when dealers arrived for work in a third stockbroking company, Donaldson, Lufkin & Jenrette, they were amazed to discover that management had hired armed guards to protect them against angry clients. Their President's peptalk, closing with the words: "Let's keep our heads cool and, maybe, we'll all get through this thing alive" did nothing to lift their spirits. Then the gong rang out and trading opened.

When the first prices flashed across computer screens the industrial index lay at 2180 – 67 points below Friday's level. Fifty million shares changed hands in the first thirty minutes of trading. Then prices started to drop slowly and steadily, while trading struck an unbelievable record. Three million stocks changed hands every single minute. After an hour, 140 million stocks had been traded and the index dropped further to 2145.

Then the real collapse started. As a dealer screamed out "Now we're going down", telephones jammed and computers started to lag further and further behind trading, in the end quoting prices over one and a half hours old. On top of all this was the widespread "computer trading". An army of computers, programmed to tally stock prices with prices on futures contracts, disgorged an endless stream of stop orders, since in periods futures prices were as far as 20% below the prices of the underlying stocks. The market dropped relentlessly minute by minute, and no-one had the slightest idea of how far down it would go. At stockbrokers Shearson Lehman, dealers put up a signboard above their desks reading: "To the lifeboats".

When 4 o'clock finally came and the saving gong rang out, a dealer's desperate cry was heard: "This is the end of the world!". Then it was all over. In the course of seven hours the American stock index had dropped by 23% to 1739, with an unbelievable record turnover of 604 million shares.

A Wave of Fear

But exchanges do not sleep for long. A few hours after the West coast market closed, the Tokyo exchange opened in an unmistakable state of shock. Within the first half hour of trading 247 of the market's 250 largest securities were suspended, and the rest were traded at plummeting prices, closing with a drop of 15%.

175

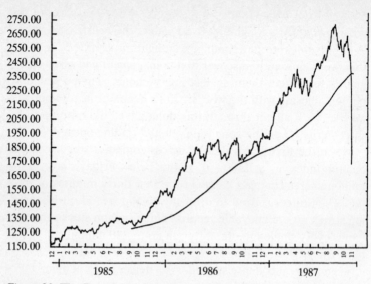

Figure 30. The Dow Jones Industrial Average on 19 October 1987. The drop on "Black Monday" was the largest ever in the history of American stock trading: Industrials fell by 23% in seven hours.

This in spite of the fact that trading in several of the large securities was suspended for up to two hours because there were not enough buyers to open.

On Tuesday the monster was also rampant in Europe. In London the index fell by 12% and in Paris the market opened with a 10% dive, at which the stock exchange's computer systems collapsed and trading was partly suspended. On the Italian exchange, from the start of trading there were 10% drops. Then several leading securities were suspended. In Spain they did not make do with the major securities, but suspended them all. Europe had capitulated and the only hope was that the USA would break the vicious circle.

When New York opened at 3.30 p.m. European time, it did not look as if this would happen. From the outset prices fluctuated wildly, and the decision was soon taken to suspend trading of almost 90 securities. But just as the President of the Stock Exchange deliberated total surrender and a closedown of the entire exchange, a hectic rally started and the index closed at 1841.01 – 6% above the previous day's level.

176

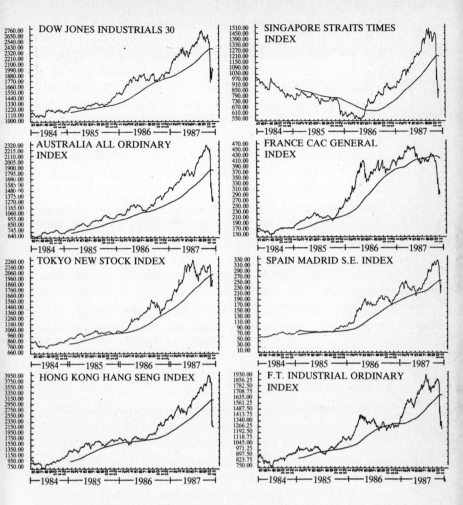

Figure 31. Eight international stock markets during the 1987 crash. The moving averages drawn in are based on 200-day prices.

On Wednesday morning it was all over. All over the world dealers reported for work on a positive market, where everything was as before. Just as suddenly as the monster appeared, it vanished again. As cleaning up after the two strangest days in stock trading history began, a strange mood spread through the markets, everybody asking one single question: "What on earth happened?"

What few really understood was that what they had witnessed was a manifestation of human psychology, the consequences of the irrational side of our imagination, the side which controls our actions more than anything else. The truth is that human decisions are rarely made on the basis of logical reasoning. Instead they arise as a consequence of more or less irrational changes in what psychologists call "attitudes". And those irrational attitudes combined with massive feedback loops are what makes our monster so monstrous.

Attitudes are the hidden needs and wishes which influence human actions, without our necessarily being aware of them. Many surveys have shown that people adopt attitudes to virtually anything, regardless of whether they are actually familiar with it. So it can be assumed that attitudes are responsible for vital functions in the human mind. Today, psychologists agree that these functions can be divided into four categories, described as "adaptive attitudes", "self-realizing attitudes", "knowledge attitudes" and "ego-defensive attitudes". (McGuire, 1969)

Adaptive Attitudes

The first of these categories, adaption, is exercised when we unconsciously develop the same attitudes as the people we identify ourselves with. How this happens can be illustrated in an experiment by psychologist Muzafer Sherif in 1937. (Sherif, 1937). In this experiment groups of people in a darkened room were told to watch a luminous spot from a metal box. They were instructed that the spot would move and that their job was to discover how far it moved. Each group quickly agreed on the distance it had moved, whereas the different groups had very different opinions.

But the interesting aspect of the experiment was that the spot in fact did not move at all. Thus the test persons' answer was a direct manifestation of pure human psychology, and subsequent interviews with individual group members showed that they were not aware of having been influenced by others. The conclusion – that unconsciously we are influenced by our surroundings – has been confirmed in many subsequent trials and is obviously also relevant for stock trading. When our banker, broker or good friend tells us that stocks will go up we develop the same opinion, not by logical reasoning but because unconsciously we adapt. If the market is in a massive trend everybody is influenced by the rising prices and by each other's reactions, and develop concurring attitudes.

If we are confronted with a conflicting viewpoint we will reject it outright by denying or even ridiculing the viewpoint's instigator. Often we will even commit the so-called "contrast error" of considering the deviating viewpoint as more deviant than it actually is, so that we find it easier to brand its instigator as a bumhead (as was the case with Babson in 1929).

One special case of adaptive attitudes is that clients have a strong tendency to punish those managers who lose money unconventionally. If, on the other hand, the managers lose money simply by going down with the general market, they are forgiven. This invites to a trend-following behavior among the managers (see Le Baron, 1983).

Nature has probably equipped us with this reaction pattern because it facilitates social adjustment (man is a social animal). But the problem with these patterns is that man is not just ensnared by various categories of collective madness in general (as described by Macay in *Extraordinary Popular Delusions and the Madness of Crowds*), but sometimes also into grotesque stock exchange calamities.

Self-Realizing Attitudes

The second attitude form is self-realizing attitudes. Most people will endorse the view that trading on the stock exchange is more "in" than being a member of a pool club. If this is why we trade, psychologists will call this a self-realizing attitude: We *do* something because it makes us feel we *are* something.

Although self-realization as such is individual, choice of lifestyle depends on collective fashion waves, and thereby on adaptive attitudes. Surveys by the New York Stock Exchange (NYSE, 1979) showed that the general standing in society of the stock exchange and stockbrokers fluctuates with share prices. When the market goes up brokers are popular. When it drops they are unpopular, and if the stock market crashes they rank equal with drug pushers in the public eye.

As a result of these attitude formations, the final phase of the bull market will suck in all the little fish, eager to strengthen their social identity.

Knowledge Attitudes

The third function of attitudes is to tackle information. As the world, and the market, offer us more information than we can possibly digest we often choose to sum up everything we know about a given topic in one simple attitude. We chunk our data in a manageable number of clusters, each of which is processed as a simple attitude: "Stocks must go up" or "Bonds must go down." We save having to study all the relevant pros and cons with all the internal conflicts this could generate. At the same time we "immunize" our attitudes by tying them to accepted norms and sources. From the moment that an attitude is formed the knowledge leading to it will quickly be forgotten, but the strength of our attitude will also gradually weaken over time.

Psychologists have tried to measure the factor in this process by hypnotizing a group of subjects to send them a postcard every day. (Orne, 1963). After hypnosis the subjects sent their postcards every day until one by one they awoke from their trance. (On the stock market, this similar awakening is sometimes described as the "riot point"). The psychologist could measure the attitude's statistical half life, experience showing that it often lies at around six months, but in other situations (depending on the nature of the attitude) it can be considerably shorter.

This phenomenon is extremely important, as it is probably the dominant reason that some of the trend indicators we will study in the next chapters have their practical forecast value.

Attitudes As Ego-Defense

The most tortuous function of attitudes is what is called ego-defense. This arises from man's strong need for harmony between what he knows and believes on the one hand, and what he says and does on the other. Imagine a little fish buying stocks in a classic bull market. As stock trading is a social process he will probably already have told his friends, his wife and his banker that "stocks will go up". His attitude will be that the market provides an opportunity for a quick profit, due not to stocks' long-term yields but because prices are rising.

Imagine further that securities start to drop shortly afterwards. After observing this for a period he will gradually lose faith in short-term profits. As there is now no longer harmony between what he has said and done and what he actually believes, he must change his attitude: The purpose of his deals is no longer short-term profits, but "long-term investment". The next to happen is that the first bad news appears in the media. As this provokes a further conflict between what our investor has said and done and his actual experience, he has to resort to attitudes again. He will now use the defense mechanisms called "selective exposure" and "selective perception". Selective exposure is a forebearing mechanism whereby he for example starts to skip negative articles in the newspaper, keeping to the positive ones which support his deals. Psychological tests indicate that the active search for reinforcing information is normal: Our little fish often calls the people he knows share his opinion for reinforcement. He seeks comfort.

Selective perception is more sophisticated: If he is nonetheless confronted with the arguments against, he distorts them unconsciously so that they wrongly appear to support his buys. Psychologists also describe this as "assimilation error". But finally his losses may be so great and his wife so mad that he is forced to take his losses. Just before this happens his attitude will change for the last time: Now he is not in it for the money but for the game. When he closes his position and takes his losses it is with a self-deprecating shrug: "What the hell – you win some and you lose some."

Another consequence of ego-defense is one of the very most important psychological phenomena in the market: transaction slip rationalizations. Anybody trading actively will know that people very often try to compensate for unwise transactions by buying at the prices at which they wrongly sold, or vice versa, on the basis of a wish to exonerate the figures on the old transaction slips, rather than evaluation of fundamental values and market dynamics. The real psychological reason is that we develop ego-defensive attitudes in order to protect ourselves against being confronted with our own mistakes. We thus become victims of our own unconscious egos.

Finally, ego-defense bears most of the responsibility for the fact that the little fish usually closes off his good positions quickly, while he allows the bad ones to carry on running. Irrational as it may appear, he considers it a personal pat on the back to see funds from closed positions flow into his account, while he does not feel corresponding defeat on contemplating current transactions at a loss. As long as the loss is not realized he does not really feel it is there, so he does not sell until he is forced to, often at the bottom of a bear market panic. This explains why turnover is normally lower in bear markets than in bull markets.

Reactions Under Stress

Although man's attitude mechanisms are extremely unfortunate in the context of stock trading, it is obvious that they are indispensable for more ordinary affairs. Attitude functions are psychological crash helmets which make us calm, well-adjusted and socially adapted, freeing us from constant back-breaking speculation on all kinds of different problems.

But there are situations (other than stock trading) which require the laid-back self-controlled individual to change his behavior. This is when he is exposed to an acute threat – like being attacked by a shark. If our little fish is exposed to a threat, his body will start to produce adrenalin, which in turn will activate a number of other enzymes in what biochemistry describes as a "cascade system". In a few minutes the cascade reaction strengthens the adrenalin's impact by perhaps 100 million, thus immediately leading to a biochemical core explosion which he can feel to the roots of his hair. His heart starts to thump, his blood pressure rises, he begins to sweat and his pupils expand. But simultaneously with these physical symptoms something more important happens: His predisposition to change his attitudes is dramatically increased.

Psychological research has shown that the dampening, stabilizing effect of attitude mechanisms on the human psyche is strongly reduced when people are subject to stress. Changes in attitudes which would normally take weeks or months can take place in a matter of hours, minutes and seconds. This is no surprise, as anybody facing a major threat obviously has to improvize at high speed.

The survey by US researcher Robert J. Schiller in 1987 indicates that this effect can be of practical importance to the market. As described on page 62, Schiller sent 2,000 questionnaires to private stock investors and 1,000 questionnaires to institutional investors from 19 to 23 October 1987. Answers were received from 605 and 284 of the investors respectively. Schiller's survey showed that on 19 October 20.3% of private investors and 43.1% of institutional investors experienced panic symptoms such as "concentration problems, sweaty palms, chest pains, irritability and high pulse". One broker, Gianna Fidanza, coincidentally on the same day was wearing a blood pressure and pulse monitoring device in connection with a stress phenomena analysis at the New York Hospital and the Cornell Medical Research Center. The apparatus monitored her stress levels every fifteen minutes. Fidanza's blood pressure and pulse fluctuated almost completely synchronously with the stock index throughout the day: The more the index fell, the more Fidanza's pulse and blood pressure rose.

In other words, price drops can provoke stress and stress provokes quick attitude changes. This results in new sale orders, which again precipitate price drops, increased blood pressure, attitude changes and price drops. The full circle is closed and the monster is unleashed.

Studying the Tracks

In the next four chapters we will study the nature of our monster more closely. We will study its behavior when it precipitates global Armageddon, as well as its everyday meals, the minidramas reflected in our price charts. We will consider these very carefully because if we cannot uncover the monster's thoughts and emotions by studying its tracks, it will be almost impossible to win on the stock exchange. And if we *can* trace the monster's tracks, we will not only get ahead when trading on the market, but also have a lot of fun in the process. Because, whatever nasty things you can say about the monster, there's one good thing to be said for it: It's never boring.

18.

When the Going Gets Decisive

Experience tells me that it is not wise to buck against what I would call the manifest group-tendency.

Jesse L. Livermoore

Let's imagine we have one isolated chart in front of us. The first question we ask ourselves is: "Can we see, just by studying a chart of historical price development, whether a trend can be expected to continue, or whether the psychology has passed the point where the market risks collapsing at any moment?" In other words: On the basis of one isolated chart alone, would we have been able to predict when the panic would start in the South Sea Company, in the infamous Wall Street crashes, or wherever? Yes, we would. The footprints in the chart tell us more about investors' attitudes than most of them are aware.

When a Trend Starts

Movements are sideways most of the time. When they climb upwards they encounter different resistance areas from which they are quickly rebuffed by chartists and transaction slip ego-defenders. Below they are met by different support areas. The small daily fluctuations between these areas are fairly noise-sensitive and unpredictable, and only scant profits can be made here.

But once in a while a market breaks through its resistance areas and starts to move resolutely upwards (or downwards – the principle is the same). In the first phase of the movement most investors see this as just a new random fluctuation, which should soon be corrected, and many therefore hurry to realize their profits, to exploit the unexpected movement. But new buyers enter the stage, and after a short hesitation, the market starts to rise again. The market sentiment changes, with previous sellers re-

184

gretting their profit-taking and starting to hope for a chance to get in again at a reasonable price. A trend is starting.

When a trend has been established it often runs far longer than anyone expects. Most investors are satisfied to get out after going along a little of the way, and then watch in increasing disbelief as the movement runs and runs. Some of these trends develop to continuing mass movements which last for years and years, interrupted only by short, temporary reactions. These are not seen very often in a lifetime, so the job is to stay with them when they happen. Regardless of whether movements span several years or less, trends are where the big money is earned, so this chapter about trend psychology is the most important of the book.

Identifying a Future Trend

How do we know whether a trend will continue? Let's look at an example.

Assume you are an investor; it is the summer of 1986 and you think gold will start to rise soon (calculated in dollars). But naturally you do not know exactly when this will happen so you decide to wait for the first rising buy signal before you do anything. After a slow summer market, where the metal traded in the 335–355 dollar range, in August it starts to climb a little and on 10 August the price reaches over 370 dollars. The day after, 11 August the market suddenly sees a massive concentration of buyers. In hectic trading the price is pushed up to 390 dollars. The chart is shown in Figure 32.

Anybody will notice this movement. Commentators rush to find explanations like "silver has risen" or "strikes in South Africa" or "demand in Japan" or "the dollar has dropped" or "computer trading". Explanations can always be found after the event and suddenly everybody can see positive arguments, and nobody the negative ones (remember the adaptive attitudes). The first thing many market operaters do on the morning of the 12th is to check out the gold price. They do so with a variety of emotions.

The Good, the Bad and the Ugly

Some investors suddenly hold really good positions. Those who bought gold before the rise (and kept it), have earned a fortune.

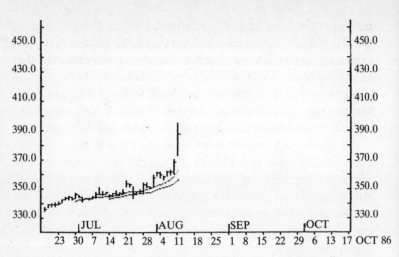

Figure 32. Gold spot price, London. The figure shows daily trading ranges and close prices for the London gold exchange. The prices are for the autumn of 1986 and the monetary unit is the dollar. The chart also shows the 10- and 20-day close-price moving averages.

Anyone buying at say 350 dollars on a 10% margin has already more than doubled his money! He can't keep his fingers off his calculator. Every three hours he works out his profit, vacillating between fear and greed. Greed tells him to stay in: "let your profits run", as they say. But they also say "you never made a loss taking your profits" and "you can always get in again if it continues". He waits and sees, but if the price does not quickly start to rise again he would now rather sell and take his profits.

Some are in a bad position: The man out of the market because he sold just before the rise. He's not less involved because he's out. It's obvious he has committed a fatal blunder. He believed in gold from the outset, got impatient, sold, and then it goes up right after! A terrible feeling, and the worst thing is that now he believes in gold more than ever before.

But he would be even dumber to go in again at a far higher price just a few days after he went out. What would his broker think? (ego-defensive attitudes!). Just one thing to do: hope the price will drop a little so that he can get in again with his honour intact.

Last comes the ugly one. The poor fellow who sold short. His emotions are fear, surprise and deep disappointment. He fears

186

his loss will be even higher and that his broker will issue a margin call. He has no urge to calculate how much he has lost (selective exposure) but he knows it's a lot. Or he is so punch-drunk that he just wants to get out as cheaply as possible (i.e. buy). Or, if he is cold-blooded, he is now on the lookout for a good price to reverse on, i.e. buy the double of what he sold, so he can lie long instead of short. Thereby he might manage to recoup his losses.

The Game of Timing

All these different market operators are staring at the gold price on the morning of the twelfth. Those with good positions are considering whether to sell while those with the "bad" and the "ugly" are speculating on when to buy. Their decisions have in fact been taken: All that is left is a question of timing. And as for us, the hypothetical "we": Like Keynes we view the markets as a beauty contest. We wait for the others' reactions, keeping our heads cool enough to postpone our purchase a few days. "It's probably a little overbought", we think.

So most watch and wait, and on 12 August and the following three days almost nothing happens. The market catches its breath, everybody watching everybody else. Whose nerves will break first? We do not have to be Freud to know that it is easier

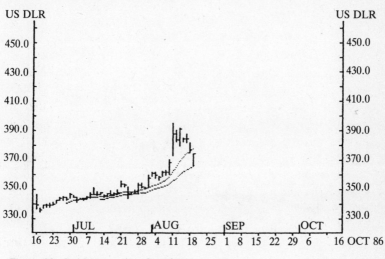

Figure 33. Gold spot price, London.

187

to take a pleasant decision than a nasty one. So the ones in the good positions react first. First a few sell, enticing a few more with them, and after another two days the chart looks like Figure 33.

Turnover is low and everybody, market operators and commentators, can see that this is only "profit-taking" for sure. But the drop was just what the poor transaction slip ego-defenders who sold in the congestion area before the rise were waiting for. And it is just the price a lot of investors wish they had bought at, the day before the rise. Now the chance is there. People buy, and the price drop stops just at the top of the old congestion area. (A congestion area is when the price does not change much for a period, while the security gradually changes investor hands. After each consolidation it can be assumed that there are some new investors).

"We" note that our beauty contest had the usual effect and the market was indeed briefly overbought. The next morning we buy at 380 dollars. Now that we are in the market we are strangely enough not as nervous as before. On the contrary, we are calmer because we no longer fear missing out on a beginning trend, while our timing appears to have been very good. Everybody can see that gold is in an initial bull market and many of those who have not yet bought panic and go in. After a month the chart looks like Figure 34.

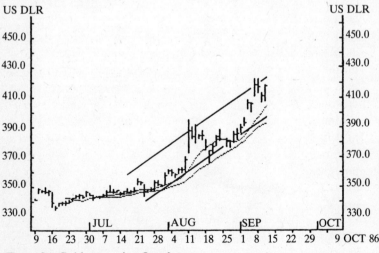

Figure 34. Gold spot price, London.

188

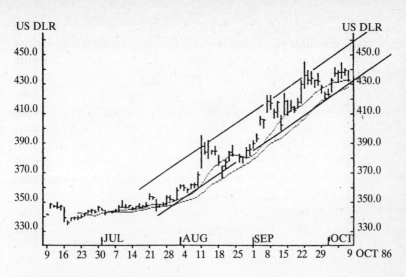

Figure 35. Gold spot price, London.

As "we" are experienced investors we try drawing a musical chairs "channel", i.e. two parallel "trend lines", on our chart. Over a few days the price has now risen by over 30 dollars and we are strongly tempted to realize our gains, particularly as we are lying at the top end of the channel we have drawn in. We sell at 415 dollars.

On 12 August a number of people may have been studying the gold price, but now everybody is doing it. Gold has become a subject for social small-talk and many are now willing to buy up at the slightest sign of weakness. Those not in the market feel ridiculous. If they are professional investors they start to fear the boss's unavoidable "backtrading": "Gold is on the move without you doing any action. Are you sitting around sleeping or what?"

Many are ready to buy and the drop is very limited before the next rise starts. This new rise is not just provoked by new investors, but also by early sellers wanting to get in again. Although nobody has tried to define what a trend is, anybody can see that on 9 October 1986, gold is lying in a wonderful rising trend (Figure 35).

Things are doing fine and there are no grounds for concern. Perhaps we should buy again? No, take a look at the chart on 26 November (Figure 36).

189

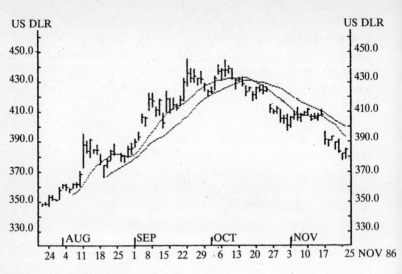

Figure 36. Gold spot price, London.

The wonderful bull trend has stopped in its tracks and most has been lost again. How could this have been foreseen?

Disappointed Expectations and Triple Shock

Let's take another look at the chart. Up to 8 October the market showed a number of abrupt rises interrupted by sideways movement in the congestion areas, previous buyers selling to take home profits, and new buyers taking advantage of an opportunity to get in. Sellers, also participating all the way up, each time noted that the market reached new higher peaks and that they should have stayed firm. Small drops were therefore used to come back in, and each increase provoked new buy interests just under the current market price.

Buyers from the outset hoping for a small increase kept postponing their decision to sell because they still saw no sign of weakness in the market. There was a dearth of supply on the market. Any supply was profit-taking, soon transformed to new buy interests – new demand from the same investors.

At the beginning of October the market missed an attempt to reach an even higher top and most of the new buyers coming in in the last double congestion area now held losses. When this happens the market sentiment changes completely. First inves-

190

tors are surprised and then uncertain and nervous. The new investors who came in in the last congestion area are in a state of shock. First the market rose strongly without them being in, and when they finally bought, the market missed an attempt to reach a new higher top for the first time. And now they are holding losses, a triple shock.

The more fortunate investors, continually postponing their sale orders all the way up, are also nervous, acknowledging for the first time that what they thought was recovered territory has been lost again. Their profits crumble away before their eyes, an extremely unpleasant experience. As for the buyers, those who for some reason must buy gold, they will now postpone their buy orders as long as they can see that the market is slipping down slowly but surely.

The Final Hesitation Before the Reversal

The market catches its breath for a period until, finally, someone takes a decision. This is the new investors, those in a state of triple shock, and naturally their decision is to go out, so they sell. If Charles Dow had been in the market at that time, he would have left, because he would have immediately noticed two things. First of all, the market could no longer achieve a higher top, and secondly, (when it fell under the previous bottom of 423 dollars) that a lower bottom would come inevitably. He would have raised his finger, saying:

> "A trend is intact as long as the price does not succeed in breaking back through the congestion areas previously formed.
> A rising trend is therefore intact for as long as there are still higher tops and higher bottoms.
> A falling trend is intact as long as there are lower tops and lower bottoms."

These are the most important characteristics of a trend. As soon as we see that the required successive series of rising tops and bottoms is broken, sentiment will change and we will go out or reverse. In a rising trend we will watch rising bottoms most closely (normally old tops), and in a falling trend, falling tops (which are old bottoms).

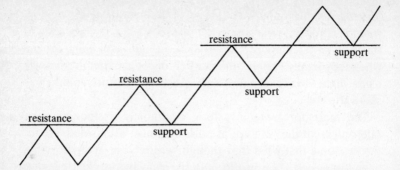

Figure 37. Resistance and support in a rising trend. When a market is in a rising trend the price curve's previous tops will often act as bottoms later. The reason is found in ego-defensive attitudes.

Support and Resistance

Here we return to Dow's third observation, concerning "support" and "resistance". When a rising movement stops Dow would say that it has met *resistance*: The market has reached a level where the big fish want to sell. When a falling movement stops it has found *support*. When old tops in a rising trend become new bottoms this means that previous resistance has now become support (Figure 37).

In the same way support becomes resistance in a falling trend (Figure 38).

Many misinterpret this pattern, believing that in a rising trend

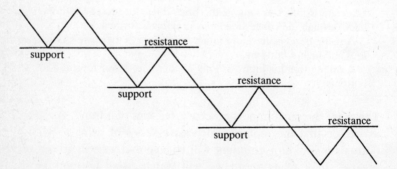

Figure 38. Resistance and support in a falling trend. When the trend is downwards old bottoms are often new tops.

the last bottom provides the greatest support. But naturally the last *top* is most important, and in a falling trend the last bottom.

When evaluating how effective a support or resistance area will be, primarily two factors should be considered. The first is how long the price has been consolidating in the area. The longer a security is traded at a given price, the better dealers will remember this price. The second factor is turnover: High turnover in a congested area will make it stronger, as many new investors have gone in at this price. Many charts lack indication of volume (on for example the currency market nobody knows the exact overall turnover). Futures contracts do have volume parameters, see e.g. Figure 23.

The best trends are those where there are no attempts to test past congestion areas, only short intervals. This regular trend is called a staircase trend and can be similar to USD/DEM from 21 June to 26 August 1986 (Figure 39).

In a trend like this a skilled chartist will never go out, as old tops and congestion areas are not broken, or even seriously tested. Dow would say: "A trend must be considered intact until the opposite is proved." A financial variation, one could say, of Newton's second law.

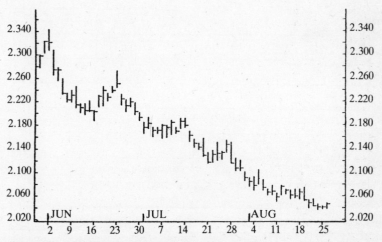

Figure 39. USD/DEM, spot price. From the summer of 1986, this chart shows a classical staircase down-trend, where there is renewed sales pressure each time the price has risen against a previous bottom. We can almost see the smiling dealer walking down the staircase on his way to the bank.

In addition to the aforementioned basic method of evaluating whether a trend is intact, there are a couple of supporting instruments which can be very useful as long as we remember to keep an eye on the underlying psychological mechanisms. The first is the so-called "moving average".

Moving Average

Moving averages are one of the most used (and abused) supporting tools in trend analysis. Let's start with the definition. Everybody knows what an average is: the sum of a series of values divided by the number of values. But with a "moving average" the calculation is new every time a new value is added. A moving average of 20 days' trading prices must be revised every day, so it is always based on the last 20 days' prices. Simple and stupid.

Let's take a look at the Dow Jones 1986 chart again, with its "Black Monday" and "Black Thursday" (Figure 26). Two popular moving averages are drawn on the chart for 90 and 200-day prices, respectively. Despite the market's turbulence these averages are moving in calm and undisturbed paths, uninfluenced by short-term fluctuations.

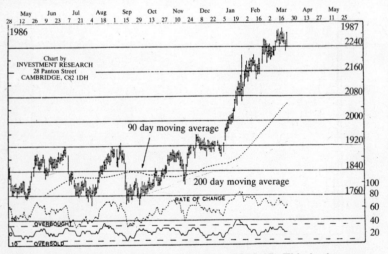

Figure 40. Dow Jones Industrial Average 1986–87. This is the same chart as in Figure 6. Note that the two strong drops in 1986 are almost unreflected in the moving averages. This indicates that despite temporary interruptions a bull market was psychologically intact. (Chart: Investment Research of Cambridge.)

194

When a chartist considers a chart like this he will interpret the averages as a good expression of the underlying trend. As he can see no indication of a weakening in this concrete situation he will continue to hold his long-term position. *So on the surface the moving average is an expression of the underlying trend in supply and demand, after peeling away the short-term turbulence.* But interpreting the moving average requires a little training. One of the most popular rules for the moving average is simply to select a specific average and then buy every time the price breaks above the average and sell every time it breaks below. The best thing to do with this rule is forget it: It doesn't work.

To take advantage of moving averages an interplay of two, possibly three, simple averages should be used. Imagine a trendless market in which we have drawn in three different moving averages. Here the price will unceasingly cross up and down over its own moving average and a "short" average based on for example three days' prices will cross up and down over a longer one, e.g. 10 or 20-day averages.

Furthermore, some of the averages will reverse upwards when others reverse downwards. The oil chart below (Figure 41), with

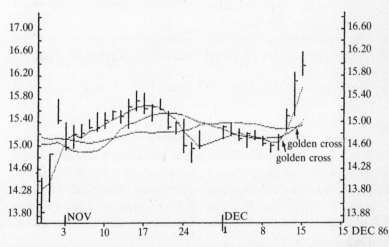

Figure 41. Crude oil futures contracts. The chart shows daily trading ranges and close prices for oil contracts on the US NYMEX exchange. At the end of the period shown (November-December 1986) the price broke upwards and a bull market was confirmed by development in the moving averages for 3-, 10-and 20-day prices. (The golden crosses shown are explained in the text.)

195

3, 10 and 20-day averages, is a good example of this. On the last day of this chart something happens: The price has broken through all averages, lying in the sequence 3, 10 and 20 days' average below market price, and all facing upwards, in the same direction. This, we say (we've left Dow behind now) is a signal to buy because:

> If a market is in a strong rising trend, all averages will lie below market price; they will all face upwards and the longest averages will lie furthest from the market price. In a falling trend the reverse is the case.

When averages cross each other to come into the right sequence for a trend, this in itself is also considered to be a buy or sell signal, provided that both slope in the trend direction. If they each slope in their own direction the average breakout is without significance, denying the movement's credibility.

– When a short rising average breaks up through a long rising average we have a *golden cross*, i.e. a buy signal.
– When a short falling average breaks down through a long falling average we have a *death cross* (the terms "golden cross" and "death cross" were coined by the English chartist Brian Marber), i.e. a sell signal.
– Average breakout, where one average faces upwards and the other down, gives a non-confirmation of an apparent trend.

This requires explanation. Let's return to the Dow Jones chart in Figure 40. As price drops on "Black Monday" and "Black Thursday" came quickly, without any preceding weakening, they had no significant impact on the moving averages. If instead the price drops had come after a longer preceding weakening of the trend, both averages would have turned downwards before the break and we would have had a *death cross*. This would have signaled a very serious situation. A prior weakening like this was seen for example at the Wall Street crash in 1929, but not in 1987.

Knowledge Attitudes and the Importance of Time

The difference is *time*. It takes time to reverse the psychology of a primary trend and if there is no golden cross or death cross this simply indicates that the sequence has reversed too abruptly and that we are facing a temporary trend interruption.

The reason lies in our knowledge attitudes. When a price moves it normally takes some time before the moving averages catch up on it. This time lag corresponds to the adaption period of the market participants – the time it takes for people to accept the new price. As in the psychological hypnosis postcard experiment, this expresses an average psychological reaction period.

One special factor illustrates this. If a golden cross or death cross come after the averages have virtually overlapped for a longer period, this usually gives a very strong signal:

> If there is a golden cross or death cross after averages have virtually overlapped for a longer period, this reinforces the signal.

The reason is that all investors, long-term and short-term, here experience the same sentiment. The rule is also related to Dow's observation that breakout from a narrow price interval gives an important trend signal. Let's take another look at the gold example. The chart in Figure 42 shows the sequence again, over a slightly longer horizon and using 20 and 50-day moving averages.

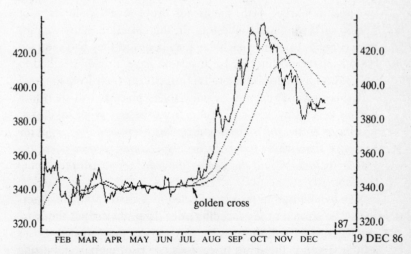

Figure 42. Gold spot price, London. This chart shows development (in dollars) in the gold price, 1986. When the bull market starts in July this is confirmed by a "golden cross". On the other hand the drop in October/November is not confirmed by a "death cross" and also turns out to be temporary.

The averages overlapped from February to July, when a buy signal was released, which proved to be effective. When a counterreaction later came in October, it did not provoke a death cross and thus proved to be temporary (the price rose shortly afterwards to 500 dollars) (Figure 42).

A special reaction, seen in many primary trends, is that the short average during the market's secondary correction phases temporarily withdraws, making contact with the long average, then again releasing without breaking through. If both averages in this situation slope in the trend direction, this in reality gives a new golden cross or death cross, with a strong confirmation of the trend's sustainability.

Distance to the Moving Average: Hope and Fear

The last rule concerning the moving averages concerns the interval between the daily price and its moving average. This rule is:

> When a market accelerates away from the moving average, this can indicate that there will be a counterreaction, so that the daily price and the moving average will again converge.

Imagine a market with significant drops over some days or weeks, surprising most investors. In this situation many will not have come out because each day they believed they had seen the bottom of the decline. These investors have already decided to sell, but hope to do so on a rally, thus cutting their losses.

If this upward reaction actually takes place it will therefore quickly be met by new sale orders from these nervous investors. *The more drastic the preceding drop has been, and the longer the period of time which passes before the counterreaction starts, the greater its impact, and the greater the tendency to sell on a small increase.*

This behavioral pattern is reflected in a chart of moving averages. The stronger the preceding price drop, the sooner the moving average will fall towards the day's price, meeting it if it rises a little. Even if the day's price does not rise, merely stabilizing for a period, it will finally be overtaken by its moving average. When this point is reached it can be taken as an expression that all hope is lost and sellers will come in again. This is naturally assuming choice of an average calculation basis, normally an effec-

198

tive indicator of the market's sentiment. It is not irrelevant whether the moving average has been based on 20-day or 50-day prices.

This example was from a falling market. In a rising market the explanation is parallel.

Self-Reinforcing Impact?

Today many professional investors use the moving averages as an investment tool, so that a certain self-reinforcing impact can be expected. Many use 10 and 20-day averages on index futures, and therefore these markets easily come to resemble those shown in Figure 43.

The idea of a self-reinforcing impact will inevitably be relevant on studying 20-day averages on international indices. Initially it is almost impossible to imagine how the market's many tests and rejections of this average can take place without some kind of global conspiracy between the world's chartists. But the problem is that the same phenomenon repeats itself if this average is plotted on charts from before the growth in popularity of moving averages. Figure 44 shows an example.

So a self-reinforcing impact is probably part of the truth, but not the whole truth. The most significant explanation must lie in investors' typical investment horizons, and in their knowledge attitude functions.

Basis for the Calculation

All rules concerning the indication derived from moving averages are naturally assuming choice of an average calculation basis, normally effective as indicator of the sentiment. The most frequently used intervals are probably as follows:

	calculation basis days
Futures contracts	3, 10, 20, 50, 200
Spot currencies	10, 20, 50, 200
Stock markets	20, 50, 200
Money rates	20, 50

This table could raise some suspicion. One might ask, "Why such fairly even numbers?" And how can several combinations be

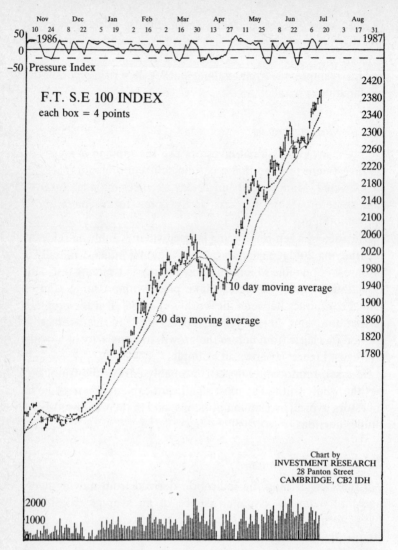

Figure 43. FTSE-100 futures contracts (English share index). This shows how a rising market is often "carried" by particular moving averages. If the price closes below these averages on a single day (as in March 1986) there are further drops before the trend may be resumed. The bottom of the figure shows daily turnover, which fell remarkably during price drops in April (a bullish sign) and the Pressure Index, explained in Chapter 20. (Chart: Investment Research of Cambridge.)

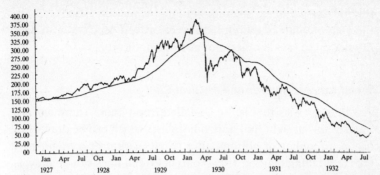

Figure 44. Dow Jones Industrial Average 1927–32. Up to the 1929 crash the US bull market was "carried" by its own moving 200-day average. When the price broke under this average it remained here until the bear market finally ended three years later. This cannot be explained by reference to the self-reinforcing impact, as use of the moving average as a technical indicator was almost unknown in the relevant period.

equally valid? The answer to the even numbers must be that even if these were not the perfect tools from the outset, people have chosen them in the lack of exact evidence. And since then, a self-fulfilling effect has made the market's behavior adapt to the tools. Regarding the various combinations of averages, this could be interpreted as fractal behavior perhaps stimulated by different investment horizons among investors.

We must not delude ourselves into believing that say the 20-day moving average is an independent statistic giving us some mystical insight into investors' attitudes and behavior. But rather, it is important to view the 20-day moving average as a given point in an overall recursive or fractal pattern. We must keep in mind that the study of moving averages only started after World War II. Without computers, limited evidence must have been available before dealers started to center their calculations around such suspiciously even numbers as 10, 20, 50 and 200 days. But as computers became available these averages have probably had an increasingly self-fulfilling effect.

We should also recall in our discussion of fractals the ocean metaphor we used to describe the relationship between ripples, waves and "super waves". In a similar manner, it is necessary to view 20, 50, and 200 moving day averages not as unrelated statistics, but rather as fractal patterns of an overall phenomenon. It

201

follows that all of the averages are dependent on a single cause, the market, and are therefore most effectively used when studied in relation to one another, not as single indicators.

Trend Lines, Channels and Musical Chairs

Another analysis tool is the so-called trend lines. These are defined as the straight, not horizontal, lines which can be drawn between a number of bottoms in a rising market or a number of tops in a falling market. If two parallel trend lines can be drawn, one between tops and one between bottoms, this is called a "channel".

Trend lines and channels are like musical chairs. There is no obvious logical explanation, but it is soon discovered that everybody is busily drawing lines on their charts. As charts are popular, our fourth rule of the market naturally has a role to play: Trend lines and channels become self-reinforcing. The rule for trend lines is:

Go out of a trend when its trend line is broken.

This rule is not universally applicable, but it is widely used on a number of markets, strengthened by the fact that it is difficult to

Figure 45. Gold spot price, USA. A staircase down-trend on gold during 1987–89. When the falling musical chairs trend line was finally broken in November 1989, an aggressive price move followed.

202

vary a straight line. If people develop a craze for drawing trend lines on their charts, most of them will draw the same lines.

Channels are just as funny as trend lines, but in both cases the natural prerequisite is that the straight line rests on maximum contacts with the market price. So:

> Trend lines and channels are the most self-reinforcing signal existing, and their significance increases with the number of contacts between price and lines.

Furthermore:

> The steeper the trend lines and the steeper and narrower the channels, the stronger the confirmation of a trend's basic sustainability. The steeper a trend line, the weaker the danger signal if it is broken.

As long as there are only two contacts it is doubtful whether the music will start, and with only three (one + two) an attempted channel can be out of step with the market. If there are more

Figure 46. DEM/CHF. The chart shows how over a number of years a market can be caught between two well-defined trend lines. When the upper trend line was broken in the spring of 1989 the price advanced to 91.69 in a few months.

contacts the signal has a rising impact until it becomes so obvious that it becomes self-destructive. The chart in Figure 46 shows an example of two strong trend lines for Swiss francs against the D-mark.

In all the examples shown the trend lines are drawn with the chart's extreme top or bottom as the starting point. However, in many cases it will be a better idea to take the immediately subsequent top (or bottom) as the starting-point, as otherwise, e.g. on a double top, the trend line can become almost horizontal.

As mentioned, trend lines and channels would be without any significance were it not for the self-reinforcing impact arising from everybody drawing the same lines on the same charts. But starting to draw them on generated indicators, e.g. the Rate of Change indicator (mentioned later in this book) is naturally like dancing to the wrong music.

Volume Confirmations

The fourth trend indicator category is volume. The best known rule of volume is Dow's principle that "the volume must confirm a trend". If the market is going up the volume will be higher on

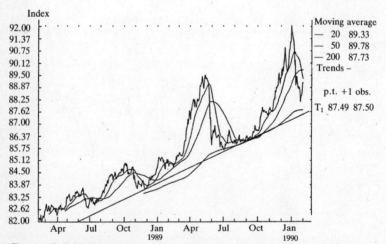

Figure 47. DEM/CHF. This chart shows what happened after the break-out of DEM/CHF in the spring of 1989. Using the trend line, the momentum indicator and the moving averages, timing this market was very easy.

rises than on falls. This can be read directly from the volume columns on a chart. The basis for this rule is very simple. When the volume is high on increases this is because investors have a great tendency to take profits too quickly (ego-defensive attitudes in reverse). But then they will regret their actions and want to buy again. Large turnover on rises thus guarantees continual demand below the current price.

Sometimes this principle is illustrated by a method called "on balance volume". By this method, launched by Joseph Granville, together with the price chart, an accumulated volume graph is drawn where volume is positive on days with rising prices and negative on days with falling prices. This visualizes the extent to which volume confirms the trend. In short-term timing volume is also an important tool, and there are three simple rules to know.

The first rule says that if the market opens differently from the last day's close price *in high volume*, there will often be a correction towards the previous close price during the day. The reason is that high volume in the morning is often due to people trading on the overnight news, which will thus be fully discounted in the price.

The second, concerning short-term trading ranges, will surprise many. In trading ranges turnover typically lies almost exclusively in the range's support and resistance areas. When the price moves between them, trading fades out. The rule is that breakout will take place at the side where volume tends to be weakest. In reality this surprising rule is just a repetition of the previous observation that the higher the volume the stronger a support or resistance area will become.

The third volume rule is the most difficult to put into practice. As we shall see in Chapter 19, typically a strong rise in volume will be expected after breakout from a congestion area. This is a reinforcing signal, but *only if it takes place after the breakout*. If the volume is high while the formation's support or resistance areas are tested during the day, this indicates that a breakout is becoming less probable. For the same reason breakouts in thin markets, e.g. up to public holidays, are often the best signals. The best trading days of the year are often between Christmas and the New Year.

What Should We Look at Most?

Now we have considered four different ways of evaluating whether the crowd psychology in a trend movement is intact:

1. The successive series of higher or lower tops and bottoms
2. Moving averages
3. Trend lines and channels
4. Volume

As previously mentioned, the first of these methods, the one with tops and bottoms, is the most important, as it is based on elementary psychology. So start by investigating this on the chart. Then look at the moving averages for supplementary indications. Remember that this requires more training than the first method. And, if obvious trend lines or channels can be found in the charts, supplement the evaluation basis with them. But remember that in reality we are here being guided by self-reinforcing nonsense. Finally, check whether volume indicators confirm the trend's sustainability. Keep an eye on whether volume suddenly declines on increases.

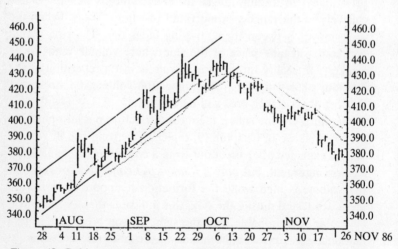

Figure 48. Gold spot price, London. This is the same chart as in Figure 36 and shows the development in the gold price against the dollar in the autumn of 1986. The chart shows the 10- and 20-day moving averages of close prices, as well as a rising channel, defined on the basis of daily close prices.

Let's see how these different methods would have functioned for our earlier gold chart. In method one we would probably have gone out the day the lower trend line was broken, because it was only here (without using the trend line) we could see that the attempt to break the old top had been abortive, i.e. out at around 430 dollars. Following the moving averages, the day after the *death cross*, we would have gone out at around 425 dollars. Going for the break in the trend line or channel we would have gone out at around 430 dollars. Finally, if we had followed the volume, we would have seen it failing in the last price increases. All in all, shortly after the market peaked, chartists would have sold out. Short-term traders might even be short.

Evaluating whether a trend is psychologically intact is the most fundamental aspect of interpreting one isolated chart. But a chart can have much more to tell. Many of its special patterns give detailed signals of how our monster is feeling. We will take a look at this in the next chapter.

19

Catching the Breath and Changing the Mind

The most important single factor in shaping security markets is human psychology.

Gerald M. Loeb

In a market moving in a beautifully well-defined "staircase trend", on which everyone trading with the trend slowly and steadily increases their profits, most of the big fish will try to stay in. But when the market makes a sudden leap, flips over and starts to zig-zag in a sideways formation, many start to doubt. What's the monster up to? Time to supplement portfolios? Get out? Reverse? There is in fact an answer to this trilemma, because if we study the movement closely, we can actually work out what is going on.

Why Dull Markets Are Not Really Dull

Take an example. In October 1986 the USD/JPY chart was as shown in Figure 49.

The dollar had fallen strongly throughout 1985 and further into 1986, in August reaching 155. Then it came to a halt, nothing happening in August, September and most of October. During these months gold soared against the dollar. Dow Jones and many other stock markets charged up and down, the pound dropped in a free fall, the dollar continued its down-trend against the D-mark and the English bond market was a battlefield. The monster was loose in many places, but USD/JPY was almost completely dead.

So what does a Japanese oil importer, in need of dollars to fund supplies, do? Previously he postponed dollar purchases as long as possible, because he could always buy cheaper later. But there are limits to how long a man can wait. When nothing hap-

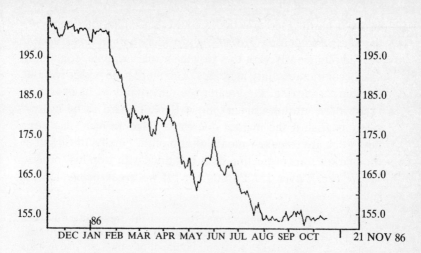

Figure 49. USD/JPY, spot price. USD/JPY is one of the world's most traded currency combinations and this combination's charts are therefore textbook examples of mass psychology. The chart shown is based on daily London close prices.

pens he will finally give up trying to buy at a lower price and instead settle his deal at the current price range. On the other hand, what does the speculator do who has sold dollars short expecting to buy them back at a lower price? He also loses patience in the end and buys back in the existing interval so he can invest in something else. And finally, what about the speculator who is out of the market, but also considering selling dollars short? Either he puts off his decision until the market starts moving again, or he finds something else to amuse him.

As time passes all these market operators get rid of limited buy orders or buy interests previously planned for below the given market price. A man who would have liked to buy at 150 finally shrugs his shoulders and buys at 154. In the same way all those with contrary expectations and interests gradually get rid of sell interests *above* market price. People hoping to sell at 160 finally shrug their shoulders and sell at 154. Over time many orders or interests which would otherwise have checked a price movement are removed.

When a market movement stops, gradually a vacuum of buy interests (support) below market price, and a vacuum of sell interests (resistance) above market price, will arise.

It is not hard to see that this vacuum means that *the longer the market is tranquil, the greater the storm at the final breakout will be*. Simultaneously with the growth in the vacuums, something else occurs: uncertainty increases. The more time passes without the market moving, the greater the uncertainty of its operators (knowledge attitudes again). So it is really hard to be aggressively bearish if the market does not budge an inch, day after day, week after week or month after month. Finally, those still in the market start protecting their positions with stop-loss orders: "If we break over 157 I'll buy" or "If we break below 153 I'll sell".

> The market's psychological uncertainty of the trend direction rises the longer the duration of a congestion area. Over time potential sell interests below market price and potential buy interests above market price will build up.

This will also contribute to an aggressive breakout when it finally comes.

Let's take out our magnifying glass and have a look at the last part of the congestion area, as shown in Figure 50.

In the final phase of the consolidation, activity almost came to a standstill. All that happened in the last month was a little musi-

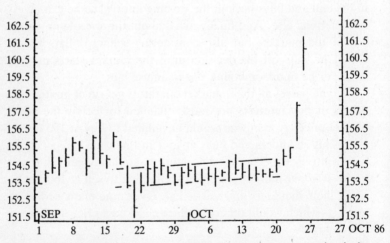

Figure 50. USD/JPY, spot price. While this market was moving in its narrow channel, buyers and sellers closed off their mutual positions. Finally one category was exterminated, obviously sellers. The chart is from the autumn of 1986.

210

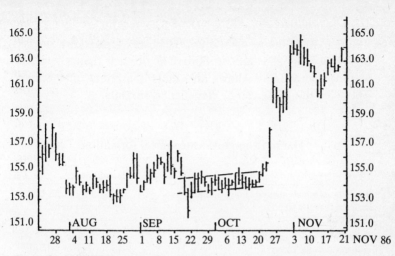

Figure 51. USD/JPY, spot price. The rise we saw in Figure 39 continued to price 165, when it stopped and the long-term down-trend was resumed.

cal chairs (note the channel), generally only of interest to brokers and interbank dealers. Everybody else left the market out of boredom or impatience. Finally, sellers were eliminated and the remaining surplus of buyers created an upward breakout into the vacuum of sellers. This trend punched up through all the self-reinforcing stop-loss buy orders, and up so high that a lot of people changed their minds, attracting many new buyers (adaptive attitudes). At a little distance the chart now appears as shown in Figure 51.

The increase continued until short-term consolidation around the 160 level. Everybody, absolutely everybody, is bullish at this point, but some will also have made so many gains so quickly that they will be tempted to realize their new profits. This desire for profit-taking gave small drops over a few days until these short-term sale orders had been absorbed. The price could continue until it found firmer sell interests at the level of 164–165.

This chart features many classical patterns, also called *formations*: In addition to a channel there is a "rectangle", four "gaps" and a "flag" and all these formations gave the signals the skilled trader would expect. However, what was virtually absent in the same period was important financial news. (We will return to this chart later.)

211

What Formations Are There?

The market refers to numerous "technical" formations, but trying to use them all would be more of an obstacle than a help. The accompanying table shows the most important phenomena, where anything else can be classified as variants.

The most important technical formations

Signal	Name	Definition
Formations which always indicate that the trend should continue	Flags and pennants	Temporary profit-taking in an intact trend.
Formations which usually indicate that the trend should continue	Gaps	A price range with a total lack of buy or sell interests.
	Triangles	A market where people are becoming more and more uncertain, or a minority are trying to accumulate or distribute.
	Rectangles	Conflict between two groups of market operators.
Formations usually indicating that the trend should reverse	Wedges	A secondary or tertiary movement where more and more players lose hope and go out.
Formations which always indicate that the trend should reverse	Double/triple peaks and troughs	Market operators give up a trend because a given level cannot be broken.
	Head & shoulders	Gradual exhaustion of a primary trend, linked to distribution or accumulation.
	Key and island reversals	A sudden shock without significance for the primary trend.

These eight phenomena are important because they occur repeatedly and often have important tips to whisper to anyone trying to understand what is going on. Although they are all based on human psychology it will be seen that these phenomena are also derived from logic which a market game must necessarily obey. In other words: They reflect not only the irrational psychology of the individual, but also the logical behaviorism performed by markets.

1. Flags and Pennants: Profit-taking

There is nothing worse than leaving a marvelous aggressive trend just because the market has taken a little time out for a couple of days. But this is just what thousands have done on many occasions.

Let's assume the market is in a very strong, almost vertical rally. This rally takes place because from the outset there is suddenly an almost total vacuum of sellers, or at least a considerable surplus of buyer interests, probably because a large number of strong positive feedback loops are in force. The fact that money can be made so quickly will lure many to take home profits, and therefore selling pressure will arise temporarily after the first aggressive movement. Suddenly the rise stops and many cash in their profits. In psychological terms, this could be expressed as adaptive attitudes needing a short consolidation to catch up with actual price movements.

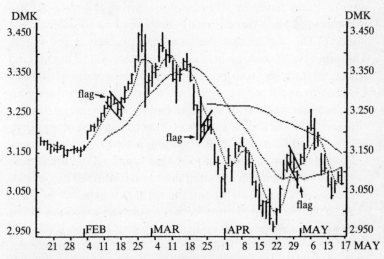

Figure 52. USD/DEM, spot price. This chart shows the dollar's dramatic top formation in 1985 before it started its dramatic slide. As will be seen, in this period there were three classical "flags". The same top formation is reproduced in Figures 48 and 55.

213

Some days pass without any significant price movements and in the end nobody wants to go out. At the same time many adapt psychologically to the new level. (The market can get used to any level at all in a most amazing way.) After the brief profit-taking is absorbed, the positive feedback loop revolves again, and the market again explodes upwards.

A flag in a rising market is a falling parallelogram and the epithet is because it resembles a flag in the face of the wind. In a falling market the flag naturally faces upwards. The USD/DEM chart in Figure 52 shows three classical flags, the first in a rising trend, the second in a falling trend and the third in a rising trend. A variant of a flag is a "pennant", the only difference being that the formation tapers out to an angle on the right-hand side. In both cases it is significant that volume drops while the formation is developing, as otherwise there would be a small top formation.

2. Gaps: Vacuum of Buyers or Sellers

A gap means that the price leaps an interval of absolutely no turnover, e.g. without the price range on one day overlapping the previous day's price range: There is a "gap" in the price. Why is this so indicative? Because it demonstrates a total vacuum of either buyer or seller interests during this interval. If a gap appears while a trend is rising, there must be no sellers in the interval. This means that the trend can proceed at full speed. The principle of looking at a chart to detect where buying and selling interests seem to be centered was essentially what Jesse Livermoore did when he ripped off the bucket shops during his teenage years. In his own words he looked for the line of least resistance. What he saw in a gap was of course an area of no resistance at all, which was naturally a strong psychological indication.

Strangely enough many will say that "gaps will be filled" and use this as a reason to leap out of the trend confirmed by the gap. The market is full of myths and the myth that gaps will be filled is a case of mistaken identity between rule and exception. Most gaps arise within one day and can therefore only be seen on a minute or time chart. This does not reduce their importance. Overall there are four types:

– common area gap
– breakaway gap

– continuation gap
– exhaustion gap

A *common area gap* arises within a congestion area, e.g. a triangle or a rectangle. This is a very normal phenomenon because most of the turnover in these formations lies at the top and bottom, not in the middle. Why? Because people trade on charts and very few will see any point buying and selling in between two strong chart points. The gap indicates the probable direction of the breakout because it reveals the significant lack of interests in the opposite direction, also if it occurs within one day.

Breakaway gaps arise on breakout from a congestion area, where a total vacuum of resistance against the movement has arisen. The gap confirms that the breakout is genuine and if there is no gap there is, in fact, reason to fear the breakout is false. The chart in Figure 53 for American Treasury bonds shows a classic bearish breakaway gap from a congestion area.

After the breakout and a trend-like movement, there will often be a further one or series of gaps, when interest is high. These are called *continuation gaps*, signaling that the movement will continue for as long as it has run since it started.

If there are several gaps the forecast becomes more compli-

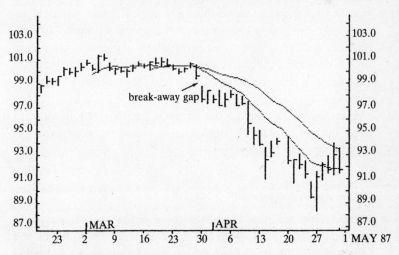

Figure 53. T-bond futures contracts. A classic "breakaway gap" here confirmed the sudden price drop at the end of March. The drop was also confirmed by a "death cross" on the moving 10- and 20-day averages.

215

cated. Imagine then what happens when you pull a piece of warm gum at both ends: It gets thinnest in the middle. Gaps indicate that resistance is thin and if there are several gaps we should look for the area where resistance appears to be thinnest. We can therefore assume that this is the half-way point of the trend and can interpolate the overall distance the trend will cover. While this method is not exactly scientific, it has proven to work. One should bear in mind that the explanation is not psychological or behavioristic, but a simple matter of statistical distribution and probability.

One complication is that what looks like a continuation gap can also be an *exhaustion gap*, a gap arising immediately before a trend is over. This is not unusual and can be anticipated if:

– the trend is expected to end soon on the basis of other indicators
– it arises in connection with vigorous acceleration in a large preceding rise
– the volume drops sharply the day after the gap
– the gap is soon closed off (the exception from the rule)

The first gap in a trend is almost never an exhaustion gap. Furthermore, exhaustion gaps are more common in bull markets than in bear markets, as traditionally there is more hysterical activity and fewer stop-losses on a top than on a bottom. But remember that gaps in a trend or breakout indicate continuation unless they are exhaustion gaps after a long trend. In the latter case there is almost always time to find other exhaustion indicators.

Conclusion: Do not go out of good trends solely because of gaps; instead, buy more (from a seller abandoning positions because "gaps will be filled").

3. Triangles: Uncertainty

Charles Dow said that if we had rising peaks and rising troughs we had a rising trend. With falling peaks and troughs we have a falling trend. But what have we got with falling peaks and rising troughs? Uncertainty! When a market goes into a triangle formation this is usually because some operators have started to doubt.

As time passes their uncertainty increases and both parties' ambitions diminish: Gradually, buyers accept buying at steadily higher prices and sellers accept selling at increasingly lower prices. As the trend has frozen, shown in the USD/JPY example, a vacuum of sell interests arises above the formation and a vacuum of buy interests below. Furthermore, more and more start to play stop-loss orders outside the triangle: Limited buy orders above and limited sale orders below. In this increasingly more unstable market state either buyers or sellers will finally be eliminated and an aggressive movement starts in the vacuum, reinforced by the many limited stop orders.

The exception is naturally when there is virtual equilibrium between buy and sell interests. In such cases the price curve moves out to the tip of the triangle and the signal is thus neutralized. A triangle is termed "symmetrical" if the support and resistance lines slope upwards and downwards respectively, regardless of whether it is actually not completely symmetrical. There is nothing in a symmetrical triangle as such to indicate whether the market's trend will reverse or continue. The formation reveals nothing before either buyers or sellers have finally been absorbed. As most congestion formations are mere interruptions in a trend, however, it is probable that the symmetrical triangle means continuation rather than reversal.

"Right-angled" triangles are considerably easier. Here there are clear arguments for the direction in which the breakout will come. A right-angled triangle has a horizontal and a sloping line and can appear as in Figure 54.

Here there was permanent sales pressure at 144, while pressure to buy steadily increased, with higher troughs to follow. Finally, rising buy interests won over sellers and the price broke through upwards. This type of right-angled triangle is described as "rising". In a minor stock or bond market it often indicates that one single major seller has placed a limited sale order (sale order at a given price) in a market with an underlying bull trend. When the major seller's securities have finally been absorbed the breakout will come and the trend continues. The line drawn in away from the triangle shows the minimum verticle objective of the breakout. It is drawn from the start of the triangle, parallel with the line opposite the breakout direction. The arguments are obvious:

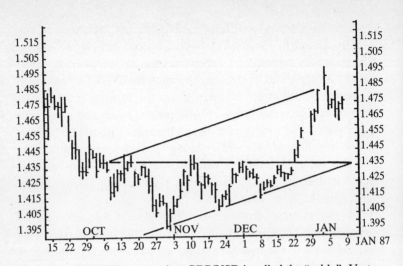

Figure 54. GBP/USD, spot price. GBP/USD is called the "cable". Up to Christmas 1986 dealers closed off cable positions to celebrate in peace and quiet. But the day before Christmas Eve the price broke up through the triangle, revealing a majority of buyers. Then a massive bull trend started.

– Firstly, it must go further away from the formation the longer time passes, because the vacuum of buyers and sellers around the formation must be increased over time.
– Secondly, its slope coefficient must reflect the shape of the triangle: The narrower the triangle, the lower trading can be assumed to be, and the smaller the difference between the number of buyers and sellers, the less aggressive the breakout.

Naturally, this line is only indicative, and must be read as a minimum objective, normally we come further. If the bottom line is horizontal this indicates increasing sales pressure against unchanged pressure to buy (possibly a large limited buy order), and the breakout can be expected to be downwards. This appears as shown in Figure 55.

A special variation of the triangle is the one starting at the tip and then expanding. This relatively rare formation is called a "broadening formation", usually indicating reversal of a major bull trend. Two typical faults in triangles must be avoided:

218

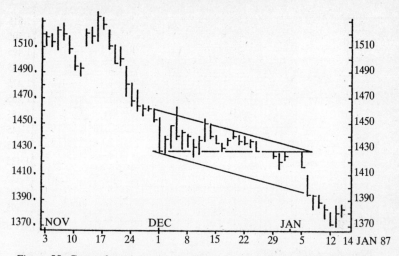

Figure 55. Cocoa futures contracts. Here we see a falling triangle where the breakout does not start as aggressively as usual, since this was in the 1986 Christmas break. When Christmas was over the formation's target was soon reached, however.

1. Trying to draw them before they are there. There must be at least two tops and two bottoms. Furthermore, the formation is not a reality before the day the breakout starts.
2. Trading on false or premature breakouts.

The second fault is difficult to avoid; read more about this in Chapter 24, Timing Tactics.

4. Rectangles: Conflict or Musical Chairs

A rectangle is a recurring forward and backward movement between two well-defined price areas. So it is trading between a horizontal line of support and an equivalent line of resistance. The chart in Figure 56 for the ASDA-MFI Group stock shows this type of rectangle over a number of years.

As in the case of the symmetrical triangle, there will be one group, e.g. the sellers, which is more powerful than the other, the buyers in this case. This will normally occur as a pure behavioristic/psychological phenomenon in a situation where the market receives few other impulses. While the relationship is not

219

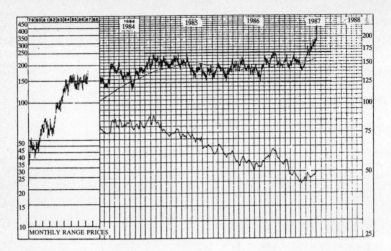

Figure 56. ASDA MFI Group. This chart shows an English share which moved in a narrow trading range over two and a half years. When the breakout finally came it was aggressive as expected. The curve also shows the 200-day moving average and a curve showing the stock's relative to total index. The latter indicator is explained in Chapter 12. (Chart: Investment Research of Cambridge).

not immediately evident, sooner or later the weaker group is eliminated and a breakout occurs in the appropriate direction. In panic trading the price breaks through the vacuum which has arisen, as well as stop-loss orders outside the rectangle.

As the rectangle fundamentally resembles the symmetrical triangle, many of the rules concerning triangles apply here. Volume and false breakout from the formation can also contribute to indicating what path the breakout will take. It should also be noted that rectangles can be very narrow (see Figure 57).

In situations like these it can be questioned whether for example buying at 161.30 and selling at 162.25 is any big deal. The truth is that this is only part of the story. The formation arises because people who are selling *anyway* wait until the top chart point, and those who are buying *anyway* wait for the lowest one. This is why many formations appear in very extreme miniature versions.

220

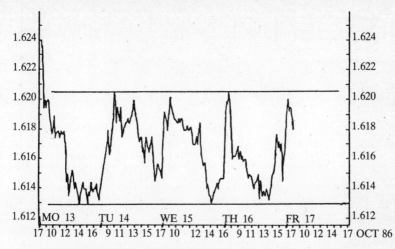

Figure 57. USD/CHF, spot price. This is an example of a very short-term trading range of a type which is very common. The chart shows prices over five days in October 1986.

5. Wedges: Rising Resistance or Support

When a trend movement stops, temporarily or permanently, to be replaced by movement in a sideways formation, e.g. a rectangle or a triangle, this is usually a case of calm before the storm. When the market explodes upwards or downwards through a vacuum new interest will briefly arise, primarily due to profit-taking. This gives flags and pennants. However, going slowly and steadily up and down in a so-called staircase trend, everything is hunky-dory. New waves of buyers or sellers follow the price along, preventing serious relapses.

But not always. There is one special movement pattern which indicates that buyers (in a rising trend) unsuspectingly move into an area of more and more resistance. The formation is wedge-like because every new upward movement is smaller than the preceding one. Finally, advances at every new top are so small that they can almost be described as a series of false breakouts in an area where there still seems to be plenty of selling pressure.

In a market like this many investors move their stop-loss orders up with every little bottom, but as they lie very close to each other, release of the first stop-loss orders will pull the price down to the following ones, and a self-reinforcing loop arises. The rea-

221

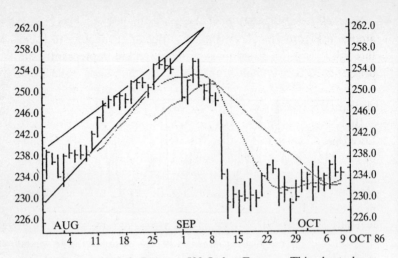

Figure 58. Standard & Poors – 500 Index Futures. This chart shows American index futures' dramatic drop on 11 September 1986. As mentioned in Chapter 6, Schiller proved that the only reason people were selling in this drop was that the market was falling. Technically this was a breakout from a rising "wedge" followed by a "death cross" on the 10- and 20-day averages.

son for this is, of course, purely behavioristic, based on the use of stop-loss orders combined with the increasing resistance.

Wedges can be rising and falling, but a falling wedge naturally signals a rise, not a fall. The difference is that while breakout from a rising wedge is normally aggressive, breakout from a falling wedge is often more relaxed in speed, if not extent. The greatest problem in trading on wedges is that they can be difficult to define. As for other formations: Wait to trade on the formation's signal until it is over and breakout has begun.

6. Double/Triple Tops and Bottoms: A Level Which Cannot Be Broken

Charles Dow wrote in an article in the *Wall Street Journal* on 20 July 1901: "Records of trading show that in many cases when a stock reaches top it will have a moderate decline and then go back again to the near highest figures. If after such a move the price again recedes, it is liable to decline some distance." He described this as the "double top theory" .

222

We saw the explanation of this phenomenon in the gold example in Figure 36. When the price does not manage to break through its last top many market operators are unpleasantly surprised and when it then breaks below the previous bottom between the two tops they get even more nervous, and the road is clear for a trend reversal.

But be careful not to see the picture before it's really there. Looking at a chart, almost any chart at all, examples will be seen of a price trying to break through a resistance or support area two or three times, finally succeeding. This is the case for rectangles and right-angled triangles. Every time this is about to happen many will shout "double top" or "triple top" before the top is finally broken, and will mistakenly reverse or go out.

A double top or triple top is important because it can signal that a longer trend is over and a counter-trend is beginning. But this does not happen very often and therefore these formations are rarer than their reputation indicates. Characteristically, the market's two or three attempts at breakthrough are clearly separated, and not just phases in a temporary slowdown. Furthermore, the second, or even third attack must be clearly weaker

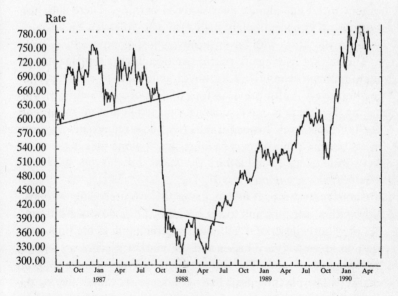

Figure 59. Siemens AG. The chart shows a double top in 1986/87 followed by a double bottom completed in 1988.

than the first, with less volume and less momentum. (We will return to the latter.) Finally, the bottom between the two tops must be broken through. Before this is the case there is no way of knowing whether the market is not just going through a temporary consolidation phase.

When a really reliable double/triple top or bottom is concluded, the signal is very strong, and the greater the preceding trend the greater the new counter-trend can be expected to be.

7. Head & Shoulders: Exhaustion of a Trend

One of the most expensive technical formations to overlook is the head and shoulders formation. Many dramatic trend reversals on the stock exchange have started with this formation, including the South Sea Company and Wall Street 1929 (Figures 4 and 5). If we are familiar with this demon we will usually recognize a very clear signal when it turns up on our chart. What happens is as follows:

The market is going up in a beautiful trend, most participants earning money. Some go out too early (and in again later), others stick, but almost everybody is earning. There has just been a top in exceptionally high turnover, followed by a somewhat smaller drop with lower turnover, just as expected.

The market rises again, reaches an even higher top, again with high, perhaps even higher, turnover, and starts to drop again at low turnover. As for previous tops this is pure and simple profit-taking. But there is one disturbing aspect: There is no support at the last top's level. Instead it falls right down to around the previous bottom. This drop is so large that it alone makes the market a little oversold and a third rise starts, *but this time with considerably lower volume.*

Shortly afterwards it breaks under the two preceding bottoms, now with lower tops and lower bottoms, i.e. a downward trend. As previously described, all investors coming in in the final congestion areas will face losses and the market psychology will be the worst imaginable. The line between the two bottoms, the bull market's last psychological line of defense, is called the "neckline". When this is broken it naturally releases a strong sell signal, but simultaneously the market can be so oversold that for a short time it withdraws, testing the neck-line from below. This is a clear opportunity to sell.

In some cases the ghost has more than two shoulders. This is without significance as long as the formation has definitively passed from a bull trend to a bear trend, i.e. from rising tops and bottoms to falling tops and bottoms. A strange tendency here is an inclination to symmetry: If there have been two left-hand shoulders there will often be two right-hand shoulders. In the same way as the other formations a head and shoulders can be upside down, thus signaling reversal of a preceding bear trend. An example can be seen in the chart for the *Financial Times* Gold Mine Index in Figure 60.

A special variation of this formation is the so-called "diamond". A poorly defined head and shoulders formation, where the neck-line has collapsed in the middle so the formation is almost rhomboid. However, this is less reliable than the classical formation.

A true story is told of a confirmed chartist who came to sit next to a man on a plane who was poring over a chart. The chart

Figure 60. Financial Times Gold Mines Index. This gold mine index is based on twenty-four South African gold mine stocks, calculated since 1955. The chart shows a reverse head and shoulders formation with a subsequent test of the neck-line before the bull market continued. The index is calculated in GBP.

showed a classical head and shoulders formation, so our chartist asked with great interest what security the chart showed. The "chart" had nothing to do with the stock market: It was a heart cardiogram, and the patient died.

Many chartists can see a head and shoulders formation where none exists, but the worst you can do is see a head and shoulders top formation in a falling trend, believing it confirms this trend. A higher top in a falling trend definitely does not confirm the trend, on the contrary, as the intervening bottoms in reality can resemble a double or triple bottom.

8. Key and Island Reversals: A Sudden Shock

Most primary trend reversals take place over a longer period. The market leaps up and down, and as time passes investor confidence diminishes. Sometimes the foundation collapses, at least for a time, on one single day, and in these situations a special intuition is needed, as trading must be fast as lightning.

The following can happen: After rising for a period one morning the market opens in strong trading, and the previous top is broken. As brokers are patting each others' backs terrible news breaks: rumors that the president is dead. Total confusion, the price hovers up and down, while people make fortunes and lose the lot in rapid succession. At the close of the day the market lies below the preceding day's lowest level.

This is a *key reversal* or key-day reversal, and it naturally indicates something very wrong with the market's values, for a time at any rate. It cannot always be seen whether the formation will hold until shortly before the market closes, and often it fails (when the attempt is made we say "they're trying for the key"). Many are so shocked by a key-day reversal that they do nothing the first day ("we never trade in panic"), but the next day they react: They sell. Therefore, react to a key reversal the same day it happens (when towards the day's close we realize something is wrong). Not tomorrow.

Another shock effect is an *island reversal*. This is a reversal characterized by two gaps – one in each direction. It is extremely difficult to profit from this reversal while it is taking place. Important is that it has one thing in common with key-day reversals: It signals a secondary, not a primary, trend reversal. The

226

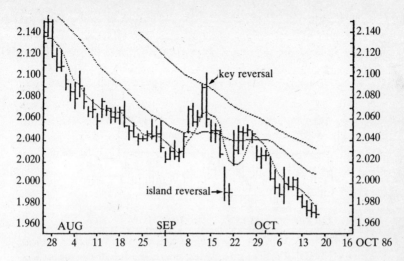

Figure 61. USD/DEM. The two reversal formations in this chart were both very short term, giving no signals for the primary trend. The chart's moving average is based on 2-, 20- and 50-day prices. (Chart: Reuter Graphics.)

chart in Figure 61 shows both formations, first a key reversal top, then an island reversal bottom. In both cases they signal reversal, but in both cases with only short-term effect.

Often a specific item of information or news releases these shock movements. Many who fail to react in time omit to do so because they do not consider the news important. This is a fundamental error because traders should never act on news *per se,* but on the market's *reaction* to the news. Do not trade because *you* have panicked, but if you can see that *others* will, you must too.

After this review of the most common formation types we can return to the first chart from Figure 49 to see whether it has anything more to tell us, viewed through "a shrink's glasses".

From August to October we lay in a *rectangle* which started with an *exhaustion gap*. In the rectangle we had a *common area gap*. In its last half we were in an almost horizontal *channel*, itself resembling a rectangle. At the breakout we saw a small *breakaway gap* and two days later a *continuation gap* before formation of a perfect *flag*. Like the middle gap the flag signaled that we

227

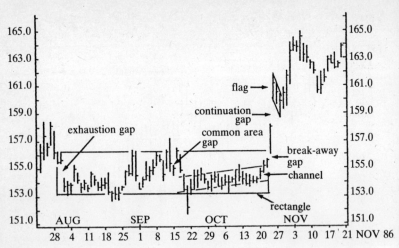

Figure 62. USD/JPY, spot price. Most charts are full of messages. This one shows the same sequence as in Figures 31–33, but now through our "shrink's glasses". (Chart: Reuter Graphics.)

were halfway through the rise. This continued shortly after, and a new top was reached, but without momentum rising equivalently. The latter was a disturbing sign, and subsequently the price also reversed.

20.

Bungee Jumping

Why do people forever try to link economy with the stock market?
Economics have nothing to do with timing – and timing is everything.

Joe Granville

There is a question which seems to nag almost everyone in the financial world. And that is whether the madness of crowds can be cracked by computers. (Just imagine one little machine crunching all the facts and figures and producing a magnificent mountain of money!) That would be genuine alchemy. Of course one should bear in mind that there are limits to what computers can do. For one thing they obviously can't go to cocktail parties to pick up titbits of delicious information. Nor can they search for lice in Ghana. Consequently the machine would have to concentrate on identifying chart patterns.

However, the awful fact is that computers are virtually blind. Even today they are so backward that if you code one to pick oranges you will soon find it stuck – trying to pick the sun. With an IQ of that magnitude, it's a bit much to trust a computer to identify a falling wedge or an exhaustion gap. So of course you can't do that. In fact the poor thing is so dumb that it's best not to use it to identify anything at all. But what you *can* do is to have the machine assist you with some simple calculations. It is for instance pretty silly to calculate moving averages by hand when a computer can do it in a jiffy. It can also calculate a few other useful indicators. And those indicators are what this chapter deals with.

Momentum: A Financial Bungee

In New Zealand they have a popular sport called "bungee jumping". The jumper springs from a high bridge with an elastic cord or "bungee" tied to the legs. Just before hitting the ground the bungy tightens, pulling the jumper up with his stomach in his throat. With our monster, we have a similar phenomena. When the monster has moved too fast, the bungy is stretched and we say the market is "overbought" or "oversold". This can be measured by a simple indicator and is called "momentum". Momentum is a statistical expression of the "knowledge attitude" effect and can thus be correlated with the moving average approach. Momentum expresses an obvious idea, best explained by the method's most banal formula:

Momentum = today's price − price × days ago.

Let us say that "x days" is 40. Now imagine that in the first month the price drops from 200 to 180 and then the following month rises back to 200. In that situation the rise in the second month is not exactly a buy signal to the market. The price has merely returned to where it has just been and buy interest is most probably due to profit-taking or "bargain-hunting". In this example momentum will be: Momentum = 200 − 200 = 0, which is naturally a neutral signal.

Now the price rises in the following two months to 250. This is neither profit-taking nor bargain-hunting, as it brings the price up to new heights. Somebody must have developed a serious interest in this stock. Now the indicator says: Momentum = 250 − 200 = 50. The higher momentum figure thus indicates that the increase is expressing something significant. Simply stated, when interest rises, momentum rises with it. Two months later we are at 350 and momentum is 100. A rise of 40% in two months usually gives a counter-reaction, so this (or another) limit warns of the impending correction.

In another scenario, after two months we lie at an unchanged 250. Momentum will then have fallen back to zero. This is one of the intervals in which the market "catches its breath" before profit-taking commences, and the drops in momentum release warning signals. So the rules are:

Rising momentum	= buy signal
Falling momentum	= sell signal
Extreme momentum value	= warning of a counter-reaction

In addition, as long as momentum stays above neutral value in a rising trend, or below in a falling trend, all else being equal, the trend is intact. On most markets basing the formula on 40-day prices gives the safest indication. Nobody has ever been able to determine why the 40-day figure is the most indicative, nor has anyone been able to calculate in advance the average time for hypnotized subjects to stop mailing postcards to the hypnotizer (cf. Chapter 17). The only thing one can do is study the market and accept its message.

Rate of Change

This is a very alluring idea, but it does have its weaknesses. In June 1978 *Commodities* carried an article by J. Welles Wilder Jr., who pointed out the obvious problems:

1. An extreme, but isolated basic price (e.g. 40 days back) can release a deceptive momentum value.
2. The scale will be individual for each single security, due solely to the different price levels.

He could have added that in all its banality the original momentum formula is quite superfluous, as it shows something which can be sensed from the chart anyhow. Instead Wilder suggested the following formula:

$$100 - \frac{100}{1 + \dfrac{\text{average of X days' rises}}{\text{average of X days' falls}}}$$

He described his calculation as the "Relative Strength Index". His choice of name was unfortunate as earlier the "Relative Strength" concept had been widely used to describe individual stocks' strength against their generic family or the stock index. Investment Research in Cambridge (UK) instead suggested the name "Rate of Change Indicator" (ROC), now preferred by many Europeans.

Let's take another look at the formula. If we for example say that ROC for a given market should be calculated for x = 10 days, ROC = 100 on ten days' successive increases, and zero on ten days' decreases. The formula thus indicates that in the relevant market it would be almost impossible for the price to move in the same direction ten days running. In other words, it would be characteristic of this specific market that in this interval people would be strongly tempted to realize profits, or buy on a sustained drop, so there would be a brief reversal in the market. If the rise or drop in market price has been extraordinarily high over a short interval, this in itself can bring the indicator close to 100 or zero. So the formula expresses what percentage price movement a market can normally bear, regardless of whether this takes place over only a very short interval. The formula is easy to use. The following rules apply:

– Watch out when ROC reaches extreme limits.
– Watch out when the price reaches a new top or bottom, without ROC doing the same.

Wilder's formula has proved extremely useful in liquid financial markets, if based on optimal horizons. The horizon which should be inserted for the formula's variable x depends on what security is being analyzed, as different markets have different psychological rhythms. The most commonly used intervals are the following:

Security analysed	Variable X
Stock index	14 or 40 days
Individual stocks	20 or 40 days
Currencies	14, 20 or 40 days
Bonds	10, 20 or 40 days
Bond futures, stock index and commodities	10, 20 or 40 days

The reason that several intervals can be indicative for a market is of course a fractal phenomenon. The limits to be considered critical also depend on the relevant market. Typically the critical value lies at 70/30 to 90/10 respectively. With a clear trend these "pain thresholds" can be adjusted asymmetrically, e.g. choosing 80/30 in a bull market, or 70/20 in a bear market. If the formula

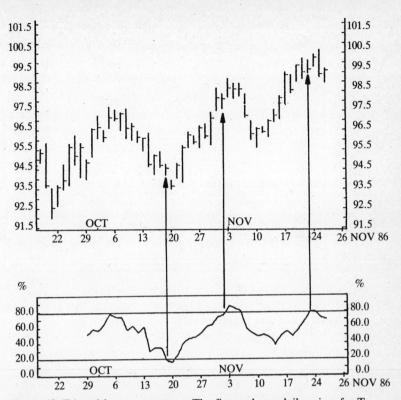

Figure 63. T-bond futures contracts. The figure shows daily prices for T-bond futures compared to the Rate of Change indicator (for 10 days). As shown, trading on overbought or oversold should normally be the day after the signal is given. Also note that each tertiary bull trend lasts for exactly 10 days. Phenomena like these mean that a 10-day Rate of Change indicator is useful in short-term timing of these contracts.

is used to support short-term timing in bond futures, the chart can look as shown in Figure 63.

The formula also works excellently if used to analyze historic stock markets. If computers had been available in 1929 and the Rate of Change formula used was with X = 14 days, it would have been the ideal timing instrument. Figure 45 shows the indicator's effect at the moment of truth, when the head and shoulders formation had been built up and the bear market started.

When the monster went wild in October 1987 many did have computers, and could see that the plummet stopped when the

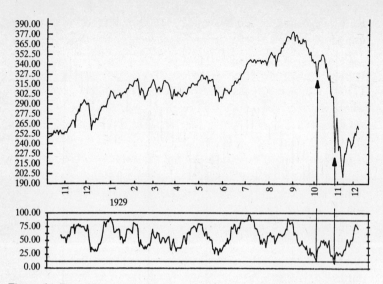

Figure 64. Dow Jones Industrial Average 1928–29. In the 1929 crash the market was oversold twice when the Rate of Change indicator for 14 days reached 12.5 and 10 respectively.

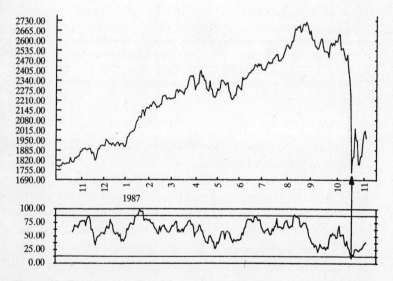

Figure 65. Dow Jones Industrial Average 1986–87. As in 1929 the panic stopped in 1987 when the 14-day Rate of Change indicator reached 10.

ROC indicator reached 10, exactly the same level as in 1929 (Figure 64).

But, most surprisingly, the indicator also functioned as intended when the bubble burst for the South Sea Company in 1720. As shown in Figure 66, the drops stopped just at the points where the indicator showed an oversold market.

Often the formula works best (i.e. in situations other than crashes) if we go out of the market the day after the critical limit is reached, and go on vacation until the indicator has shifted 10 points from the critical value. At this point a temporary consolidation will often be over and the breakout's direction from this congestion area will indicate the direction of the market's next major movement. If caught in a panicking market, ROC can be used to evaluate when *not* to sell. Don't sell if ROC = 10.

The rule that ROC should confirm new tops and bottoms is naturally linked to the fact that a new top can be a red herring if not accompanied by rising enthusiasm in the market. Simply, if a

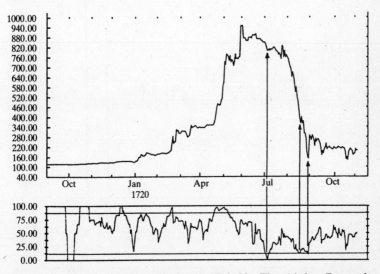

Figure 66. The South Sea Company 1719–20. The 14-day Rate of Change indicator shows how the South Sea Company braked its fall three times when it was "technically oversold". Because of the company's unchallenged dominant position on the stock market at that time it can be reasonably compared with a stock index. The extreme Rate of Change values in September/October 1719 are due to the fact that the indicator does not function in markets without any movement.

235

new top is not confirmed with a high ROC it must be read cautiously. This rule is not certain but usually gives a good forewarning of a coming trend fluctuation (although it has nothing to do with real trend reversals).

If trading on the long term, as a general rule ROC should only be used as a supplementary timing instrument for those transactions one would make anyway. Then the rules are:

– Use an extremely high ROC in a rally against a primary bear trend to sell short.
– Use an extremely low ROC in a secondary reaction against a primary bull market to buy.

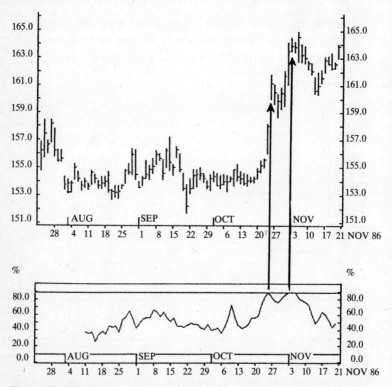

Figure 67. USD/JPY spot price. When the price has concluded a new top without the Rate of Change indicator (here for 14 days) reaching higher than the last top, the rise is often approaching its conclusion. The top on the chart shown was definitive and shortly afterwards the dollar resumed its primary down trend.

– Ignore ROC if the market has made a breakout from a large base formation.

So Rate of Change can be used for short-term and long-term deals. Trading in the very short term, another popular formula, called the "Pressure Index", can also be put to good use. This formula was developed by Investment Research in Cambridge.

Pressure Index

The calculation for the Pressure Index is a little complicated as it involves the Rate of Change formula. The link between them is as follows:

Pressure Index = STI (Short-Term Indicator) – ROC

STI can be defined as follows: Start by taking the highest trading price in the last ten days (H), the lowest trading price in the last 10 days (L) and the last day's close price (C). Then define the two variables:

Range = (H – L)
Close position = (H – C)

On this basis the formula is calculated in three stages. The first is:

$$STI(A) = 10 \times \frac{\text{Close position}}{\text{Range}}$$

This stage is calculated for the situation "today" and "tomorrow" (i.e. highest price preceding yesterday, etc.). Then the result is used in the following way:

$$STI(B) = \frac{STI(A) \text{ today } + STI(A) \text{ yesterday}}{2}$$

Then STI can be calculated:

$$STI = 10 \times (10 - STI(B))$$

Now close by inserting STI in the top formula, which gives the Pressure Index. Pressure Index fluctuates in the interval $\pm$ 100, in practice seldom reaching beyond $\pm$ 50. Like ROC the formula expresses the market's enthusiasm, but from a more short-term angle. It is therefore often primarily used for short-term timing on futures markets, traditionally very hectic, and where even the short term can seem like an eternity. Here the formula's rules are as follows:

In a bull trend:

A Pressure Index over 25 indicates great enthusiasm and is therefore a reinforcing signal. A signal under −25 indicates oversold and is therefore a buy signal.

In a bear trend:

A Pressure Index over 25 indicates overbought and thus gives a sale signal. A signal under −25 indicates great seller enthusiasm, thus confirming the trend.

In a sideways trend:

A Pressure Index over 25 or under −25 indicates overreaction, so a reversal is probable.

21.

What's *Really* Going On When a Trend Reverses?

Anyone taken as an individual, is tolerably sensible and reasonable – as a member of a crowd, he at once becomes a blockhead.

Friedrich Schiller

When a market is on the brink of a major trend reversal, as already described, this can often be read from classical chart formations. The patterns we see are not always according to the textbook, however, so it is just as important to be familiar with their background: What is *really* going on? To understand this we should first be aware of what "the market" actually is. The market's inner core is just a small select group of professionals. These people will monitor every event and price tic at the closest range. A majority of the market's tertiary movements originate from this selective world of dealing with the shortest possible time frame.

One of the best known examples of how this can evolve was the famous events released by two single brokers' trading in Northern Pacific stock. This took place on the New York Stock Exchange way back in 1901 – the year before Charles Dow died.

A "Corner" on Northern Pacific

On 6 May 1901 the New York Exchange opened calmly, except for one single security. From the start of the morning's trading, one of the dealers, Eddie Norton, started buying all Northern Pacific stock in sight. The stock started at 114, jumping at the second sale to 117. One of the men on the floor of the stock exchange on that morning was Bernard Baruch. He had noticed that Pacific stock was lower in London than New York and therefore, hardly surprisingly, planned to buy the stock in London for later sale in New York. But one of his colleagues discretely asked him to refrain from this, and he also got wind of what was brewing: Two different speculators, Harriman and Morgan would duel for control of Northern Pacific. As the good colleague he was, Baruch refrained from buying the stock. Instead he did something quite different: He sold a broad selection of other securities short.

The next day the two brokers continued their rival buys and throughout the day the stock rose steadily, closing at 143. With these major price rises a problem began to emerge: Traders lying short in Pacific met growing difficulties in re-purchasing securities to close off their contracts at the agreed time. In other words, a "corner" was developing.

On 8 May panic started to spread among short sellers and in some cases brokers believed to hold Pacific stock were virtually attacked by those about to be shut off in short positions. In some instances fullscale fights erupted in the struggle to get to the occasional few Pacific sellers. At close of trading the stock was listed at 180.

The next morning there was total panic from the exchange's opening. After just an hour the price of the much-coveted securities had risen to 400. At that time, Jesse Livermoore – the boy plunger – entered the game. Just like Baruch had done three days earlier, Jesse sold short across-the-board (except of course Northern Pacific). Shortly before lunch Northern Pacific reached 700, and after lunch the stocks were traded at 1000, at which they finally peaked.

The most interesting thing about these events was not what happened to Northern Pacific. It was the impact of this on the rest of the stock market. In order to cover contracts at these inflated prices short sellers had to sell off other securities across the board, with the consequence that the entire market plummeted, the panic ending late in the afternoon of 9 May only three days after it started.

During the afternoon, Jesse, who did not operate from the floor as he was still inexperienced in trading the market, gave orders to close his positions. To his surprise, he ended up with a great loss. Jesse didn't realize until it was too late that the tape was far behind the market. Actually, he had sold short at the bottom and bought back at a higher rate. Baruch, however, closed his deal faster. When he covered his position during the

240

day he scored the largest and quickest profit ever in his entire career on the stock exchange.

Intermittent Skirmishing

The day after, 10 May, the New York Exchange opened in good order and it was hard to imagine the tumultuous scenes of only the day before. The market soon recovered its previous losses and for most ordinary investors it had all happened so quickly that they neither bought nor sold before all had returned to normal.

This is the point. If General von Clausewitz had been interested in stock trading he would probably have described this short-lived activity as "intermittent skirmishing". In these skirmishes the only traders are the small inner circle. These have already decided what they intend to do (or, as in the example, are forced to do) and therefore their only variable is *timing*. As soon as either the buyers or sellers in this small group have been absorbed (the short sellers in the example), the market returns to normal. The same applies for classical congestion formations, such as for example triangles or rectangles.

But while this brief conflict takes place, none of the other market operators – long-term investors, pension funds, mutual funds, and odd-lotters – manage to do anything at all. *All these market operators will be influenced and decide to trade only if the price shows very significant movement over a longer period.* When this finally happens it is no longer a question of intermittent skirmishing. It becomes the key battle.

On the subject of major key battles Clausewitz wrote that "the effect is more to kill the enemy's courage than his soldiers". The conclusion of a major trend is also a battle requiring the combined forces of courage and psychology. When looking for the reversal of such a trend we should look for movements which can have a serious impact on the entire market.

The Market's Key Battles

A bull market usually starts with a few people detecting signs of a brighter future. They buy, thus revealing their standpoints to others. When the prices rise, the media and the general public get interested. "There must be a reason for such price rises," they think. Adaption attitudes come into play and many without the slightest interest in stock trading start to dabble in the market. If this goes well they tell their neighbors. The neighbors in their turn decide that stock trading is the thing to do (self-realizing attitudes) and jump on the bandwagon.

With the prices breaking through a number of chart points, new buy orders are triggered off. At the same time price gains give a surge in financial liquidity, generating new buy orders, increasing media interest and provoking publication of a series of post factum rationalizations of the bull market. As price rises reach a certain level, it turns out that companies get easier access to capital through the stock exchange, which means their actual value increases. Public valuation of the stock increases as buyouts become common.

In this way the market functions like a series of interconnecting turbochargers, where each increase stimulates a new positive feedback loop, which again sends the price up. As the bull market continues, this gives rise to new extreme parameter impacts, leading the market through bifurcations and provoking increasingly greater instability. At this point many who have sold short on the basis of fundamental economic arguments are forced to buy back their positions in panic, which can release a so-called "blow-off top", a very dramatic acceleration immediately before the final reversal. At the same time, more and more odd-lotters are sucked into the mania, leading to an exponential increase in the number of speculators.

But then, at a certain stage, the big fish will sense something is wrong. They may feel that prices are too high in relation to the fundamentals; perhaps their bullish consensus sounds the alarm, and perhaps their rate of change indicator reaches an extreme level. So they start selling off their major positions and the market is thrown back in enormous jerks. New amateurs see this as an interesting opportunity to buy: "Buy today while securities are cheap". Many of the professionals use the new rises to unload and the market takes a few more leaps up and down which are very different from the preceding trend movement.

The key battle is being fought and the process which Charles Dow termed "distribution" is in full swing. While the large stock operators are distributing their stocks in the market, the less competent fail to recognize the warning signals, partly due to in-

242

ferior analytical systems and partly due to the function of ego-defensive and knowledge attitudes. The continuing upward and downward fluctuations spread uncertainty, however, and doubt makes more and more amateurs decide to sell again. (Note: It is seldom the major operators' sales alone which provoke the reversal. Often this does not come until distribution is over and the first of the small market operators also start to sell.) When distribution is over there are no more buyers and the market collapses, and all the positive bull-market loops start working in reverse.

So one of the first characteristics of the primary trend reversal is distribution or accumulation.

But How Do We Recognize Distribution?

On the small stock markets of previous decades selling a dubious security was often a difficult process. The difficulty is expressed in the story of broker Beit's distribution. During the period prior to the historic crash of the South African gold mine stock in 1895, many brokers had the foresight to get rid of their securities before the fall. The English broker Beit was one of these.

Beit started the process by sending his mother, living in Hamburg, a sealed package containing gold mine stock. He wrote to her that this stock would soon rise ten-fold but that she was on no account to open the package and check the name of the security. It had to remain a secret as he intended to buy some stock for himself "while the price was low". His tactics worked. Consumed by curiosity she immediately opened the package and shortly thereafter (swearing them to secrecy) told her girlfriends the story. Word spread like wildfire and soon half of Hamburg was buying up the stock. What they did not know was that the seller was broker Beit in London, using this method to distribute his securities.

Today's ample statistical material and close media coverage make it possible to recognize an initial distribution phase with reasonable certainty. The general signals are the same as they have always been: a strong increase in the number of mutual funds, "bubbles", excessive euphoria, a confirmed belief that the market trend will continue forever, and more and more amateurs in the market. The chart shows this phenomenon as acceleration,

243

irregular fluctuation and unusually high volume. A broker can also recognize the last phase of a distribution from *the absence of limited sale orders above the current price*: When that happens, the big fish are through with selling their stocks.

The Mystery of Volume

There is a small mystery involved in trend reversals: When the price finally breaks out from the distribution area and collapses, *volume is high*. In the media, this will be referred to as massive sales, but in fact *as many securities are bought as are sold*. People had a reason to buy before, but what is the explanation *now*?

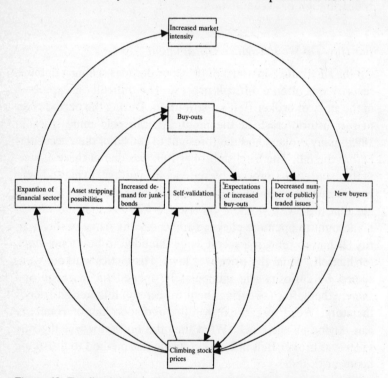

Figure 68. Feedback loops stimulating a rising stock market in the long term. The chart illustrates three important loops. The first one appears as a bullmarket leads to an expansion in the brokerage sector. More dealers get employed and marketing efforts to sell stocks are consequently intensified. The second loop concerns buy-outs. A good environment for asset stripping and financing via junk bonds stimulates take-over activity and buy-outs. The third long-term feedback loop is the self-validation effect, as described in Chapter 1.

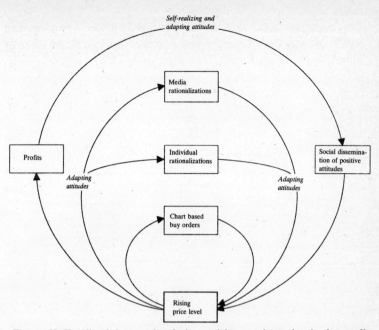

Figure 69. Feedback loops stimulating a rising stock market in the medium-long term. The first of these phenomena is the social feedback loop, where rising prices lead to social contamination. This is of course an exponential phenomenon. The second element is the widespread post facto rationalization in the media, which can lack price changes by one day to several months. Finally, chart-based buy orders will typically lack price movements from a few minutes to several days.

The immediate reason is very commonplace. It is quite simply that on a day like this the market moves through a very wide price range and therefore absorbs a lot of buy interests on its way. But the *real* problem is why so many stick to their buy interests when the market has clearly started on a falling trend? There are various reasons. One is that investors are very different. Some do not understand price movements. Many have *chosen* not to watch them (a much better strategy than watching without understanding them). Many watch the price but not "daily fluctuations". And finally, many short term traders have never fathomed the difference between trading on trends and congestion ranges: As a matter of principle they buy up on all price falls and supplement stocks "to improve the average price". We have, in other words, conflicting views between short term traders and long term trend hunters.

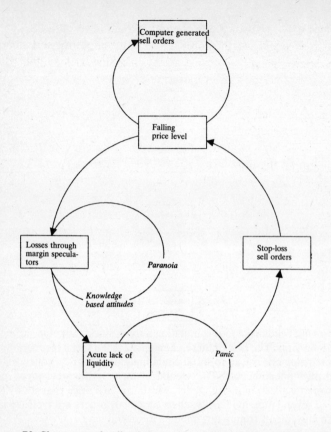

Figure 70. Short-term feedback loops in a falling market. When a market falls beyond a critical "trigger value", a very aggressive set of feedback turbo-chargers can accelerate events dramatically. At first, the falling prices will lead to paranoia (ego-defensive attitudes) among many investors and because of this the losses will surpass what was initially imagined possible. After a while, an acute liquidity crisis will lead to panic for the investor as well as his broker. In a matter of minutes, margin calls are met with stop-loss sell orders. At the same time, hedging activity will trigger computer-trading sell orders typically lacking events buy one to two minutes. These aggressive short-term loops are the major reason why bear markets in equities tend to move much faster than bull markets.

The Significance of the Time Factor

In the short term many will buy on a weakening, or are unaffected by the price movement. Others misinterpret it, resulting in the aforementioned high volume. In the long term there is another aspect. If a stock is bought at 300 on the grounds of a belief that it is really worth more, and it falls smoothly and steadily over a year, there is no great alarm on selling back at 300. Alternatively, if we buy good investment stock for our pension nest egg and it starts churning like the South Sea Company, we will soon wish to sell back on the next rise, just to see how things go.

Some market operators react at lightning speed while others dawdle. As we saw in the interpretation of moving averages and momentum the time factor is extremely important. This factor is related to knowledge attitudes and it alone can reverse a primary trend. This happens when a slowdown extends over months, or even years, when the market is "dead" and trading comes to a standstill. When activity starts up again the trend could have reversed, even though accelerations and shock movements have been seen. So the market can reverse solely because of the passing of time, but this is relatively seldom.

Characteristics of a Major Trend Reversal

All primary trend reversals are different. However, we can draw the conclusion that almost all primary trend reversals will have all or some of the following four characteristics:

1. *Acceleration and volume.* A sudden acceleration of the trend indicating exponential influx of new buyers; possibly connected with an exhaustion gap. Furthermore, unusually high volume, indicating distribution, signifying that a new "generation" is buying securities, which again means that almost everybody will run into losses on only a small decrease.
2. *Trend violation.* Serious interruption in the trend's pattern of rising or falling peaks and troughs, as for example seen in head-and-shoulders and double-top formations. To be "serious" the violation must have movement on a certain scale and over a long enough period for the psychology to suffer serious damage (knowledge attitudes).
3. *Shock movements.* Significant movement against the trend, making many insecure. This churning is often seen in wedges, key reversals and island reversals. Without numerous repetitions over a certain period, however, the time element is ab-

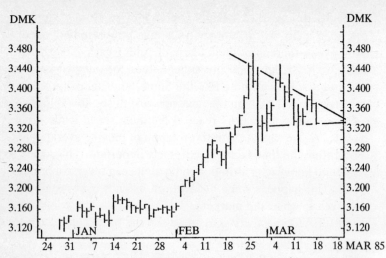

Figure 71. Dollar/D-mark, spot price. This formation clearly shows the important patterns that are drawn on the basis of close prices, not intra-day ranges. The day after the end of the chart the dollar broke through, starting one of its greatest free falls ever.

sent and the movement lacks credibility. Only secondary trend movements reverse.

4. *Time and momentum.* The trend comes to a standstill for so long that gradually long-term investors lose all patience and abandon positions. This is reflected in the price curve's falling momentum (cf. Chapter 20).

The tulip mania, the South Sea Company and the Wall Street crashes were classic examples of these phenomena. But in fact they occur all the time, e.g. in the case of the chart in Figure 52, showing the end of the dollar's bull market in the spring of 1985. Let's take another look at this market, as it appeared immediately before the final trend reversal (Figure 71).

There was strong acceleration with high volume followed by alarming shock movements. The entire top formation took almost a month to form, thus meeting the necessary time criterion for a primary trend reversal. The only thing lacking was serious interruption of the bull trend's pattern of rising peaks and troughs. This came after 18 March with the first close prices under 3.32, after which a falling trend was a reality. Barely three years from this date the dollar had dropped to 1.57, losing over half its original value vis-à-vis the D-mark.

248

VII

Beating the Gun

It's easy to make money on Wall Street. All you have to do is – buy when the price is low. Then, as soon as it goes up, sell and take your profit.

Mark Twain

22.

Strategy and Tactics

It requires a great deal of boldness and a great deal of caution to make a great fortune.

N. M. Rothschild

We have now dealt with the challenge of analysing the markets. The last section of this book concerns the no less interesting task of beating them. The first part of the problem is to determine just how effective our analytical tools actually are. The second half of the challenge is to determine which tactics are feasible given such an analytical system. Let's return to our initial framework of subsystems:

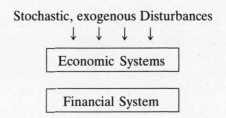

Exogenous Disturbances

For a start we could consider the disturbances, the noise. We had originally decided to disregard the noise as an analytical tool as the markets are transparent and it is instantly manifested in the price level. But to ignore the noise as an analytical tool in no way means we should bypass it altogether. Noise can be described as good or bad news flowing in an unpredictable sequence. The important fact is that the positive and negative factors are unlikely to counterbalance in the short term. Consequently, they could add an unwelcome twist of chance to the task of predicting market behavior. But fortunately, noise does not accumulate over time. Quite the contrary: The good and the bad must be expected to even out in the long run. The law of averages reigns and exogenous noise becomes just noise.

Chaos – The Wall of Unpredictability

While noise is a short-term complication, the contrary applies when we consider positive feedback loops and deterministic chaos. Feedback loops have fairly predictable effects in the short run. But over time they build up a forum of butterfly effects. The loops are accumulative – in fact, many of our timing signals (like breakouts) are derived from the feedback loops. Compounded over time they constitute an invincible barrier to prediction. They become the strongest component in our "dark forces of time and ignorance".

The Economic System

So noise disturbs the short-term signal and chaos disturbs the long view. But somewhere in the middle we can see. Whatever we see there must come from signals given by our two systems. Let's first consider the economic subsystem – the business cycle. This system is rather lethargic. Take, for example, the Kitchin cycle. The *average* cycle duration here is 41 months (although with great variation). This leads money rates, long bonds, stocks, commodities and precious metals to turn twice during each 41 month cycle, giving approximately three market reversals a year.

Three reversals a year is not a very dramatic process and certainly nothing to justify daily or weekly forecast revisions. With such a weak signal it becomes quite obvious that the signal-to-noise ratio will be very poor in the short term. For dealing with a time horizon shorter than one month, this model loses all relevance. On the other hand it also becomes very inefficient in the very long term, and for two reasons.

First of all, the only thing this business cycle model provides is the sequence. If one market reversal is not correctly predicted, then the rest of the forecast will have to be revised. It is therefore pointless to use this model for predicting anything more than the next market turn. On average this will only be two months into the future, rarely more than six.

The second factor limiting the forecast horizon is the economic chaos effect. Owing to the friction in the real world, however, chaotic effects are probably not a significant complication when we limit our predictions only to about two months ahead.

So all in all, the business cycle can lead us to draw a rough pattern of the future, say, once to three months in advance. Not less and not much more.

The Financial System

Unlike the economic subsystem, the financial subsystem generates some very strong signals which make it possible to forecast with precision in the short term – the signal-to-noise ratio permits even intra-day forecasting. But because of the strength of these positive feedback loops, chaos is a much bigger complication here. You can say that you have hit the wall of unpredictability much sooner than in the economic subsystem. Chaos makes it very difficult to predict behavior generated by the financial subsystem more than a few weeks in advance.

One aspect that should be noted, however, is that many of our best analytical tools are derived from trend psychology. Once the markets are locked into specific trends, they become very easy to forecast. When, on the other hand, the markets are trendless, our short-term signal-to-noise ratio worsens drastically and price movements approach a true random walk. It is for this reason that trading on trends will receive high priority in our tactical framework.

The conclusion regarding our financial subsystem is, in part, that it permits fairly accurate forecasting in the short term – say two hours to four weeks, but contributes very little to decisions covering a longer duration. Additionally, our hit record will be significantly better if we trade on trends rather than in trendless markets.

So What Is Our Visibility?

Within a time frame ranging from a few hours to a month we can often make extremely accurate forecasts of market timing and price levels – at least when trading on trends. From one to six months we can form qualified assumptions about overall market sequences.

Assuming no one forces us to take long term positions, the basis of our tactics should be to respect our long-term business cycle in a defensive sense – don't fight it. But active decisions – when to open a trade, when to close, how much investment should be headed to short-term signals generated by the financial subsystem – that is what we call our tactics. As we have seen, the financial system generates many signals – from liquidity indicators and bullish consensus to chart formations. But as we have shown in Chapter 21, the common denominator and the most important publicity agent of all market dynamics is price movements. It is only because of the price dynamics that there are positive feedback loops in the financial system. For this reason, although we shall always consider all our indicators, the ultimate, tactical framework can be based on price movements.

Tactics Are Two Things

When speaking of stock market tactics, the key distinction should always be between two elements:

– exposure tactics
– timing tactics

Exposure will always be the starting-point and these tactics primarily depend on risk aversion, i.e. the "financial pain threshold". Exposure can be defined as follows:

> Exposure is the largest worst case loss which can be reasonably imagined in any given transaction.

Exposure is always based on the investor's own situation and the assets being managed. Only when exposure tactics have been hammered into place can we turn to *tactical timing*, where we should concentrate solely and exclusively on the market.

> Tactical timing means trying to act in a market solely on the basis of what we think it will do.

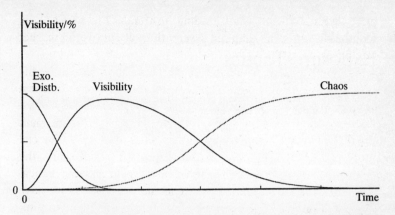

Figure 72. Noise, chaos and visibility. The chart gives a suggestive, idealized presentation of how noise, chaos and visibility (the residual) may look over time. In real life, the curves will not of course be smooth – chaos, for instance, will be composed of financial short-term effects and economic long-term effects.

This tactic should not be influenced by gains and losses already made.

So the idea is to achieve a state of mind of complete separation of exposure tactics and trading tactics. When trading we keep our fingers off the calculator and refrain from engaging in risky attempts to "recoup losses" (like Churchill) or "improve average prices" by repeatedly buying up in a falling trend. Nor do we close off a deal just because profits are good. If we believe in the market, we stay with it and go for a home-run.

To sum up, tactics are a question of disciplining actions and suppressing personal emotions. Good tactics are a mental crash helmet against irrational fear, doubt and greed. The next chapters will consider how to put simple tactics into practice.

23.

Exposure Tactics

Don't gamble; take all your savings and buy some good stock and hold it till it goes up. If it don't go up, don't buy it.

Will Rogers

Planning exposure tactics should always start with an element of realism, with answers to the following three queries:

1. *With your hand on your heart: How large is your overview?*
   The more different markets you can study, the greater the chances of success. In fact, a broad-based international market overview is the very most important criterion for success. Why is this so? Because it enables us to listen to the markets' cross-talk and because it helps us to be more discerning. Monitoring many markets, we will find it easier to keep our hands off the 95% unsafe investments, instead concentrating on the 5% which are obvious possibilities. So we must decide how many markets we can take on and, most important, how we will keep tabs on the relevant information.
2. *Is the paperwork under control?*
   Many investors succeed in planning market strategies worthy of first-class generals, only to see their troops frustrated by administrative impediments. Undeniably, administration is a prime bottleneck to exposure breadth.
3. *What about tax provisions?*
   After the close of the financial year, hopefully a tax has been incurred on profits earned. From this date an amount corresponding to this liability should be placed in a safe investment, thus reducing exposure correspondingly.

When these questions have been answered satisfactorily the next task is to distribute resources to bring exposure under control. A good general rule for the initiate (after many years of unbroken success, risk can be concentrated gradually) is to place one half of the capital in prudent liquid investments and the other half in something a little more "lively". A simple structure:

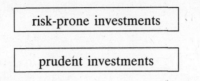

Prudent investments can be short-term bonds, bank deposits or suchlike. This is the structure's foundation, which must never be smaller than the superstructure. The superstructure, which is the interesting half, must be spread further. Depending on temperament, overview and resources, the rule can be made that no deal may exceed one-third, or for example one-fifth, of the total exposure of the more exciting investment pool. So we are not talking about "money" any more, but "exposure". If we have a million dollars for the more interesting deals, "one-fifth exposure" corresponds to a set-up where losses over 200,000 dollars are very unlikely.

When spreading exposure we should first think in terms of probable losses and then decide on a position size corresponding to this maximum loss. So we choose to "gear" many positions with borrowed funds to adapt the risk level of different transactions to varying extents. But what if there are not enough exciting deals available to meet the selected framework? Then we place the funds as bank deposits until something really good turns up. The risk-prone exposure level is a maximum, but not an absolute necessity. So the prudent exposure policy can be summed up as follows:

> Divide available funds into two equal portions, one for prudent placements and one for more risk-prone transactions. Then decide what maximum proportion of total exposure one individual deal may account for. Finally: Stick to this policy always.

If short-term transactions show a profit the risk-prone limit is increased by one half of the profits, while the other half is added to the "prudent pool". With a loss, do the opposite.

"Pyramiding" and "Reverse Pyramiding"

If the more exciting activities go well, on the basis of this exposure strategy we can go into "pyramiding" in single good transactions. We increase investments as we make profits, *but by diminishing amounts*.

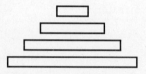

4th investment
3rd investment
2nd investment
1st investment

"Pyramiding" while profits are flowing in is relatively innocuous, but a more consistent and elegant model does exist.

Anybody good at reading charts can divide the exposure level in one deal category into three levels: primary, secondary and tertiary.

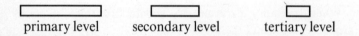

primary level   secondary level   tertiary level

The simple idea is that at the primary level we keep to the primary trend, and ignore everything other than technical indicators of the primary trend. Correspondingly we control the secondary level according to secondary movements, and the tertiary level according to short-term buys and sales on small daily fluctuations ("scalping"). Together the secondary and tertiary levels must correspond to the primary level. As a consequence, the net result will be "square" (out of the market) when secondary and tertiary signals point against the primary trend, but exposed at full strength when all indicators point in the same direction.

Often the problem with this exposure tactic is getting started. Starting with a newly established trend, initially it may at times be hard to see whether the movement is primary, secondary or tertiary. So we can start by assuming that it is secondary and from the outset operate only with the secondary level. If we later realize that we have found a primary trend we rename the positions "primary" and allow ourselves a new secondary and tertiary level.

Why This Strange Exercise?

Because it will always prevent net exposure against the primary trend, and psychologically it aids holding a long-term position, even if short-term warning signals appear at frequent intervals.

Let's conclude this chapter on exposure with a suggestion of how, as an absolute certainty, to lose every cent on the stock exchange. This system is called "reverse pyramiding" and means that in a highly geared investment we increase exposure by continually reinvesting all profits in the same security. The model appears as follows:

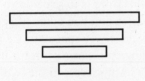 4th investment
3rd investment
2nd investment
1st investment

This structure looks very unstable and will finally collapse when one of Dow's unavoidable reactions against the trend finally commences. After the reaction the investor will be under the table and the party will carry on without him. This method is popular among first-time speculators, and the results are so astounding that their first transactions are very often their last.

Hybris, Nemesis and Nothing Left

Finally, when considering the exposure problem, we should not forget the life-time element. History shows that more than a few extremely competent players, after many years of unbroken success, suddenly lose all. One notorious example of this was our friend Jesse Livermoore.

Since his first gains in the bucket shops, Jesse kept on throughout his life reinvesting all his money, keeping none in reserve. Jesse was known for his bearish bias and made a killing during the 1929–30 crash. At the start of 1931, his total private fortune was around 30 million dollars. But then – at the age of 56 – he suddenly lost his grip. The explanation was probably the discovery that his wife, who was then an alcoholic, was having an affair with a prohibition agent. Whatever the reason, Jesse managed to lose everything he had in just two years. On 4 March 1934 he filed for bankruptcy, with a total debt of more than two million dollars.

He never managed to stage a come-back. On 28 November 1949 he went into the bar at the Sherry-Netherland Hotel. He drank two martinis and took out his note book where he wrote his last words: "My life has been a failure. My life has been a failure. My life . . .". Then he went to the men's room, drew a pistol and killed himself.

The lesson to be learned from this story is to scale down exposure slightly as your fortune increases and you come of age. Although it's the game that matters mostly to speculators – rather than the money – the habit of scaling up exposure forever implies a significant risk of sooner or later losing access to the battlefield as well as the money.

24.

Timing Tactics

Your average Wall Streeter, faced with nothing profitable to do, does
nothing for only a brief time. Then, suddenly and hysterically, he does
something which turns out to be extremely unprofitable. He is not a lazy
man.

Fred Schwed

Money is made by sitting, not trading.

Jesse Livermoore

Tactical timing should always start with a simple diagnosis. We
could call it the "10 feet test". Find the chart you want to evaluate, hang it on the wall, step back 10 feet and take a look at it.
Then ask yourself what you see:

1. An intact trend?
2. An initial trend reversal?
3. A trading range?

This study is very important as each of these three situations requires its own set of very different tactics. Should you be in
doubt turn the chart upside down and do it again. If still in
doubt, check what you see with the signs described in Chapters
17–21.

Trading on Trends

Let's start by assuming that you have identified the pattern as a
trend. Most money can be made from trading on trends (although not for the broker, as trend trading does not give much
turnover). What is special about trends is that often we don't see
them before they've run for some time, which is the reason for
the following strange rule:

When trading on trends, buy on strength and sell on weakness.

Read it again. You must buy when the price *has* gone up (when it has broken up through a congestion area) and sell when it *has* gone down (when it has broken under a congestion area).

The sensible type will naturally consider it pretty dumb to buy after the price has risen on Monday, and then sell after it has dropped on Tuesday. But this type of situation is accidental and is naturally not what it is all about. Buy on Monday's rise because you believe in positive feedback loops: Because you think that strength leads to more strength and more strength to a trend. If you sell after a drop on Tuesday this just means that (because of the drop) you have changed your mind and no longer have faith in the trend: The move did not trigger the loops.

Let's assume that the market actually ignites. The next stage will then be to evaluate whether the trend we have accepted is a primary trend, which can run for very long, or a secondary trend, which is more likely to last for a few weeks or months. This is important for how we consider the chart:

> The larger the trend, the longer, more comprehensive, the chart we should be looking at, and the more is needed before the trend is no longer considered intact.

In practice, what we should consider primarily are congestion areas: What level should be penetrated before the trend is no longer psychologically intact? When should we take a stop-loss?

Bulls Die Hard

Any experienced trader will know that it is much easier to enter a position at the right time than to abandon it at the right time. When you buy, you are completely free to make your decision. But once you're in, you *have* to decide when to get out again. The problem can be solved only by defining a clear stop-loss policy. Let's first consider the most obvious method:

1. *Stop on breakout from congestion area.* Exercise the stop-loss (this term is used regardless of whether a profit or a loss is made) if the price "resolutely" breaks back through an important congestion zone previously formed.

The logic is obvious. If we break through an earlier congestion area, according to Dow's theory the trend is no longer intact, so we should get out. But in practice the situation is as follows. Liquid Laboratories Inc. has risen steadily over a few years, now at 210. Smith bought this stock two years ago at 140 and has raised his stop-level on several occasions as the price rose. The last congestion area was between 200 and 206, so he has put his last limited stop-order at 198 ("If we break through 200 I'll get out"). Jones has no Liquid Laboratories stock and is hungry to buy, but only if he can get out cheap if the trend breaks. In other words, he wants to buy at 200 (so he can get out at 198, if 200 should be penetrated). If the price does *not* drop to 200 he won't dare buy. If the market, in addition to the usual small sale orders, consists only of Smiths and Joneses (as it often does) the price will unavoidably drop to 200, when Jones will buy and Smith will get very nervous. So:

> If obvious stop-loss levels can be defined in the market it is very probable that the price will reach them. *Stop-loss levels attract the price.*

So Smith's stop-loss levels attract the price and consequently his nerves must be tested again and again. In addition he can very easily be shoved out of the market on short-term false stop price breaks. Even worse: If a genuine breakout finally comes the whole market will often want to execute stop-loss orders simultaneously, so the market makes a break-away gap and he won't be able to sell until 170 (or thereabouts). When this has happened enough times he will probably choose another stop policy. He might use the following method:

2. *Stop in the middle of a congestion area.* He puts his stop in the middle of the above congestion area and so gets out a little earlier than in method 1.

The reason is that bitter experience of charts over many years has taught Smith that on testing of a congestion area one of the following three things will almost inevitably happen:

- Either the price will be refused at the start of the congestion area without penetrating it at all (surprisingly, Jones buys at 206).
- Or it penetrates without problems (down to for example 170).

– Finally, often it will penetrate the congestion area, continue on the other side in a short false break over one day, then reverse and resume its original trend movement. (It falls to 198, Smith sells in panic, Jones surprises Smith by buying, and it rises to 300.)

If the price penetrates below 206 Smith will sell at 203, and can sit back and watch what happens next. If it dives he is considerably better off than usual (where he gets out at 170) and if the bull trend is resumed he can buy back as soon as it breaks over 206.

So, the problem of placing a limited stop-order for Liquid Laboratories Inc. stock can be solved here. But there is one special situation where stop-orders must be placed according to another principle. Imagine that Castles in the Air Inc. stock is traded at 50–70 over six months and then breaks up aggressively in an unbroken, almost vertical, rise, giving fears that the price curve will eventually fall backwards. After four months it lies at 300. But

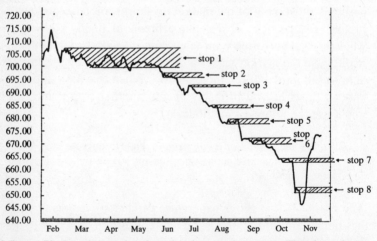

Figure 73. Stop-loss orders based on congestion areas. The chart shows the DEM/ESB price throughout 1987, a falling price expressing a rising peseta. A pesetas buyer (DEM seller) on the breakout from the spring's congestion area of 700–707 could place the first stop-loss in the middle of this range (stop 1). As new congestion areas were terminated this stop could be moved downwards (stops 2–8). Only when the price finally rose up through stop 8 did the stopout come.

the last congestion area is still in the range of 50–70. So we can imagine the following strange conversation:

Investor: "How are Castles in the Air Inc. doing today?"
Broker: "Around 300."
Investor: "O.K. I want a limited stop-order. If they drop under 50, then sell."

This would indeed be a rare conversation. Instead you should use what is called a "trailing stop".

3. *Trailing stop*. A stop-loss which shifts with the price when it moves in the trend direction. The stop is selected on the basis of the largest reactions against the trend so far. The distance to the stop is made a little larger than this.

If the largest drop so far in this situation has been 20 (perhaps in the congestion area 50–70) the trailing stop will for example lie

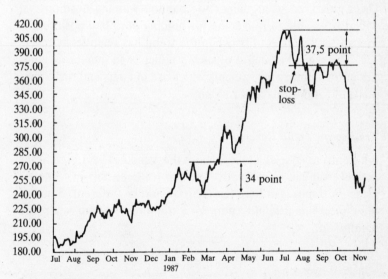

Figure 74. The trailing stop-loss. In 1987 British Petroleum started to rise so aggressively that a moving stop-loss would have been a good idea, with the starting-point the largest setback the stock had faced in this trend movement. This took place in February 1987, and was 34 points. In such a case stop-out would have been in July, when the stock dropped from 407.50 to 370.00, a decline of 37.50 points. This stop-loss policy should only be used in very aggressive trends.

22 under the current price and will thus be 278 if the current price is 300. If the price continues to rise the stop level is raised equivalently. If it drops the stop level naturally stays unchanged.

Financial Stops

The alternative to the three aforementioned stop methods is the tactic using *financial stops*. When financial stops are used, it means that exposure policy and trading tactics are being mixed and that something is seriously wrong.

If we buy a position to keep it in the long term, and then close it again as soon as we have earned 10%, *solely because we have made 10%*, we have cashed in a financial stop-profit. If anybody asks why, the explanation will be something like this:

> "Must leave a piece of the cake for the next man" or
> "Shouldn't be too greedy".

Using this kind of argument to abandon winning positions we will also be able to find some for holding onto bad positions as though they were profits, when the trend has relentlessly reversed. The typical evidence of such a policy is an increasing number of involuntary investments which are old pets and rusty remnants of former financial romances.

Trading on Trend Reversals

All trends reverse at a point, and if the trend has been significant the reversal can be dramatic. We can trade on this just like we trade on trends, but here the tactic should be different. Some of the typical financial indicators for a trend reversal are as already mentioned:

- lack of breadth
- insider sales
- extremely bullish sentiment
- strong acceleration
- trend violation
- shock movements
- loss of momentum

266

as well as the classical trend reversal formations:

– head-and-shoulders formations
– double/triple tops

(As mentioned, island reversals and key day reversals rarely reverse major trends). Considering these phenomena, and their conclusion with breakout from the congestion level or formation, the position can be opened, bearing in mind a very important rule:

> The larger the preceding trend and the larger and more dramatic the reversal formation, the more significant the movement after the reversal.

So we should look for something big. If we find a small head and shoulders formation in a very large trend we should just hang onto any long-term trend position.

After opening a position on a trend reversal, and approaching the first goal, the tactics are very simple: Hold onto the position until the reversal's minimum signal is reached, and then evaluate whether the movement has attained trend characteristics. If this is the case, hang onto it and then treat it as a traditional trend deal. But please bear one detail in mind: The first phases of a newborn trend are choppy. In the beginning it pays to trade more actively while later it's better to just stay put. What doesn't pay is of course to trade against the trend.

Many investors change psychological track in the middle of a trend, and then see every interruption and every congestion area as a trend reversal, even though the required characteristics are not present. "We're seeing the last panic-ridden convulsions", they say and take a position against the trend. A few weeks later, when they go out again, with enormous losses, they are suddenly the panicky ones themselves.

Trading on Congestion Areas

When trading on trends or trend reversals, we do not go in until the market has already moved a little in the trend direction. So we give away some of the movement in exchange for extra certainty in decision-making. Trading on congestion areas, the reverse applies.

When trading on congestion areas, buy on weakness and sell on strength.

Although this can appear more obvious than trading on trends, it is in fact more difficult.

When trading on congestion areas we try to identify a limited trading area, e.g. a triangle or rectangle, and then quite simply buy at the bottom of the formation and sell at the top. (If the interval is very narrow this is called *scalping*.) In both cases we place a stop-loss order outside the formation. This trading would be easy and simple were it not for the following problems:

1. Often we do not recognize the pattern until it has been running for some time, so the risk is that it dissolves just as we go in.
2. Secondly, at the final breakout we will just have taken an opposite position (e.g. bought on the bottom, after which it breaks out from this bottom) so that the breakout gives an unavoidable loss.
3. Thirdly, we must tackle the previously mentioned false and premature breakouts, which can tempt us to sell just when we should buy and to buy just when we should sell.

Can we do anything about these problems? Yes, we can – two things:

1. Primarily evaluate breakout on the basis of the close prices.
2. Only take positions in the direction from which we expect the final breakout from the congestion area to come.

Many overlook these methods, even though they can be very important when trading in ranges.

Evaluation of a Breakout's Sustainability

Trading ranges often have small false breakouts. This is particularly true of smaller markets where an increase in volume is often a safer signal than a breakout. To evaluate a breakout's sustainability it will often be a good idea to wait until shortly before the close price before taking a stand. Experience shows that the result is far more certain if based on the market close price. For breakout on a very significant level with a strong trend signal we should be even more cautious: Wait for confirmation of the breakout in two days' close prices before changing from range-trading tactics to trend-trading tactics.

Can We Predict the Breakout's Direction?

Following the traditional tactic of buying at the bottom and selling at the top of a formation, by definition we will lose out when the final breakout comes. As the loss cannot be limited by placing a stop-loss right up to the formation (where it will inevitably be activated on false breakouts), we have seen there is only one alternative: Make do with taking positions in the breakout direction.

How do we know what direction the breakout will take? Look for signs of a fundamental imbalance between buyers and sellers. This can often be found using the following indicators:

1. *The overall trend.* The most important signal is the preceding trend. This gives a strong indication, as by far most congestion areas prove to be intermittent skirmishes in a continuing trend. Mere statistics indicate that the breakout conforms with the trend direction.
2. *Formation.* We know that most formations give a trend signal. This often gives a very important indication.
3. *Volume.* Remember that "volume follows the trend". If we know the turnover in the rises and falls within the formation, we can find an indicator for the breakout direction.
4. *Gaps.* If there are gaps in a drop, e.g. within one day, this indicates buyers' weakness, just as gaps in a rise naturally indicate sellers' weakness. Gaps, or mere sudden shifts in one direction indicate a breakout in the shift's direction.
5. *Trial breakouts.* There are two types of trial breakout: premature and false. False breakouts are so called because they are immediately followed by a (genuine) breakout in the opposite direction. "Immediately" means within a few days or even

hours. If this does not come after an abortive trial breakout, it is premature: The final breakout will come in the same direction as the premature one.

6. *Commonality*. As mentioned, signals from related markets can often tell us a great deal about what a specific market will do.

If we can sense a breakout direction this will make tactical trading on congestion areas a considerably safer pastime.

25.

The Road to Ruin

I've worked myself up from nothing to a state of extreme poverty.

Said by *Groucho Marx,*
who lost 250,000 dollars in one day in the 1929 Wall Street crash.

We are now approaching the end of our tour. We have peeped through windows, door cracks and keyholes and taken a look at cycles, information flows and attitudes. Perhaps to our surprise we have found that present-day stock trading, with its battery of modern technology and regulations, is not very different from when it all started. We have made the discovery that there is one constant factor, and from our consideration of the market's innumerable excesses and eccentricities it is hard to overlook that this constant is human psychology. It is, in other words, ourselves.

We may not have found a simple recipe for How to Make a Million from stock trading but we have at least identified a few of the things we ought *not* to do. We can bypass the Road to Ruin with the corollary that if we swim upstream, we will not suffer the fate of the great majority.

And we can sum up *The Road to Ruin* something like this:

1. Choose to specialize in a small number of markets, and trade on them all the time.
2. Base information collection on these markets on a random hotch-potch of newspapers, economic statistics, straight tips, rumors and titbits of good advice from banks, brokers, acquaintances and taxi-drivers.
3. Listen to everything, since if information is good, more information must be better. But have most faith in the information you want to hear.

4. In particular, pay a lot of attention to economists.
5. Even though there is no doubt that you "are pretty good at economics yourself".
6. But pay little attention to liquidity flows, as "historically M2 has been a poor indicator".
7. Buy when the man next door and everybody else seem to be buying, and sell when the market has collapsed.
8. Nobody likes being out of the market, especially selling short. So for this reason most of the time you think the market will rise.
9. Make sure you receive lots of snippets of information, but never in perspective.
10. Cultivate the practice of considering prices haphazardly (on computer screens or stock lists) instead of in perspective (on charts).
11. If you use charts they must be sophisticated, with five moving averages and seven secondary indicators. The only problem is, it's hard to see the price.
12. As a chart user you are a chartist, but not if important news breaks. Then you have no faith in charts.
13. As a chartist you take a position on a head and shoulders formation even though it doesn't conform with its general characteristics. Studying the more detailed psychological basis is best left to the "theoreticians".
14. Trade on a signal which is only half developed. "Have to be quick", you think.
15. Trade on your own feelings, not the market's. Call "the others" "hysterical old women" and develop a taste for positions against an intact trend.
16. Perhaps because you never consider what "an intact trend" actually is.
17. Or because you think you already know how far a trend will go.
18. You have no particular exposure policy, and like taking chances.
19. You close off long-term investments after a week because they have given a profit.
20. And keep short-term investments if they give losses, renaming them "long-term investments".
21. Or use reverse pyramiding instead when things are doing

well. In which case you also replenish stocks to "improve the average" in a falling trend.

22. You use the same tactics regardless of whether the market is in a trend, a congestion area, or making a trend reversal.
23. You move stop-loss orders when the market is against you because you live in hope of a reversal.
24. You hide losses with hedges instead of realizing them.
25. You consider historical market cycles to be irrelevant. "Today's situation is different".
26. So you don't show much interest in the market's cross-talk.
27. You think it's easy.
28. You think it's enough to be smart.
29. You think the others aren't out to make a profit.
30. You forget this is the world's toughest market.

Keeping these thirty rules in mind, before getting too immersed in the market, take a good look at yourself and remember the old proverb: "If you don't know who you are, the stock exchange is an expensive place to find out."

Enjoy!

Figure 75. An ill-starred speculator, Walter Thornton, New York, put his sports car up for sale on 30 October 1929. (Kindly lent by the Granger Collection, New York.)

273

Appendix 1:

Characteristics of Typical Chart Formations

Flags and pennants:

Definition:
Short counter-reaction in a steep trend. Typically lasting a few days to three weeks; exceptionally up to five weeks.

Characteristics:
Resembles a flag or a pennant on a flagpole. Often slopes against the trend. Takes place in a gradually falling volume.

Variations:
A.   Flag: parallelogram
B.   Pennant: small triangle
Exceptionally the formations can be horizontal or slope with the trend.

Signal:
The trend movement has reached only halfway. It has stopped due to profit-taking but will continue aggressively. The signal is released as soon as the price breaks out of the formation.

Warnings:
Loses credibility if more than five weeks pass or the volume does not decrease.

When these formations arise a good deal of money can be made (or lost). They are also some of the most reliable signs we have and are therefore Very Good to Know.

Gaps

Definition:
Price leap without turnover, arising from a total lack of either buyers or sellers in a given price range.

Characteristics:
Any "gap" in the price within one day or between two days.

Variations:
A.	Common area gap:	Within a congestion area
B.	Breakaway gap:	On breakout from a congestion area
C.	Continuation gap:	In a trend
D.	Exhaustion gap:	Immediately before interruption or conclusion of a trend

Signal:
General signal: Total lack of buyers or sellers; confirms a movement. However, exhaustion gaps are the exception.
A. Indicates probable breakout direction
B. Confirms breakout
C. Indicates middle of a trend
D. Indicates impending stop or reversal

Warnings:
If the gap is filled the continuation gap hypothesis is denied. This indicates an exhaustion gap instead.

Triangles

Definition:
Triangle-like formation with at least two contacts at both top and bottom lines. The formation is provoked by general uncertainty or isolated distribution or accumulation in an intact trend.

Characteristics:
Independent of previous movement. No time limits. Often, but not always, with a steady fall in volume before the breakout. Right-angled triangles have greatest volume in the movements

pulling against the horizontal limit. At an upward breakout there is normally a considerable rise in volume. At a downward breakout the volume normally rises two or three days later.

Variations:
A.   *Symmetrical*. Rising line of support, falling line of resistance.
B.   *Rising, right-angled*. Rising line of support, horizontal line of resistance.
C.   *Falling, right-angled*. Falling line of resistance, horizontal line of support.
D.   *Broadening formation*. Reverse triangle, i.e. starting from the tip.

Signal:
A.   Typically signals continuation of the trend, but not always.
B.   Upward breakout.
C.   Downward breakout.
D.   Indicates reversal in bull markets, but not in bear markets. The minimum prognosis for breakout of triangles is to a line drawn parallel with the opposite border of the triangle from time of first contact.

Warning:
Symmetrical (but not right-angled) triangles relatively often have premature, false breakouts. Breakouts without volume characteristics can be false. Breakouts give the strongest signal around one-third from the tip. In order for the breakout to be significant, it must occur in the first three-quarters of the triangle. If breakout is one-quarter from the tip or later, the signal is canceled. If breakout in a right-angled triangle has not come closer than one-quarter from the tip, it is often the opposite of the formation's traditional signal.

Rectangles

Definition:
A horizontal channel with at least two tests of channel bottom and channel top. The formation is generated by the conflicting opinions of two groups or as a self-reinforcing chart game.

Characteristics:
Independent of previous movement, with no time limits.

The volume falls smoothly in the formation's lifetime, but surges at upward breakout, less at downward breakout.

Variations:
None.

Signal:
Often indicates continuation of the trend. The breakout will at least correspond to the formation's height, but is greater the longer the rectangle has lasted. Around 40% of all breakouts give pull-back to the break line before the movement continues.

Warning:
Relatively often there are premature breaks in the rectangle. A premature breakout attempt from a rectangle indicates with reasonable certainty that the final breakout will be in the same direction. On the other hand, dangerous false breakouts are somewhat rarer occurrences.

A large volume on breakout from a rectangle does not have the same signal value as breakout from other congestion areas, the reason being stop-loss orders from scalpers (people trading on short-term fluctuations). Often breakouts at low volume are the most reliable.

Wedges

Definition:
Rising or falling wedge-shaped formation with at least two tests of both support and resistance lines. Arises when a trend encounters rising resistance.

Characteristics:
Typically last three weeks to three months. Normally continue to at least one-third from the formation's tip; sometimes past the tip of the wedge and a little further, before the trend reversal begins.

Volume almost always drops through the formation, rising strongly at breakout.

Variations:
Rising wedge.
Falling wedge.

Signal:
On breakout there is a withdrawal extending at least to the formation's start. Breakout is strongest in terms of both speed and volume for rising wedges.

Warning:
A wedge can arise because an old support or resistance area is met. If this is broken before the end òf the wedge it will probably mistake its signal.

Double/triple tops and bottoms

Definition:
Two or three clearly separated tests of the same top or bottom, followed by a breakout in the opposite direction through the intermediate level.

Characteristics:
There must be a clear separation of individual attempts, possibly up to several months.

The volume of the second, or even third test, must be declining. The volume between the tests must be very low.

Top formations often conclude primary bull markets, while bottom formations typically conclude secondary bear markets.

Variations:
A.	Double top
B.	Triple top
C.	Double bottom
D.	Triple bottom
The only significant difference is that distance requirements between each attempt are lower for triple formations than for double formations.

Signal:
The signal is not confirmed finally before breakthrough of the "neck-line", the bottom between the tested tops or the top be-

tween the tested bottoms. This breaks the most important trend criterion (for triple tops/bottoms the neck-line is drawn as a straight line between the formation's bottoms or tops). The signal is a reaction at least corresponding to the distance from the rejected tops or bottoms to the neck-line – often far longer. The neck-line is thus the last line of defense of the bull or bear market.

Warning:
Easy to confuse with other formations. If in doubt, break in the neck-line will continue to indicate a trend switch. Often there is a pull-back to this line after the break. This is an attractive trading opportunity, not a threat.

Head & Shoulders

Definition:
Formation of three tops, called head and shoulders, of which the middle one is highest and the intervening bottoms are at approximately the same level, but under the first top. Then break below the straight line between the two bottoms.

A bottom formation is the reverse.

The formation expresses a large distribution or accumulation process.

Characteristics:
Large volume in the first two rises, less in their fall. Clearly less volume in the third rise. Only occurs after a major preceding trend movement.

Variations:
A.   *Top formation*: As described above.
     Top formations are more clearly delineated, occurring in higher volume than bottom formations.
B.   *Bottom formation*: Volume characteristics deviate from top formations in that the decline to the head normally takes place at lower volume than in the first shoulder and that volume in the slope from the head is greater than in the first shoulder's slope. Also high volume at break of neck-line (between the formation's peaks).

C.   *Several shoulders*: Two or three shoulders, often symmetrical. Does not deviate significantly from the basic model.

Signal:
The breakout signals movement with an objective at least corresponding to the distance from the neck-line to the top, but often far more. The objective line is drawn parallel with the neck-line.

Warning:
Head and shoulders without a preceding trend is meaningless. Sometimes there is no strong movement after break of the neck-line. This does not change the signal, which is only cried off if the price again rises above the last shoulder's top.

Key and Island Reversals

Definition:
Key: Breakout from old top, later the same day close price below preceding day's bottom (reverse in bottom formation).
Island: A reversal delimited by two gaps within the same area.

Characteristics:

Key:	– During the day breaks through the preceding day's top in a primary or secondary trend movement.
	– Unusually high turnover.
	– Trading closes below preceding day's bottom.
Island:	– Extremely high turnover, indicating accumulation or distribution.

Variations:
Key reversal can last two days.

Signal:
Short-term trend reversal; objective cannot be defined.

Appendix 2:

Leading, Coincident and Lagging Indicators

Leading Indicators

1. Average work week of production workers (manufacturing)
2. Index of net business formation
3. Index of stock prices (SP 500)
4. Index of new building permits, private housing units
5. Layoff rate, manufacturing (inverted)
6. New orders, consumer goods and materials
7. Contracts and orders for plants and equipment
8. Net change in inventories on hand and on order
9. Percentage changes in sensitive prices, wholesale price index of crude materials excluding foods and feed
10. Vendor performance, percentage of companies reporting slower deliveries
11. Money balance (M1) 1967 dollars
12. Percentage change in total liquid assets

Coincident Indicators

1. Number of employees on non-agricultural payrolls
2. Index of industrial production
3. Personal income less transfer payments, deflated
4. Manufacturing and trade sales, deflated

Lagging Indicators

1. Labor cost per unit of output
2. Commercial and industrial loans outstanding
3. Manufacturing and trade inventories
4. Average duration of unemployment
5. Ratio of consumer installment debt to personal income
6. Average prime rate charged by banks

Appendix 3:

Warning Signals of a Stock Market's Peak

The following list shows the typical warning signs of an imminent stock market top – excluding chart formations such as accelerations, exploding volume, trend violations and other stock movements.

Phenomena	Indicators
1. *Irrational attitude changes in the individual*	
1.1 You concentrate on liquid stock which can be easily resold	Narrow index rises more than the broad index
	Advance/decline line drops while narrow index rises
	Net new highs drop while the narrow index rises
	Diffusion drops while the narrow index rises
1.2 You concentrate on self-reinforcing buy signals	Related markets move in close tandem
	Self-reinforcing indicators function extremely efficiently
1.3 You accept the most optimistic expectations	Junk bonds have long been rising more quickly than AAA bonds
	Bond yield exceeds equity yield
	Price earnings exceed 20
	Price-book value exceeds 2.5
	Equity yield for blue chips drops below 2%
2. *Epidemic spread of irrational attitude changes*	Price rises accelerate after long-standing steady rises. Volume explodes
	Bullish consensus reaches the critical value
3. *Disquieting objective information is beginning to disseminate*	Media are extremely positive while insiders switch from net buying to net selling

Phenomena	Indicators
4. *An increasing shortage of liquidity*	For a period the money market interest rate has been rising and now long interest rates are following
	Yield curve narrows or becomes inverted
4.1 Total financial liquidity has long been falling	Velocity of money is rising
	Debit/loan ratio is falling
	Bank investments are falling
	Net free reserves are falling
4.2 Financial supply increases	Strong rise in number of issues
4.3 "The financial battery" is discharged	Time saving deposits are low
	Brokers' cash accounts are empty
	Mutual funds are fully subscribed
5. *A market cyclical phase shift is taking place*	CRB futures are in an intact bull trend
	Gold, silver, platinum and palladium have reversed their bear market trends. F.T. Gold Mines rise *faster than* other stock indices
	Laggers outperform leaders (e.g. metals and minings versus utilities)
	60–100 months have passed since the stock market's last peak.

Appendix 4:

List of Historical Financial Crises

Here the most important source is Charles P. Kindleberger. The list excludes currency crises, due to their number.

Year	Country	Speculation in:	Peak	Acute Crisis
1557	France, Austria, Spain, (Habsburg Empire)	Bonds	1557	1557
1636	Holland	Primarily tulips	Summer 1636	November 1636
1720	France	Compagnie d'Occident Banque General Banque Royale	December 1719	May 1720
1720	England	South Sea Company	July 1720	September 1720
1763	Holland	Commodities, based on kite flying	January 1763	September 1763
1773	England	Real estate, canals, roads	June 1772	January 1773
1773	Holland	East India Company	June 1772	January 1773
1793	England	Canals	November 1792	February 1793
1797	England	Securities, canals	1796	Feb.-June 1797
1799	Germany	Commodities, financed by kite flying	1799	Aug.-Nov. 1799
1811	England	Export projects	1809	January 1811
1815	England	Exports, commodities	1815	1816
1819	USA	Production enterprises generally	August 1818	November 1818 – June 1819
1825	England	Latin American bonds, mines, wool	Beginning of 1825	December 1825
1836	England	Wool, railways	April 1836	December 1836
1837	USA	Wool, land		September 1837

1838	France	Wool, building sites	November 1836	June 1837
1847	England	Railways, wheat	January 1847	October 1847
1848	European Continent	Railways, wheat, real estate		March 1848
1857	USA	Railways, land	End of 1856	August 1857
1857	England	Railways, wheat	End of 1856	October 1857
1857	European Continent	Railways, heavy industry	March 1857	November 1857
1864	France	Wool, shipping, new enterprises generally	1863	January 1864
1866	England, Italy	Wool, shipping, new enterprises generally	July 1865	May 1866
1873	Germany, Austria	Building sites, railways, stocks, commodities	Fall 1872	May 1873
1873	USA	Railway		March 1873 September 1873
1882	France	Bank stock		December 1881 January 1882
1890	England	Argentinian stock, stock flotations	August 1890	November 1890
1893	USA	Silver and gold	December 1892	May 1893
1895	England, Continental Europe	South African and Rhodesian gold mine stock	Summer 1895	End of 1895
1907	USA	Coffee, Union Pacific	Beginning of October 1907	1907
1921	USA	Stocks, ships, commodities, inventories	Summer 1920	Spring 1921
1929	USA	Stocks	September 1929	October 1929
1931	Austria, Germany, England, Japan	Miscellaneous	1929	May-Dec. 1931
1974–1975	Global	Stocks, office buildings, tankers, aircraft	1969	1974–75
1980	Global	Gold, silver, platinum	January-February 1980	March-April 1980
1985	Global	Dollars	February-March 1985	February-March 1985
1987	Global	Stock	August 1987	October 1987
1990	Japan	Stock, currency	December 1989	February 1990

Glossary

A

Acceleration. Unusual increase in the speed of a price movement.

Accumulation. A market process where generally small traders are sellers while large traders are buyers, thus "accumulating" securities.

Advance/decline line. Formula stating the ratio between the number of stocks in a country which have advanced and declined respectively. The formula may include issues which are unchanged.

Analysis. Generic expression covering breakdown of a problem into its sub-elements, normally related to submission of proven hypotheses. See also "Technical analysis" and "Fundamental analysis".

Arbitrage. Transaction to profit from price differences by simultaneous purchase of one security and sale of another.

B

Bar-chart. Chart showing the day's (or e.g. week's) highest and lowest price, and usually the close price.

Bear market. A market with an overall downward price trend. Also *bear positions*, sale in anticipation of falling prices. When we think a market will go down this is often called being *bearish*.

Bear trap. See under "corner".

Bifurcation. A system which alters its behavior on a given value of a given parameter, giving it several alternative equilibrium states.

Blind issue. Issue of new stock from an inactive company, or a company with very vague plans for the future.

Blow-off top. Primary bull market top closing with strong acceleration.

Book-value. Expresses by how much equity exceeds share capital. Book-value is calculated by dividing the share capital into the net assets.

Bourse. Marketplace for trading of securities (stock exchange), commodities, precious metals or currencies. The name originates from the Dutch Van der Beurs family, whose home in Bruges in the 16th century was a center for local stock trading.

Breadth. Volume of securities or assets within a limited financial market, following the same price trend, e.g. a rising trend.

286

Breakout. A price movement out of a defined congestion area.

Broadening formation. Chart formation where the price fluctuates in an increasingly wider interval.

Broker. Person or company trading securities on a commission basis.

Brokers' cash accounts. Cash deposits to clients' accounts with their brokers.

Broker's cash loan. A loan provided by a broker for a client's margin deals.

Bull market. A market where the overall price trend is upwards. Like bear markets there are *bull positions* and *bullish*.

Business cycle. The relatively regular fluctuation of the level of economic activity between the following stages: Boom, economic decline, slump and economic expansion.

Butterfly effect. A system's extreme sensibility to initial conditions.

C

Cash & carry. Simultaneous purchase of a security and sale of its future (or the reverse) to exploit price discrepancies.

Channel. Two parallel trendlines.

Chart. Diagram showing price and turnover trends.

Chartist. Anybody who tries to predict price trends from reading charts.

Close price. Price on closing of the exchange (or currency market). For stocks and bonds often the last bid price or traded price and on the currency market often the average of the last three prices.

Computer trading. Stock trading based on computer-based decision-making systems.

Confirmation. The phenomenon that several markets or securities confirm each other's trends by mutual logical or parallel price movements.

Congestion area. Price movement in a relatively narrow interval over an extended period.

Contrary opinion. Systematic exploitation of situations where a very high degree of public consensus indicates a concluded distribution or accumulation process in the market.

Corner. A market where short sellers have difficulty in covering their positions due to lack of supply. As corners are often the result of manipulation, they are increasingly prohibited by exchange rules and legislations.

Crash. Exorbitant price drops in a panicking and disorderly market.

Cyclical movements. Price fluctuations in which a systematic frequency can be identified, or with a systematic shift in sequences between different markets. In chaotic markets, cyclical influences can be present even if they are not readily detectable in the chart patterns.

D

Death cross. A falling short moving average (e.g. 20 days), crossing below a falling long moving average (e.g. 50 days).

Debit/loan ratio. Private and commercial bank deposits divided by commercial credits.

Deposit interest rate. Interest rate for interbank cash deposits.

Deterministic chaos. A deterministic process that generates behavior which mistakenly appears random during statistical tests such as spectral analysis and auto-covariance functions.

Diamond. Head-and-shoulders formation where the neck line is "broken" so the formation is rhomboid in shape.

Diffusion. Percentage of a market's securities lying above a specified moving average of its own prices.

Distribution. The market process where major market operators generally sell securities to minor operators.

Double top. Reversal formation with two clearly defined tops at the same price level.

E

Effective rate. Indexed currency rate against a weighted basket of other currencies representing the country's most important trading partners. Calculated for major currencies by, among others, the Bank of England.

Efficient market. Market immediately capable of discounting all new information in prices.

F

Family. Limited group of stocks, considered to be related and comparable due to their business area and structure.

Feedback loops. A process where one event affects others which in turn re-affect the first. If the feedback amplifies the first, it is called "positive". If it dampens the first, it is called "negative".

Feigenbaum cascade. A successive series of bifurcations.

Financial liquidity. Difference between the liquidity created by the banking system and that absorbed by the commercial, private and public sectors.

Flag. Formation showing short-term counterreaction in an aggressive trend.

Formation. A visual pattern on a price chart, one of several standardized descriptions.

Forward contract. Financial transaction with effect on a specific agreed future date. Started on French commodities markets in the 12th century with forward contracts for cloth, wine, fish, timber and metals. Unlike futures contracts, forward contract settlement dates are fixed by the dealers in each case; not by the stock exchanges.

Fractals. Systems that repeat behavior in different scales. Such systems are sometimes described as "self-simulating".

Friction. Term often used to describe the total sum of practical problems making up the distance between decision and action in the business world.

Fundamental analysis. Analysis of securities' true value or expected future yields.

Futures contracts. Standardized stock exchange contracts committing the owner to buy a specific commodity on a specific future date. This phenomenon was first introduced on the Chinese rice markets of the 18th century.

G

Gap. Price interval without any trading.

Gearing. Trading on the margin.

Golden cross. A rising short moving average (e.g. 20 days) breaking up above a rising long moving average (e.g. 50 days).

H

Head and shoulders formation. Formation in which three tops, the middle being the highest, indicate a primary reversal of a bull trend. Can also occur as three bottoms, thus indicating the reversal of a bear trend.

Hedger. Person who tries to cover a commercial risk with a financial transaction.

I

IMM. Abbreviation for International Monetary Market, a division of the Chicago Mercantile Exchange (CME).

Index future. Futures contract where the underlying security is a broad selection of a country's stocks.

Insider. Person with special access to information on a stock exchange listed company's activities. In the USA the term is also used to describe persons holding over 5% of a listed company's stock.

Interest rate arbitrage. Currency arbitrage where a high-yield currency is bought against a low-yield currency to profit from the difference in interest yields.

Intransitive systems. Systems with several alternative equilibrium states.

Island reversal. Trend reversal delineated by two gaps.

K

Key reversal. Trend reversal where on the same day the price breaks above its previous top and later closes below the preceding day's trading range (in a bottom the opposite applies).

L

Leaders/laggers. Stocks rising most in relative terms in the early and late phases of the business cycle, respectively.

Leading indicators. Key economic figures used to indicate trends in economic activity.

Limit orders. Trading orders to be effected only at (or above, or below, respectively), specific price levels.

Line charts. Ordinary line diagrams.

London basis. Prices based on events during normal trading hours on the London exchange.

Long positions. Term used for buying in the market (in contrast to short positions).

M

Manipulation. Individual market operators' or institutions' attempts to influence the price of a security.

Margin. Pledge of security for part of the actual exposure in a stock exchange transaction.

Margin call. Request for additional collateral due to an investor's losses on margin trading.

Member. Member of the stock exchange, i.e. stockbroker.

Momentum. Strength of a trend movement expressed by the price's percentage fluctuation over a specific period.

Money market. Market for simple bank or inter-bank liquidity placements. Interest rates charged on such placements are referred to as "money rates".

Moving average. Continually updated average of prices over a specific interval. If different time periods are used an average based on a few days' prices is "short" and one based on more prices is "long".

N

Neck line. Critical psychological price level which can be drawn on head-and-shoulders and double-top formations. Neck lines are often referred to as the "last lines of defense".

Net free reserves. The Central Bank's excess reserves less discount window borrowings other than extended credits to banks.

New highs/new lows. Proportion of stocks in a given index lying at the so far highest, or lowest, level over a specific interval.

Newsletter. Publication with specific decision-making oriented recommendations.

O

Odd lotter. Term covering deals of under 100 stocks (odd lots), or persons making such deals. Generally assumed to represent the actions of the less qualified investors.

Open interests. Net outstanding contracts on a futures market. If 1,000 contracts are bought and 1,000 sold short, the open interests are 1,000 contracts.

Option. Stock exchange contract which gives the right, but not the obligation, to either buy or sell a specific security at a specific future price. If the option can be traded on the exchange it is called a *traded option*. Option trading can be traced back to the Dutch market of the 17th century.

OTC-list. Over The Counter, covering securities not included in ordinary price lists, and therefore not subject to the same strict stock exchange rules of conduct.

Overbought/oversold. A market state where price rises or drops over a limited period have been so significant that it is unusually vulnerable to a correction.

P

Pennant. Variation of a flag, formed like a small triangle.

Physical Delivery. Actual delivery of the commodity specified in a futures contract.

Point & Figure. Chart system where rises are indicated with an "X" and drops with an "O". The charts have no actual time axis.

Pressure index. Technical support calculation expressing a market's enthusiasm and overbought and oversold.

Price fixing. The exchange's indicative price fixing of a security.

Primary trend. The ruling trend over a number of years.

Profit taking. Wave of sale orders in a rising trend or bear cover in a falling trend, due to realization of profits.

Pull back. Temporary reaction back to a congestion area after previous price breakout.

Pyramiding. Continuing increase in exposure in a market, but by degressive amounts. If exposure is added in increasing amounts, this is called "reverse pyramiding".

R

Rally. Temporary rise of a market in an intact long-term downtrend.

Random walk. A theory essentially stipulating that there is no systematic link between historic and future price movements.

Rate of Change. Technical indicator expressing the market's oversold and overbought states as a function of percentage price movements over a specified interval, combined with the number of days in a given period in which the price has moved in the same direction.

Rectangle. Consolidation between two well-defined price levels. Also called "trading range".

Relative to total index. Indicator of a stock's strength based on its relative price trend in relation to the country's overall index.

Resistance. Price level where a significant concentration of sale interests can be identified.

Response. Any reaction in a broad selection of a market's stocks to isolated price movements in leading securities.

Resulting factors. The direct price-determining factors arising from primary economic events.

S

Scalping. Tactic using short-term transactions to exploit the market's tertiary oscillations.

Seasonal cycle. Cyclical price fluctuation related to the calendar.

Secondary trend. Trend extending from a few weeks to several months.

Short covering. Buys to cover short positions.

Short position. Bear position, i.e. securities not covered have been sold for future delivery.

Spot trading. Trading with immediate effect (in contrast to forward trading).

Staircase trend. Well-ordered series of higher and lower peaks and troughs, respectively.

Stimulating factors. Primary events which can ultimately influence the value of a security.

Stock. A portion of a company's share capital.

Stock index. An indexed value of a specific number of shares. In many markets different total indices are used, the "narrow" index often based solely on the largest stock companies, while the "broad" index covers a larger number of companies.

Stop-loss order. Limited trading order serving to limit losses if the market moves against investors.

Support. Specific price area where a large concentration of buy interests can be identified.

T

Tapewatching. Psychological trading based on constant continual monitoring of price trends.

Technical analysis. Analysis of the stock market itself, i.e. market operators' activities and motives.

Tertiary trend. Trend extending from a few days to several weeks.

Time-saving deposit. Time limited binding of liquidity on a bank account at a specifically agreed interest rate.

Timing. Attempt to optimize the time of execution of deals which have been decided on.

Trend. The overall long-term development in a price movement.

U

Underlying securities. The specific securities (or other assets) to which a future or option is related.

V

Vacuum. Price interval in which a general lack of buy or sell interests can be identified.

Velocity of money. GDP/M2 (= Gross Domestic Product divided by Money Supply).

Volatility. Price fluctuation trend.

Volume. Stock exchange or currency market turnover.

W

Wedge. Wedge-shaped reversal formation.

Y

Yield curve. A diagram showing the annual yields on different fixed interest rate securities and money rates as a function of maturity time. A "normal" yield curve shows lowest yields at the shortest maturities. An "inverted" yield curve shows short rates that are higher than those of for example 20-year government bonds.

Bibliography

Ayres, Leonard P.: *Turning Points in Business Cycles*, Augustus M. Kelly, USA, 1967.

Babson, Roger W.: *Business Barometers Used in the Accumulation of Money*, Babson Institute, USA, 1910.

Bakken, H. H.: *Futures Trading – Origin, Development and Present Economic Status*, Mimir Publishers, USA, 1953

Baruch, B. M.: *My Own Story*, Odshams Press, USA, 1958.

Bieshaar, N. & Kleinknecht, A.: "Kondratieff Long Waves in Aggregate Output? An Econometric Test", *Konjunkturpolitik*, Vol. 30 (1984), pp. 279–303

Bernstein, J.: *The Handbook of Commodity Cycles*, John Wiley & Sons, USA, 1981.

Bolton, H.: *Money and Investment Profits*, Dow Jones Irwin, USA, 1967.

Brock, W. A. & Sayers, C. I.: *Is the Business Cycle Characterized by Deterministic Chaos?*, University of Wisconsin, 1987

Brock, W. A.: *Chaos and Complexity in Economic and Financial Science*, Social Systems Research Institute, University of Wisconsin-Madison, 1990.

Chiarella, C.: *The Elements of Nonlinear Theory of Economic Dynamics*, PhD Thesis, University of South Wales, 1986.

Commodity Exchange Authority: "An Analysis of Speculative Trading in Grain Futures", *Technical Bulletin* No. 1001 U.S. Department of Agriculture, Commodity Exchange Authority, October 1949.

Drew, Garfield A.: *Drew Odd Lott Indexes Daily 1936–1958 Inclusive*, Boston Drew Investment Associates, USA, 1959.

Edwards, R. D. & John Magee: *Technical Analysis of Stock Trends*, John Magee, USA, 1957.

Ellinger, A. G.: *The Art of Investment*, Bowers & Bowers, England, 1971.

Galbraith, S. K.: *The Great Crash 1929*, Houghton Mifflin, USA, 1955.

Giffort, E.: *Money Making Matters*, Commodity Syndicate, England, 1981.

Gleick, J.: *Chaos – Making a New Science*, Viking, USA, 1987.

Granville, J. E.: *A Strategy of Daily Stock Market Timing for Maximum Profit*, Prentice-Hall, USA, 1960.

Hadady, R. E.: *Contrary Opinion, How to use it for Profit in Commodity Futures*, Hadady Publications, USA, 1983.

Hamilton, W. P.: *The Stock Market Barometer*, Harper & Brothers Publishers, USA, 1922.

Hooker, E. E. Jr.: *You Can't Win in Wall Street*, Hooker Company, USA, 1927.

Keynes, J. M.: *The General Theory of Employment, Interest and Money*, Hartcourt, England, 1936.

Kindleberger, C. P.: *Manias, Panics and Crashes*, Macmillan Press, USA, 1978.

Kondratieff, N.: *The Long Wave Cycle*, Richardson & Snyder, USA, 1984.

Kroll, S. & I. Shishko: *The Commodity Futures Market Guide*, Harper & Row, USA, 1973.

Laszlo, E.: *Evolution: The Grand Synthesis*, USA, 1987

Le Baron, D.: "Reflections on Market Efficienty", *Financial Analyst's Journal*, May/June 1983, pp. 16–23.

Lefevre, E.: *Reminiscence of a Stock Operator*, George H. Doran Company, USA, 1923.

Livermoore, Jesse L.: *How to Trade in Stocks*, Duell, Sloan & Pearce, USA, 1940.

Loeb, G. M.: *The Battle for Investment Survival*, Simon & Schuster, USA, 1957.

Lorenz, E.: *Predictability: Does the Flap of a Butterfly's Wings in Brazil Set Off a Tornado in Texas?*, American Association for the Advancement of Science in Washington, 1979.

Lorenz, E.: "Strange Attractors in a Multisector Business Cycle Model", *Journal of Economic Behavior and Organization*, Vol. 8 (1987), pp. 397–411.

Lorenz, H.-W.: *Nonlinear Dynamical Economics and Chaotic Motion*, Springer-Verlag, Germany, 1989.

Malkiel, B. G.: *A Random Walk Down Wall Street*, W. W. Norton & Co. USA, 1973.

McGuire, W. J.: *The Nature of Attitudes and Attitude Change*, Handbook of Social Psychology, 2nd ed. Vol. 3, Addison Wesley, Reading, Mass, 1969.

May, R.: "Simple Mathematical Models with Very Complicated Dynamics", *Nature* 261, 1976; and R. May & G. F. Oster, "Bifurcations and Dynamic Complexity in Simple Ecological Models", *The American Naturalist, pp. 573–599, 1976.*

Moore, G. H.: "Generating Leading Indicators from Lagging Indicators", *Western Economic Journal*, Vol 7, No. 2 (June 1969), pp. 137–144.

Murphy, J. J.: *Technical Analysis of the Futures Markets*, Prentice-Hall Co., USA, 1986.

Neill, H. B.: *The Art of Contrary Thinking*, Caxton Printers, USA, 1954.

Notes and Queries, 4th Series 11, 1868, p. 375, England.

NYSE: *Public Attitudes Toward Investing: Marketing Implications*, 1979.

Orne, M. T.: "The Nature of Hypnotic Phenomena: Recent Empirical Studies", *American Psychologist*, Vol. 18 (1963), p. 431.

Ping Chen: *Mode Locking to Chaos in Delayed Feedback Systems*, Center for Studies in Statistical Mechanics, University of Texas at Austin, 1986.

Ploeg, F. Van der: "Rational Expectations, Risk and Chaos in Financial Markets", *Economic Journal*, Vol. 96, suppl. (1985), pp. 151–162.

Pring, M. J.: *How to Forecast Interest Rates*, McGraw-Hill, USA, 1981.

Pring, M. J.: *International Investment Made Easy*, McGraw-Hill, USA, 1981.

Pring, M. J.: *Technical Analysis Explained*, McGraw-Hill, USA, 1985.

Rasmussen, D. R. & Mosekilde, E.: "Bifurcations and Chaos in a Generic Management Model", *North European Journal of Operational Research*, Vol. 35 (1988), pp. 80–88

Rasmussen, S. & Mosekilde, E.: "Empirical Indication of Economic Long Waves in Aggregate Production", *North European Journal of Operational Research*, Vol. 42 (1989), pp. 279–293.

Rhea, R.: *Dow Theory*, Barrons, USA, 1932.

Rothschild, Lord: *The Shadow of a Great Man*, Steller Press, England, 1982.

Sayers, C. L.: *Chaos and the Business Cycle*, Department of Economics, University of Houston, 1989.

Schiller, R. J.: *Survey Evidence Regarding the September 11–12 Stock Market Drop*, Yale University, 1986.

Schiller, R. J.: *Investor Behavior in the October 1987 Stock Market Crash: Survey Evidence*, Yale University, 1987.

Schiller, R. & Siegel, J.: "The Gibson Paradox and Historical Movements in Real Interest Rates", *Journal of Political Economy*, Vol. 89 (1987), No. 5.

Schultz, H. D.: *Bear Market Investment Strategies*, Dow Jones-Irwin, USA, 1981.

Schumpeter, J.: *Business Cycles*, McGraw-Hill, USA, 1939.

Schwed, F.: *Where are the Customers' Yachts?*, Simon & Schuster, USA, 1940.

Sherif, M.: "An Experimental Approach to the Study of Attitudes", *Sociometry*, Vol. 1 (1937), pp. 90–98.

"Smith, Adam": *The Money Game*, Random House, USA, 1967.

Soros, George: *The Alchemy of Finance*, Simon & Schuster, USA, 1987.

Sowards, J. K.: *Western Civilisation to 1660*, St. Martins Press, USA

Sperling, J. G.: *The South Sea Company*, Baker Library, USA, 1962.

Sprinkel, B. W. & R. J. Genetski: *Winning with Money*, Dow Jones Irwin, USA, 1977.

Touchey, J. C.: *Stock Market Forecasting for Alert Investors*, Amacon, USA, 1980.

Volcker, P. A.: *The Rediscovery of the Business Cycle*, Free Press, USA, 1978.

Watling, T. F. & J. Morley: *Successful Commodity Futures Trading*, Redwood Burn, England, 1974.

Wilder, J. W.: *New Concepts in Technical Trading Systems*, Trend Research, USA, 1978.

Index

Acceleration   242, 247, 282
Accumulation   77, 164
Advances/declines   121, 282
Analogies (market)   123, 127, 128, 131, 133
Attitudes   82, 178–182, 186, 192, 196–197, 205, 213, 242, 245, 246

Babson, Roger Ward   28–30, 43
Bank investments   107, 283
Bar-charts   20
Barometers (the markets as)   28–30, 33–34, 70, 78, 90
Baruch, Bernard   150, 239–240
Bear market   21
Beauty Contest Metaphor   63, 157
Bifurcations   53, 54, 242
Blind issues   40, 97
Blow-off top   242
Book value   11
Breadth (the market's)   118, 122, 123, 125
Breakout (false, premature)   269–270
Broadening formations   218, 276
Brokers' cash accounts   109, 283
Brokers' security loans   109–110
Bruges   9
Bubbles   40, 245
Bull market (bullish)   21

Bullish consensus   159–164, 242, 266, 282
Business cycles   74–83, 87–91, 93–102, 283
Butterfly effect   49–51
Buy-outs   244

Capital International   120
Cartel   15
Cash & carry   120
Central banks   114, 169
Channels   63–64, 189, 202–204
Chaos   47–59, 147, 252
Charts, chartists   20–21
Churchill, Winston   150
Clausewitz, Carl von   139, 241
Close price   20, 63, 268
Cohen, A. W.   82–83
Commodity Research Bureau (C.R.B. Futures Index)   128
Compagnie d'Occident   39
Computer trading   120, 246
Congestion   193, 262–265
Contrary opinion   82–84, 158–170
Corners   22, 239–240

Death cross   81, 196–198
Debit/loan ratio   107, 283
Diamond (formation)   225
Diffusion   123, 282
Distribution   77, 164, 242
Double/triple tops (double/triple bottoms)   222–224, 278–279

Dow, Charles Henry (Dow
  Theory) 75–78, 83, 191,
  242
Drew, Garfield A. 82, 83, 158

Economic activity 95–98, 104–
  105
Edwards, R. D. & J. Magee 81
Euromoney 12
Exposure tactics 154–160

False liquidity 97, 110–111
Family (stock) 119
Feedback loops 47, 51–52, 58,
  62, 71–72, 244–246, 250–
  251, 262
Feigenbaum cascade 53
Financial inflation 105
Financial liquidity 96–98, 105–
  116, 242, 283
Fisher, Irving 29, 43–45
Flags 213–214, 228
Formations (chart) 211
Forward contracts 23, 125
Friction 30
Fundamental analysis 10, 71
Futures 23, 120, 124, 126, 128,
  131–132

Gaps 214–216
Golden cross 81, 196–198
Granville, Joseph 164

Hadady, R.E. 83–84, 159–160
Hamilton, W. P. 28–29, 44,
  78, 83
Harvard Economic Society 29–
  30
Head & shoulders 224–226,
  279–280
Hedgers 22,156
Homing pigeons 138
Hoover, President 44–45
Hunt, Bunker 169

Index futures 23, 120
Industrial Index (Industrial
  Average) 76

Information dissemination 139
Insiders (large stockholders)
  154–155
Interest rate arbitrage 127–128
Interest rate trend 124
Intransitive systems · 54
Investment companies 43
Investment Research of
  Cambridge 231, 237
Island reversal 226–228, 280
Issues 108, 283

Joseph effect 87
Juglar, Clement (Juglar cycle)
  79, 88

Kaufman, Henry 12–13
Keenes, James R. 78
Key battle 241–243
Key reversal 226–227, 280
Keynes, John M. 15–16, 59,
  62–63, 156–157
Kitchin, Joseph (Kitchin
  cycle) 79, 83, 91, 252
Kondratieff, Nikolai
  (Kondratieff cycle) 80, 83,
  89–91
Kostolany 27

Lagging indicators 33, 281, 283
Laszlo, Ervin 54
Lawrence, Prof. 29
Leaders/laggers 101–102
Leading indicators 32, 281, 283
Leontief, Wassily 11
Limit orders 62, 246
Line charts 20–21
Linear models 51
Livermoore, Jesse 121, 152–
  154, 259–260
Loeb, Gerald 17
Long (positions) 22
Long-term investment 14
Lorenz, Edward 48–50

Mackay, Charles 38, 179
Malkiel, Burton G. 148

Manipulation 28–29
Margin 109–111, 246
Market rotation 95, 100
May, Robert 52–54
Media 96–98, 164–169, 282
Metereological forecasts 48–50, 54
Mississippi scheme 39
Mitchell, Charles 44
Mode-locking 88–89
Momentum 229–231, 248, 266
Money managers 149
Money supply 90, 103–105
Movements (the market's three) 76–77, 88
Moving average 194–202

Neck lines 41, 45, 224–225
Neill, H.B. 82–83
Nelson, S.A. 78
Net free reserves 107, 283
New highs/new lows 122–123, 282
News 27, 143
Newsletters 159, 161
Noah effect 143–144
Nonlinear models 51
Northern Pacific 239–241

Odd-lotters 82–83, 158–159, 242
On balance volume 205
Open interests 161, 163
Options 10, 23, 37

Pennants 213–214, 274
Perception 181, 246
Phase sequence 92, 95, 98–99
Point and figure charts 21
Pressure Index 237–238
Price fixing 130–131
Price inflation 105
Profittaking 188, 213
Pyramiding 258–259

Random walk 10, 51, 146–147, 251

Rate of Change (Relative Strength Index) 231–237
Rational expectations 32
Rectangles 219–221, 276–277
Relative to total index 119
Response 117
Resulting factors 142
Rhea, Robert 78
Rothschild, Nathan Mayer 137–138

Samuelson, Paul 149
Scalping 268
Schumpeter, Joseph 30–31, 80
Schwed, Fred 155
Selective exposure 181
Selective perception 181
Self-validating (price movements) 14
Shiller, Robert J. 61–62, 82, 183
Short (positions) 22
Short sale 22
Sibbet, J.H. 84
South Sea Bubble 38–43, 235
Speculators (major) 156
Staircase trends 193
Stimulating factors 142
Stochastic exogenous disturbances 69, 251–252
Stop-loss orders 62, 246, 262–266
Support and resistance 192

Tactical trading 161–170
Tapewatchers 147–148
Technical analysis (definition of) 17
Time factor 196–198, 241, 246–248
Time saving deposits 109, 283
Tops and bottoms (peaks and troughs) 77, 192–193
Transportation Index (Rail Average) 76

Trend reversals 190–191, 206–207, 239–248, 282–283
Trendlines 202, 204
Trends 184–207, 261–266
Triangles 216–219, 275–276
Tulip mania 36–38

Unpredictability 16, 51–52, 252

Vacuums 209, 214, 217–218, 220
Velocity of money 107, 111

Volume 77, 204–207, 214, 224, 244–245, 269

Wall Street crash of 1929 29–30, 42–46, 201, 234
Wall Street crash of 1987 62, 173–177, 183
Wedges 221–222, 277–278
Whispering candles 75
Wilder, J.W. 81

Yield curve 113–114, 283